TH
HIDDEN PL

of

Norfolk and Suffolk

Written by
JOY DAVID

Acknowledgements

This book would never have been compiled without the dedicated work of the team, to whom the editor offers a sincere thank you. There have been many times when so much has been done by so few beyond the call of duty!

OTHER TITLES IN THIS SERIES
The Hidden Places of North Yorkshire
The Hidden Places of Devon and Cornwall
The Hidden Places of Somerset, Avon and Dorset
The Hidden Places of Southern and Central Scotland
The Hidden Places of Hampshire and the Isle of Wight
The Hidden Places of Yorkshire
The Hidden Places of Cumbria
The Hidden Places of Sussex

AVAILABLE SHORTLY
The Hidden Places of Wales
The Hidden Places of Gloucestershire and Wiltshire
The Hidden Places of Warwickshire, Northamptonshire and Leicestershire
The Hidden Places of Shropshire, Staffordshire and West Midlands
The Hidden Places of Kent

ISBN 1-871815-10-X
First published 1989. Reprinted 1990.

Dolphin House, Sutton Harbour, Plymouth, Devon PL4 0DW.

Originated and printed by Sawtells of Sherborne Ltd.

Introduction

THE HIDDEN PLACES is designed to be an easily used book. Taking you, in this instance, on a gentle meander through the beautiful countryside of Norfolk and Suffolk; however, our books cover many counties and will eventually encompass the whole of the United Kingdom. We have combined descriptions of the well-known and enduring tourist attractions with those more secluded and as yet little known venues, easy to miss unless you know exactly where you are going.

We include hotels, inns, restaurants, caravan parks and camping sites, historic houses, museums, gardens and general attractions throughout East Anglia; together with our research on the local history. For each attraction, there is a line drawing and a brief description of the services offered. There is also an A-Z index of all the towns and villages mentioned, and finally, a reference guide giving you full details of all the hotels, inns, etc., detailed.

We do not include firm prices or award merits. We merely wish to point out *The Hidden Places* that hopefully will improve your holiday or business trip and tempt you to return. Should we succeed in our intent, then please do greet your host or landlord and thank them for our pleasure which inspired us to prompt your visit.

THE HIDDEN PLACES
of
Norfolk and Suffolk

Contents

Erwarton Hall and Gateway

Foreword

How many times have you heard someone say "I don't know why we keep going abroad on holiday every year, when we haven't begun to explore or get to know our own country."

And it's true, Britain as a whole is full of the most wonderful countryside and coastline, and whether it is in the far west peninsular of Devon and Cornwall or in the Orkneys, we have some of the world's finest natural treasures. But it's the hidden nooks and crannies, the quiet places, and the unexpected that hold much of the true charm of any region.

Being a local helps, they have known about such places for generations. But the visitor may pass them by, and so miss many of the real pleasures.

So these books are by way of a privilege. Bringing you access to places county by county, you may never have seen before. So enjoy, and perhaps understand why those of us fortunate enough to have been born here think of it as being God's own Kingdom.

ANGELA RIPPON

Hunstanton
& North West Norfolk

Holkham Hall

Area covered in Chapter 1

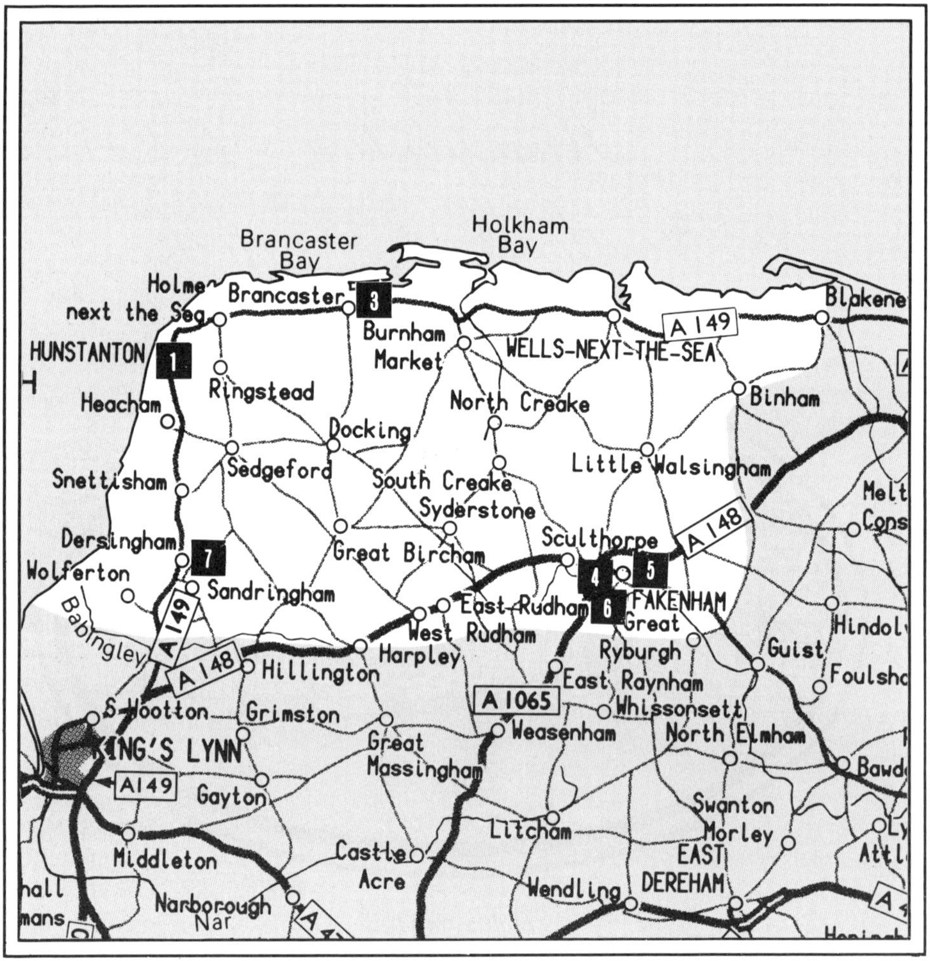

- **1** Baggy Anne's Restaurant *(Hunstanton)*
- **1** The White Cottage Guest House *(Hunstanton)*
- **3** Titchwell Manor Hotel *(Brancaster)*
- **4** Henry IV *(Fakenham)*
- **5** Fakenham Garden Centre *(Fakenham)*
- **6** Thursford Collection *(Fakenham)*
- **7** The White House Guest House *(Dersingham)*

CHAPTER 1

Hunstanton & North West Norfolk

For some years we have wanted to come back to Norfolk and re-discover the delights of this unspoiled country which like Cornwall is fiercely protective of its own identity. So many people think that Norfolk is flat. How wrong they are. It has as many variations of height and depth as other countries, and a wild beauty of its own that is unsurpassed. There is a small corner of this region stretching from Hunstanton abutting the Wash, to Wells-next-the-sea, and south to Fakenham, that takes in the marshland and farmland, and captures the flavour, richness and greatness, not just of East Anglia but of a country.

Hunstanton is a very English resort, with fine sands and striking cliffs, noted by geologists for their striped appearance, a layer of red chalk separating white chalk at the top, and brown and yellow stone at the bottom. You must pronounce the town's name "Hunston", incidentally.

We chose to stay in **The White Cottage Guest House**. The proprietor, Mrs. Burton is a very amiable, understanding lady who was recommended to us by the Royal Society for the Protection of Birds. This part of Norfolk is an ornithologist's haven, but it does take a very sympathetic hotel or guest

The White Cottage Guest House

house keeper to put up with the odd hours that enthusiastic bird-watchers keep! Mrs. Burton takes it all in her stride. Nearby are Holme, Snettisham and Titchwell, all Wild Bird Reserves, so the location is excellent.

For those of you who do not share our enthusiasm for ornithology, do not be put off. The White Cottage is quiet and relaxing. Very comfortable and all the bedrooms have superb views over the sea and a golf course, so you do not even have to step outside to enjoy the panorama.

The Golf Course is only two minutes walk from the house, and a quiet round of golf is a marvellous relaxation. The White Cottage has spacious grounds of its own, and lies in the lovely village of Old Hunstanton. The beach has protective sand dunes, and just a stone's throw away coastal paths and Roman walks provide the opportunity to enjoy some breathtaking sunsets.

Hunstanton offers plenty of entertainment for all the family. There are donkey rides on the sands, boat hire on the Marine Lake, band concerts, dancing at the Kit Kat Club, discos and dinner dances. The shows in the Princess Theatre are always entertaining.

The local big house is a moated Tudor Hall, which belonged to the Le Strange family for hundreds of years. Sir Roger Le Strange became an early journalist in Milton's time, and he attacked him fiercely. He started one of the country's first newspapers, the *Public Intelligence*. He also translated Aesop's Fables — quite a task.

Do you like deep sea fishing? We had a wonderful day out in a boat doing just that. The weather was kind to us, and from the moment we left North Promenade we knew it was going to be a good day. The skipper of the boat we hired had the patience of a saint and did not mind that we were totally inexperienced. Sometimes worrying about whether you are going to make a fool of yourself stops you from enjoying a new experience. Do not let such a feeling deter you in this instance. If you do not want to fish you can enjoy a sea trip to Seal Island. These trips are available every day in the summer.

Water ski-ing was not for us, but watching the skill of people skimming along the water's surface gave us a great deal of pleasure. Power boating seems to be another sport which gives a lot of enjoyment at Hunstanton. More peacefully there is tennis and croquet! We are not sure we would describe croquet as being safer — the mallet is a lethal weapon, if your opponent is the aggressive, competitive kind!

Looking for somewhere to get a meal, we found **Baggy Annes** in Le Strange Terrace. The art of pasta making is rarely seen. To be able to watch it being prepared in an open kitchen whilst you are sitting at a restaurant table is an experience. This is just what you will find at Baggy Annes. We were full of admiration for their culinary skills. Whenever we have tried to do it ourselves we get into the most terrible mess. We can remember trying to make raviolo with a meat filling for a dinner party once — the result was indescribable! Horrible lumps of heavy pasta from which all the filling had oozed out and stuck to the bottom of the pan. If we remember correctly our guests ended up with a take-away from the nearest Kentucky Fried Chicken House. Not so at Baggy Annes. Everything is skilfully and freshly prepared. Pizzas come together before your eyes with a variety of different toppings. There are traditional Italian dishes or well-cooked English ones. If you wish you can choose a three course meal at a fixed price of £6.95. Vegetarians need not fear, there is a menu for them. Fish in all its forms is available, simply fried or cooked in exotic sauces. There is also an extensive steak menu. Baggy Annes is a busy, vibrant place. At night it is a haven for the cast of whatever production is playing at the Princess Theatre. The bar has an extension every night, so if you too have visited the theatre this is a good place to choose.

Baggy Annes Restaurant

The restaurant was rebuilt three years ago, but has not lost character. The arched ceiling and the saddleback chairs live comfortably with the open planned modern kitchen. Eat here at any time from 10.30 am until midnight all the year round. The Sykes family who run it welcome people as warmly for morning coffee as they do for afternoon tea or a late supper. There is a children's menu, and traditional Sunday lunches are served (with special portions for pensioners).

We were shown over the almost completed all-weather Sea Life Centre which opens this coming summer. It is situated right on the promenade in Hunstanton. British marine life is presented in new, fresh and spectacular ways using the latest technology.

Beneath the waves lies a fascinating underwater world, which until now has remained a mystery to those who stay on shore. The Sea Life Centre invites you to explore this world. Each step offers unequalled opportunities to view from above, below and in the Ocean Tunnel from inside!

Tens of thousands of gallons of water will surround you as you come face to face with hundreds of sea creatures, from the intriguing octopus to the sinister conger eel. There are 'Living Touch' pools that are a delightful rock pool environment, where you can observe and handle a rich variety of creatures. You can take a cliff walk and see a world usually only experienced by underwater divers. An audio-visual presentation, giving you an insight into man's involvement with the oceans, is entitled 'Ocean Story' and is both entertaining and exciting. You can just imagine man's impact on the marine environment when you are peering out as though you were in a sunken vessel. It is open all the year round and we are sure you will find it interesting, educational and relaxing, but most of all it is fun for all age groups.

Two and a half miles south of Hunstanton is **Heacham**. The church there has an impressive 13th century tower which sadly has lost its transepts, and bulk buttresses have taken their place. The seats round the 13th century nave pillars are worth looking out for, as is the perpendicular clerestory and the handsome rood screen. The church attracts many American tourists because there is a colourful piece of local Jacobean history commemorated in a modern memorial to the Red Indian Princess Pocahontas, who married the squire of Heacham, John Rolfe in 1614. It is especially interesting to Americans because a descendant of the Princess, who settled in the U.S.A., married President Woodrow Wilson.

While you are in Heacham you must visit Caley Mill, the home of **Norfolk Lavender**. It is England's only lavender farm, and to get the best out of your visit we would suggest you join one of the information tours. These take place daily from the end of May to September. The times are posted on the notice boards at the entrances. It is a most remarkable place. The National Collection of Lavenders enables you to study the different colours and sizes of the lavender varieties. Some of them have been bred at the lavender farm and others have been obtained from other gardens, nurseries and enthusiasts. We were told that Caley Mill aims to establish the definitive plants for each variety.

Norfolk Lavender Farm

There is a wonderful herb garden, which has been laid out to show the many varieities of interesting herbs in popular use today. It includes culinary, aromatic and decorative plants. Most of them are available for purchase either as plants or seeds in the conservatory shop.

In keeping with lavender, the farm has a purple kiosk in the lay-by which has a wide range of lavender gifts and souvenirs but the Conservatory is the only place where you can buy some of the many varieties of specially selected lavender plants bred at Caley Mill. They stock an interesting range of books on lavender and on herbs.

The Millers Cottage Tea Room is very popular after a tour of the farm. They really do make some delicious home-made cakes and scones. The aromatic smell of fresh coffee mixes tantalisingly with the scent of the lavender. You can sit inside and eat your tea under the old beams, or on a fine day take your tea down to the riverside garden and watch the ducks. You might even see a kingfisher or a heron.

It is only a short distance from Heacham to **Snettisham**. L. P. Hartley describes the church of St. Mary here in his book The Shrimp and The Anemone. We realised from reading this that we would find the church stunning, but we did not expect it to make quite so much impact on our souls. There is so much to see. It was originally a cruciform church. The magnificent tower and spire stand at the east end, without the chancel which once extended 40ft. beyond. The west window has the most equisite decorated tracery flowers, creating a wonderful front together with the side turrets and porch. We loved the seats circling the tall nave pillars. There is a perfect 13th century saunce, or sanctus bell. The wafer oven is still there, which once was used for baking the communion bread. In amongst all this beauty is the collection of Jacobean brass. The church is open from 0930 am – 1900 pm Monday to Saturday and from 0800 am – 2000 pm on Sundays.

Snettisham has a charming water mill built about 1800, where you can see them actually grinding corn. There are several demonstrations during the course of the day. The gardens are a delight to walk in with a waterfall and a millpond complete with ducks. You will find it on the road to Snettisham beach, just follow the brown signs.

You can spend a happy day at the **Park Farm** just off the A149 in Snettisham itself. Easy to find you just follow the signs. Children love it here. There are safari rides, a red deer herd, cattle, sheep and pigs and three farm trails to enjoy. It is open every day from 10.30 am – 5 pm except Saturdays.

Going south again we came to **Dersingham** and met Dawn Nightingale, a friendly lady who runs an excellent guest house called **The White House**, in Hunstanton Road. The house was built in 1901, and was once part of a

The White House

farm owned by Edward VII. It is comfortable and well-furnished, with a friendly family feeling about the house.

Dawn has been running the business for five years, and has many visitors who come back again and again. We have no doubt it is because she makes them so welcome, and gives them a very well-cooked and substantial breakfast. If you stay with her during the winter months you can count on being warm; the house has full central heating. The bedrooms have tea and coffee-making facilities; always a boon wherever you stay. Every bed has the luxury of an electric blanket.

If you prefer to have a downstairs bedroom, for whatever reason, this is possible. The rooms there are en-suite.

Dersingham is half way between King's Lynn and Hunstanton, and is only $1\frac{1}{2}$ miles from Sandringham and a lot of other interesting places to visit, including the world renowned Bird Sanctuary.

If you enjoy garden centres, then take a look at Thaxters Garden Centre while you are in Dersingham. They invite you to inspect their huge selection of bulbs, heathers, ornamental trees, magnolias and many more. All the shrubs and trees are container-grown, so they can be moved all the year round. They stand in small beds surrounded by concrete slab paths, which makes for easy access and saves you getting your feet wet and filthy.

We enjoyed a visit to Dersingham Pottery while we were there. It is only a tiny place but there is something very rewarding about watching a craftsman at work. You will find the pottery in Chapel Road and they open daily all the year round.

From Dersingham, Sandringham is only a stone's throw away, but we intend to take you there in Chapter 3, so we will ignore it for the moment. We do hope that it is not unreasonable to suggest ignoring the Monarch. We can assure Her Majesty that we are ardent royalists!

Going across country lanes to the east of Dersingham, we made for **Houghton**. The village was rebuilt in the 18th century and now has a straight avenue of limes and discreet whitewashed cottages nestling in pairs, which lead the eye to the white-painted wrought-iron gates of **Houghton Hall** built in the 1730s by the first Prime Minister of England, Sir Robert Walpole. He commissioned architects of course, Colin Campbell and Thomas Ripley, but Sir Robert left his own mark on the outside with its four little turrets. Inside his own influence is even stronger, but he did give William Kent his first big architectural job. The ceilings, mouldings, doors, state beds, tables and chairs are almost all by William Kent. It is one of the first houses where mahogany was used to any great extent. The house was once offered by the Walpoles to King Edward VII but he chose Sandringham instead. Subsequently the house has never been sold, and the present owners are directly descended from Robert through his daughter, Mary.

The family fortunes were not always sound. Sir Robert's grandson, the eccentric Earl of Orford, was so deeply in debt that the original collection of pictures was sold to Catherine of Russia to put matters right. This deeply upset Lord Orford's uncle, the famous Sir Horace Walpole. Since then other pictures have found their was to Houghton, and today there is a fine collection. You will find rare Mortlake Tapestries by Francis Poyntz, fine 18th century book bindings and many other beautiful things. The stables of carrstone, with a courtyard and a fountain, are very attractive.

The Park is beautifully landscaped and in it you will find St. Martin's Church, which was partly rebuilt by Sir Robert Walpole in 1729, but has no monument to him nor to Horace Walpole who, however, was buried there. The Church contains a coffin lid with a carved effigy of a prior of Coxford (1307), box pews in the aisles and a west gallery. There are hatchments, and in the chancel some fine Jacobean woodwork. The house is open to the public in the summer.

Houghton Hall

Great Massingham, just two miles south of Houghton, is a totally different place. It has a feeling of timelessness. The little village encircles a green whose ponds could well be the fish ponds of an Augustinian priory established in the early 13th century. You will find remains of the priory in Abbey House, which only dates from the 19th century, but has a mediæval doorway, lancet window and buttress. The church of St. Mary has an absolutely beautiful 13th century south porch with a roof of arched braces to colar beams. Inside the church the 14th- and 15th century unite with the lovely font of the earlier century complimenting the 15th century screen. You can even see fragments of original mediæval stained glass in the tracery of the chancel.

You could combine a visit to Houghton Hall with a little time taken out of your day to see **Great Bircham Windmill**, just off the B1153. It is probably Norfolk's finest corn mill. The setting is lovely. Beautiful, totally unspoilt countryside. It has been used for wind-milling since the 1700s. Be brave and climb the five floors to the top so that you can view the milling machinery which is in working order. There is a Bakery Museum and a gift shop, but most of all after that climb, a cup of tea in the tea rooms will be high on your priority list. It certainly was on ours. It is open daily from May 20th until the end of September, except Saturdays. From Easter onwards you can go there on Sundays and Wednesdays.

Great Bircham Windmill

When we went we continued on to Houghton Hall for a second visit for several reasons. The palladian house is very special, and the parkland where peacocks, Egyptian geese and fallow deer roam is reason enough to go back. In addition this time we wanted to take more time to look at the display of state harness and coaches in the stables. Lord Colmondeley's collection of some 20,000 model soldiers, paintings and militaria, said to be one of the finest in the world, is exhibited in the picture gallery. We did not have time on our previous visit to see all these things.

We made Hunstanton our base for our entire visit to this part of Norfolk. Why move anyway when you are comfortably housed? We did however go to Le Strange Arms Hotel for dinner one evening. It is a fine country house hotel with lawns that sweep down to sand dunes and the sea. It is a very well run hotel and we enjoyed both the food and the service. Our main reason for going there was to see if it would make a suitable venue for a small conference. The answer was definitely Yes.

For example the Palace Suite is 50ft long, 17ft 7ins wide with a floor area of 879 sq. ft. Theatre style, you could use it for 90 people, Classroom 48 and Boardroom 46. There are four conference areas all told, and the accommodation if you wanted a residential conference offers you 28 bedrooms, all en-suite. Apart from the hotel restaurant it has the Ancient Mariner Inn right down by the beach and the Galley, another attractive spot. Audio-visual equipment is available for hire together with all the other requirements needed for a conference. We thought it was a first class spot, and if you have any thoughts in this direction do ring Mr. Wyllie the Director on (04853) 34411. He is a very helpful man.

Have you ever tried clay shooting? The Norfolk Gun Trading Company at 14 Greevegate invite you to try it. They say, "Complete beginners especially welcome", and they mean it. It is different and it is fun. They will supply you with whatever equipment you need.

Even if you are not an ornithologist please do not miss a visit to the **Titchwell Marsh RSPB**. The reserve was purchased in 1973 and has now become one of the RSPB's major reserves and is of national importance with many species of bird breeding on or around the reserve, including avocet, marsh harrier and several species of the terns. The reserve comprises some 420 acres of reedbeds, freshwater and brackish marshes, saltmarsh and beach. This variety of habitats encourages many species of birds, especially wildfowl and waders, to be present throughout the year and these are easily seen from the three public hides. The reserve is just five miles east of Hunstanton on the A149 coast road. It is open all year. We spent four hours there, but we are told that people spend anything from 1–4 hours generally. There are no catering facilities but ample toilet facilities. The good news is that two of the hides are easily accessible by wheelchairs.

Titchwell Marsh

In between Hunstanton and Wells-next-the-sea are several places of great interest and steeped in history. Holmes-next-the-sea is linked by an ancient track called Peddar's Way to an inland area, the Breckland. These lonely, isolated saltings run on to **Brancaster**, where we went to stay at **The Titchwell Manor Hotel**. It is not quite in Brancaster, and it is a charming country house which would be best described as a country house hotel by the sea. The Titchwell Manor Hotel is run by Ian and Margaret Snaith, who make sure that you feel a sense of freedom and welcoming informality the moment you walk through the door. Important ingredients for any holiday.

There are ten bedrooms, eight with private bathroom, and each with radio, tea and coffee-making facilities and a baby listening service. It is fully licensed and open to non-residents. There is a TV lounge and ample car parking.

You will find the food is good English fare, using fresh produce and local game and sea food in season. Marvellous oysters too, from the local oyster beds of Titchwell. You will enjoy the a la carte menu which is extensive, or you can just have an attractively-presented bar meal.

The Snaiths pack an excellent picnic lunch, which you can take with you whilst you explore this lovely part of Norfolk, with all its history and natural beauty. The bird life is full of interest all the year round. The beaches are sandy and very clean. Brancaster is a marvellous place for sailing, which can easily be arranged for you. There are championship golf courses nearby, and horse-riding. On top of all this there are superb walks, and because the county is flat, cycling is an excellent way of getting about. It is easy to visit Sandringham House, Holkham Hall and Houghton Hall from here and they are all musts on your visiting list.

Titchwell Manor has a wonderful walled garden with marvellous views of the beach and the sea so if you do not feel like going anywhere you can just laze in the garden.

Titchwell Manor Hotel

Burnham Thorpe we must tell you about. There are several Burnhams: Deepdale, Market, Norton and Overy, before you get to Burnham Thorpe from Brancaster. Here, where his father was rector, that greatest of all English admirals, Horatio Nelson was born.

Burnham Thorpe is a Mecca for all admirers of that naval genius, and they can sit in a pub where Nelson himself once sat. Everywhere they will be reminded of him, for there is a huge collection of Nelsonia. The landlord who restored the Lord Nelson Inn became an authority on Nelson. You will find mementos of the victory and its admiral in the church, where the lectern is built from timber from the victory.

Nelson was thirteen years old when he entered the Navy in 1770, and he was only 47 when he died after wiping out the French fleet off Cape Trafalgar. He was a rear admiral at 39 and a national hero a year later after the Battle of the Nile.

It was at the Lord Nelson Inn, as it is now called, that he held some of his celebration dinners, and it is in the churchyard that members of the Nelson family still lie.

Still in this small corner of East Anglia we come to the home of another great Englishman, to whom modern agriculture owes so much. When Nelson went to sea as a small boy, 16 year old Thomas Coke lived in a great house nearby, **Holkham Hall**.

Coke was to transform the countryside and revolutionise farming throughout the land, making as considerable a contribution in his own way as Nelson. He inherited three thousand acres of barren land, where is was said two rabbits fought over one blade of grass.

His great uncle had built the mansion in the style of an Italian palace, and had reclaimed many acres from the sea. His descendant, who was to be enobled and take the title Earl of Leicester, was to put them to good use.

The trouble was that the topsoil was infertile. But underneath was a rich clay marl which Coke dug up and spread on the ground, enriching it and giving it body. He then planted great crops of turnips, using the expertise of another Norfolk agriculturalist pioneer, "Turnip" Townshend, and this was the foundation for the whole country's reputation for good farming.

Sheep cleared the roots, their manure enriches the soil further, wheat and barley were grown for the first time, and now herds of cattle could be kept. It was the start of mixed farming.

Coke was a farming evangelist. He invited farmers and landowners from all over England and abroad as well to look at his experiments. At one visitation to his annual sheep shearing he entertained 7,000 guests. It was fortunate he was a rich man. He had become very much richer as his rent roll increased enormously in value, but he literally ploughed the money back into the land.

Thousands still visit Holkham Hall but today they go, as we did, to visit this 18th century palladian mansion. It was built between 1734 and 1762. The architectural style is the result of the combined talents of Thomas Coke, Lord Burlington, William Kent and Matthew Brettingham. It was constructed mainly of local yellow stone and, perhaps because it is a trifle heavy in classicism, the outside has never been much admired by the neighbours. The entrance hall is magnificent with its pink marble pillars. In the long line of state rooms which occupy the first floor there is much original furniture by William Kent, and on the velvet and damask hung walls are pictures by Van Dyck and Gainsborough amongst others. The house reflects Thomas Coke's natural appreciation of classical art developed during his Grand Tour. There is a gold and white library full of beautifully bound books, and a famous collection of illuminated manuscripts, folios and psalters, as well as all kinds of other records. The long sculpture gallery has antique statues brought from Italy by Thomas Coke, and said to have been packed in ilex seeds, which may account for the unexpected number of these dark evergreen trees, which are such a beautiful feature of the estate, both along the roads and grouped in the park.

A tour of the house can last for 30–90 minutes, depending on yourselves, but on leaving you will pass Holkham Pottery started in 1951 by Elizabeth,

Countess of Leicester and today supervised by Viscountess Coke. A highly skilled team produce this fine range of pottery. During the season various demonstrations can be seen which are thoroughly enjoyable.

Beyond the pottery are the 19th century stables which house the Holkham Bygones collection of Victorian and Edwardian agricultural tools and domestic equipment. There are something like 4,000 items which range from working steam engines, vintage cars and tractors to craft tools and kitchenware. We found it fascinating, particularly having found out so much about the history of the family.

Holkham Park consists of almost 3,000 acres of parkland, agricultural land and timber, and includes a large Deer Park, where there are approximately 600 head of fallow deer. The lake near the Hall is almost one mile long, and throughout the year many species of wildfowl can be seen. There are some very attractive walks, and we cannot conceive of anyone not enjoying a visit to Holkham Hall.

Holkham Hall

Wells-next-the-sea was once a busy port, but now the sea is some way off across the marshes. These little coastal villages were once very wealthy from exporting wool and catching fish, and their churches reflect their former prosperity. Nor are they lacking in the signs of today's affluence.

Wells-next-the-sea is quaint, much loved by those who discover it. Take a train journey on the Wells and Walsingham Light Railway through this delightful countryside. The railway runs from Wells through scenic countryside, and halts at Warham St. Mary and Wighton before it reaches **Walsingham**, famed for centuries as a centre of pilgrimage. With the regular service you will have ample time to explore Walsingham with its shops, restaurants and inns, as well as the famous shrine, before catching the train back. The station at Wells has a charming restored signal box which sells refreshments and souvenirs. The unique Garratt steam locomotive was built in 1986 especially for this line.

It is worthwhile in Walsingham to take one of the guided tours. There is so much history in the little town that on your own you may well miss out something special. If you ring Scilla Landale on Walsingham 250 she can arrange special tours on Wednesday afternoons from June to September. The tour leaves the Shirehall, Common Place at 2 pm and it takes $1\frac{1}{2}$–2 hours. Her charge for the tour when we took it was £1.50p for an adult and £1.00 for children and senior citizens. Little Walsingham has been a place of pilgrimage since 1061, when the lady of the manor had a vision of the Virgin Mary. Henry VIII paid bare-foot homage, and hundreds of thousands of pilgrims have made their way here from far and near. Today's shrine is built on the site of a much earlier one.

In the 12th century the Augustinians set up a priory and the Franciscans followed with a friary in 1347, both of which prospered until the reformation, when they were demolished. The largest survival of the priory is the gatehouse, which consists of two slender towers supporting an arch, while one chamber of the priory has been built into a house and its vaulted ceiling is still preserved.

The friary stood outside the village on the road to Houghton; just two cloisters and parts of the living quarters remain. There is little left of the church.

Great Priory Gatehouse at Walsingham

The great priory gatehouse stands at the east side of the High Street, and the village has a number of attractive old houses, a 16th century octagonal pump house set atop with a beacon brazier in Common Place, and a market. There is an old grammar school and the College of Priests. The church of St. Mary was virtually gutted by fire in 1961, but much restoration work has been carried out on the interior. In the North Chapel you will find Epstein's statue of the Risen Christ. The exterior thankfully still displays good 14th- and 15th century work.

The **Slipper Chapel** at **Houghton St. Giles** got its name because pilgrims approaching Little Waslingham from the south showed their devotion and humility by completing the last mile of their journey barefooted, leaving their footwear in the chapel.

Every county has its share of unusual and enchanting names. Here in West Norfolk we have **Great** and **Little Snoring**. The most interesting feature of Great Snoring is the opulent 16th century rectory with its octagonal turrets and fancy Victorian chimneys. The mediæval church of St. Mary has a large 17th century commandment board with the last Four Things: heaven, hell, death and judgement; as a warning!

We like the Norman church at Little Snoring, which has a beautiful carved Norman font, and a detached round tower which is thought to be Saxon. There are only about 170 round towers in England, and Norfolk has 119 of them. The reason for this is because of the intractable nature of flint as a building material. Where square corners are required they must be of freestone or brick built into the flint walls. A round tower has no corners, and can consequently be built entirely of flint.

There are so many delightful places to visit in this area. It is difficult to know which one to choose. There is the little village of North Creake just a few miles from Little Walsingham. The beautiful mediæval church of St. Mary the Virgin must delight anyone's eye. It has a very handsome perpendicular tower, and the restored chancel is the envy of many churches. It was built by William Careltone in 1301, and retains to this day the richly crocketed, curved and cusped sedilia, piscina and Easter Sepulchre. The hammerbeam nave roof has the most wonderful detail and is bordered by angels. It is thought that the brass figure near the altar, which holds a church, may be the benefactor of the 15th century rebuilding, one Sir William Calthorpe. If you look very hard you may be able to make out the Doom painted above the chancel arch. The church is open every day from 0800am - 1800pm.

One mile away are the remains of Creake Abbey. Founded by the Augustinians who lived there for many years, it came to a sad end when all its monks died of plague in one week. I have read that perhaps it was a good thing, for it saved Henry VIII the trouble of dissolving the Abbey in later years.

The Slipper Chapel at Houghton St. Giles

There are two super villages close to Wells; Blakeney, which is very beautiful and somehow breathes the spirit of Betjeman's England. To add to its charm it has a well-known bird sanctuary.

And now to nearby **Stiffkey** (pronounced 'Stewkey'). You can buy the most marvellous shrimps and whelks here. Try to buy the whelks straight from the boiler, they are absolutely delicious. Stiffkey is a lovely little village, which became a hotbed of gossip and scandal between the wars because of the antics of its rector. He was much concerned with rescuing 'fallen women' in London's West End, and his involvement with these young ladies, ranging from waitresses to actresses, got him into hot water with the ecclesiastical authorities. For years he was rarely out of the headlines of the popular press, and achieved such notoriety that as many as five hundred people would pack into his church to see him preach, and hundreds more would stand in the churchyard.

Eventually the Rev. Mr. Davidson met a bizarre fate. He lost his living, joined a travelling show and was shown at Blackpool sharing a cage with a lion. Finally the lion, which obviously had no sense of humour, killed this little man. So died a true English eccentric.

We have almost completed this journey through North West Norfolk, that has taken us through the centuries and through much of the history of England. We hope you have enjoyed meeting some of the people of whom we have been writing. So many of them have helped to give England its unique flavour.

Norfolk has given flavour not only to England but it has made a sizeable contribution to life in North America. Captain Vancouver of King's Lynn has left his name in Canada. Captain Mason, also from King's Lynn, and John Rolfe, made their mark in America.

Thousands more were to leave this peaceful area and cross the Atlantic. There were mass emigrations in the 1830s of Norfolk folk. They went steerage for just over £6.50! The next wave paid nothing! They were the many local girls who married American servicemen in the 1940s and settled in the States. American servicemen were everywhere in this part of Norfolk, as they were, and still are, in so much of East Anglia.

The people of Norfolk, once they had got used to them, found them fascinating, with their relaxed, free and easy manner, their high standards of living, their generosity, and the echoes they brought of Hollywood, skyscrapers and wide open spaces. Their impact was considerable.

From the air base at Sculthorpe, just outside Fakenham, American aviators flew their missions and airmen and ground crews breezed into the towns and villages to give life an unique flavour in the 40s and 50s.

Fakenham is a sturdy agricultural centre, with a well-known National Hunt race course. It is a busy little market town which we wanted to take a look at, so we decided to stay at **The Henry IV** in Greenway Lane. Malcolm and Pat Fleetwood, the proprietors, are a super, friendly couple who made us very welcome, as we are sure you will be if you decide to stay at the Henry

IV. It is quite a new building, and has been designed for comfort. The rooms are pleasantly furnished and roomy. The main bar has fine high ceilings with good furnishings. There is another little bar known as the Foyer Bar which also has a retail counter. The restaurant, which will seat 40, was unusual for a modern building. The walls were panelled with some remarkable English walnut, something you rarely see today. The menu was remarkable too. Have you ever been offered Transkei Mud in Norfolk? We have. It is the most delectable mixture of caramel and whipped cream, with a subtle flavour of mint chocolate and layered with biscuit crumbs. The menu was quite extensive, and very reasonably priced. Children, who are very welcome, can have a main course for as little as 95p, whilst you can have a five course dinner, including Transkei Mud of course, for £9.95. Whether you just call in for a drink, a meal, or to stay a day or two as we did, the Fleetwoods will certainly look after you. It is only ten miles from the sea, and a super area for walking or cycling.

The Fleetwoods believe that their pub is the only one in England named the Henry IV. Do you know of one? If you do, let us know and we will pass the information on to them.

The Henry IV

If you are a keen gardener you will thoroughly enjoy a day out at **Fakenham Garden Centre**. Perhaps, like us, you know little about gardening but love to potter. If this is so then here you will find a vast amount of understandable information. Sometimes choosing plants or shrubs can be a nightmare can't it? Especially if you are lacking in knowledge. Basically it is the inability to plan properly isn't it? We never know how to judge the layout of our small plot, but with the enthusiastic help we got from Fakenham Garden Centre and from Gordon and Brenda Turner, the owners, we feel quite confident that our garden will be a delight this summer.

The Garden Centre is 5,000 square feet of well laid out areas. There are plants, shrubs, trees, water plants; the list goes on for ever. The quality of everything we saw was of a very high standard.

Undercover we found an Indoor Plant House, and a book selection which ranged from highly technical publications to simple books for idiots like ourselves.

We had a super time there, and children will love it too. There are rabbits and gerbils, fish and birds to look at.

At the end of your visit you can reward yourselves, with a very welcome cup of tea or coffee, in the pleasant eaterie.

Fakenham Garden Centre

If you take the A148 to the east of Fakenham you will come to a left turning almost opposite the B1354. This will lead you to **Thursford** and **The Thursford Collection**. Frustration sets in with us when we want to write extensively about some of the very exciting places we visit, and cannot do so because of space. Visiting The Thursford Collection comes under this heading. No one visiting East Anglia should miss out this extraordinary exhibition. Thursford might not seem the most likely place for a museum of fairgrounds and steam, but in fact, looked at properly the place would be an almost inevitable choice. East Anglia has many vital relationships with the history of festival and its objects, and the real Norfolk traditional art is not water-coloured painting but the practice of festival. There have been fairs all over Norfolk for over a thousand years. The counties of East Anglia are full of stories and rituals based on the idea of folk entertainment, so that the development of the industrial fairground much later is not really so surprising.

Norfolk is full of living folk history in which fairs were significant events for isolated communities, and had an agricularally based life, from which steam power quite naturally, and of necessity, evolved. When you think about it, the engineering of the farms is exactly that of the fairground, and the machinery is a parallel form of the same thing. Just as the traction engine in the fields needed to be adaptable from the many varied tasks required of it, so the showman's engine, and the modern fairground vehicle, needed to adapt as generators, haulers of materials, cranes etc. It is hard for us to imagine now the effect which the visit of a fair would have had on the

Little Walsingham – Conduit

separated villages in Norfolk, in the late nineteenth and twentieth centuries. Out of the plain landscape came these exuberant vehicles and their mechanical mysteries with carved monsters and swinging chairs, and all of them painted and polished in a style of power and colour. The cinema too had its beginnings in the fair, with the huge bioscopes which travelled between 1896 and 1914, some of them with room for 1,000 people.

Above all else the fairs brought electricity with them, at a time when most towns and villages themselves would have only had gas lighting! For many people therefore this would have been the first sight of electric light; more magic than anything Aladdin could have brought. Families would walk miles to see these things, because in a pre-television era this was the place where the truly spectacular could be seen and, more importantly, shared.

Among the scattered groups who went to the fair was one small boy, GEORGE CUSHING, who instinctively understood these things, and has retained the image of it all his life to make The Thursford Collection a show for us to see and enjoy.

George Cushing was caring for and collecting steam engines when most men would not have given you £5 for one. Without his perceptive honesty the museum would not exist. All the exhibits have one thing in common, which is that they are beautiful objects made by craftsmen who knew their work, and some of them have at one time or another fallen into disregard. George Cushing's real love for these things has a countryman's sense of the intrinsic value of the objects, to bring together this collection, to see through the blindness or carelessness which allowed traction engines, for example, to go for scrap, and to re-make for all of us one of the best arrangements of steam engines and organs in the world. More than the skill, more than the money which it has taken to make the museum, it has required his vision and enthusiasm.

The Thursford Collection

Having given you a potted history of Thursford, let me tell you why we think it is one of the brightest spots in Norfolk and will surpass all your expectations. Firstly, the museum. It's not just a museum but a total experience. Music: live music shows starring Robert Wolfe in the Wurlitzer show, plus music from nine mechanical organs. Shops: housed in renovated farm buildings, offering a wide and varied selection of goods, many locally made. Food: cream teas on the lawn, light snacks in the genuine Norfolk barn, home-made ice-cream from the parlour and to top it all there are enough activities including a Savage Venetian Gondola ride, to complete a wonderful visit.

More seriously the museum exists solely for the benefit of the people of Norfolk and the nation at large, and is of accepted national, historical and educational importance. There may be individuals or organisations reading this book who have items of related interest for which they have no space, which they do not wish to sell or see destroyed, or which they would like to see exhibited. It is now possible for such items to be placed on permanent or extended loan, or donated to the Thursford Trust in the sure knowledge that they will be safe for all time. Anyone who is interested is invited to contact the museum.

Sheringham, Cromer & North East Norfolk

North Norfolk Railway

Area covered in Chapter 2

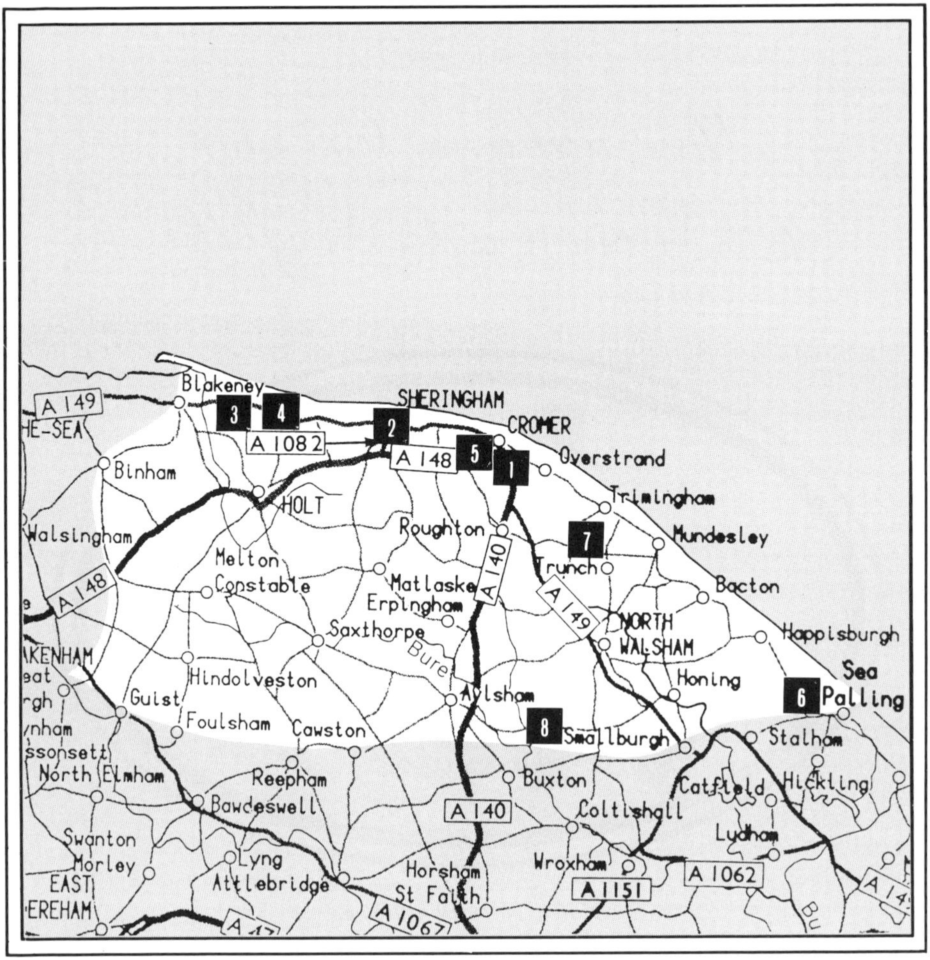

1 The Dagmar Hotel & Restaurant *(Cromer)*

2 The Anser Guest House *(Sheringham)*

3 The Swiss Restaurant *(Weybourne)*

4 The Muckleborough Collection *(Weybourne)*

5 The Dolphin Free House & Restaurant *(Cromer)*

6 The Hall Inn *(Sea Palling)*

7 Church Farm Guest House *(Southrepps)*

8 The Weavers Arms *(Swanton Abbott)*

CHAPTER 2

Sheringham, Cromer and North East Norfolk

From Blakeney Point to Mundesley, North Norfolk will delight people who are interested in fossils and geology. Don't groan those of you who find this a dead bore. The whole area will offer you a wonderful variety of things to do and see. But back to fossils and geology where, in these parts, you will find miles of shingle banks just waiting for your inquisitive looks.

The pebbles and shingle come from three main sources: flints laid down in ancient warm seas, deposits from the time when the mighty Rhine's estuary reached this area, bringing with it mud, silt, stones and a whole series of glacial deposits, some of which had their origins in Scandinavia. Rocks and minerals abound. If you search carefully you will find gneiss, granite, porphyries, quartz, calcite, serpentine, schists, gabbro, iron pyrites and iron stone nodules. The list is never ending.

The stretch of beach around **West Runton** provides a rich hunting ground for fossil collectors. Fossilized sea urchins can be found in the flints on the beach. It is incredible to think that some echinoids, sea urchins to people like us, are known to be between 425–500 million years old.

We were walking along the shore one evening, where the pebbles were still wet from the sea, and we found a cornelian. Amber used to be found in fairly large quantities in the Cromer area, but not so today. If you are to find any it is most likely to be where the shingle meets the sand, and in rock pools.

Our hotel for this part of our travels was **The Dagmar Hotel and Restaurant**, just 500 yards from the beach at **Cromer**. It is a well appointed and very well run hotel, specialising in good food, comfort and hospitality. All the twelve letting rooms are light and airy. Sufficiently spacious too, so that if you have need of a family room you will not feel cramped in any way. Each room has central heating, colour TV and tea/coffee making facilities. A very good English breakfast is served in the restaurant from 8am – 9am after which the restaurant, which is fully licensed, opens from 10.30am – 4pm for snacks and meals with a difference! Liv Pugh who owns the Dagmar is Norwegian, and on the menu you will find Norwegian dishes as well as English. You will enjoy the Smorgesbord — it is great. The restaurant opens for dinner from 7 pm – 11 pm, with last orders taken at 9.30 pm.

Cromer is a super place for a holiday, with excellent golf courses and wonderful wild life for bird watchers. People who love walking will be in their element. For your evening entertainment Cromer has the ever popular Pier Show, and one minute from the Dagmar is a club where hotel guests and their children are very welcome. They have live entertainment every evening.

The Shire Horse Centre

As you come into Cromer you pass a sign which says 'Gem of the North Norfolk Coast'. It is a gem, and brings many people back year after year. The town became fashionable as a seaside resort over one hundred and fifty years ago, and has retained its popularity ever since. It is not a big place, which probably contributes to its charm.

Cromer crabs are legendary throughout the country, and you will not have to look far before being able to tuck into a delicious feast. Fishing has declined in recent years but a good number of boats still sail out and bring back regular hauls of shellfish, sole, plaice, mackerel and much more.

Take a look at the lifeboat museum at the bottom of the gangway. Cromer is as famous for its lifeboatmen as it is for its crabs. You will find models and photographs there which make you realise the bravery of lifeboatmen of days gone by and of the present crews who use the modern lifeboat.

The Cromer Museum, housed in a late Victorian fisherman's cottage, will tell you more about the history of this area. There are displays of all kinds: history, geology and natural history.

In the centre of Cromer there is a fine church, St. Peter and St. Paul. You cannot miss it because it dominates this pleasant resort.

The nicest thing about staying in Cromer is that you can choose delightful places to visit, either to the east or the west, and know that at the end of the day you can return. We wandered extensively whilst we were here.

Just ten minutes from Cromer, on the Norwich Road, we spent a memorable day amongst lovely things and friendly people at **Alby Crafts**. The craft centre is housed in a large set of mellow brick and flint farm buildings, excellently restored and flanked by gardens which were being extended.

In the Alby Lace Museum we gazed at the best collection of lace we have ever seen outside London. Some of it was over 300 years old. We talked to Lesley Thomas who works in, and cares for, this museum. We watched bobbin lace being made, and had some of the intricacies explained to us. The speed and deftness of the nimble fingers enthralled us. You can buy handmade lace, books and lacemakers' requisites if you wish.

The **Charles Matts Furniture Showroom** was obviously a favourite haunt for visitors to Alby Crafts. There were a surprising variety of distinctive, imaginative and original designs. Local grown hardwoods: oak, elm, ash, wild cherry, yew and walnut are kiln dried and made into super furniture at their Thurgarton Workshop. Marianne Matts told us that clients come from far and wide to buy or commission furniture. Exhibitions are held regularly throughout the year, and there is bound to be something special for you to see. If there is not then we are sure you will be more than content to watch sculptors, stained glass designers, woodcarvers, glass engravers, a silversmith and a ceramics expert at work.

Taking the A149 west towards Sheringham you will come to **The Norfolk Shire Horse Centre and Countryside Collection**. It is majestic to watch the Shire Suffolks and other breeds of draft horses demonstrated working. You can see this twice daily at 11.15am and 3pm. We loved these gentle giants. There is much more to see. You will find a good picnic area there and a tearoom.

Dagmar Hotel and Restaurant

The Shire Horse Centre is also the home of the West Runton Riding Stables, which is open all the year round. The Riding School offers, for the novice or experienced rider, either riding instruction in a covered all-weather riding school, or accompanied rides through pleasant coastal countryside.

Sheringham is a delightful old seafaring village. Visitors here can still enjoy the delicious catches that fishermen bring in. A cluster of old cottages, some with lofts for mending nets, are reminders of the old ways of life, before the charming place became so popular with visitors. It is very neatly laid out, and has a splendid golf course along the cliffs. You can imagine how exhilarating a game of golf is here. The promenade is pleasant, and to the south the ground rises steeply to a stretch of beautiful heath and woodland. From the spot called, somewhat inadequately, 'Pretty Corner' there is a superb view of the countryside.

The old railway station has been taken over by the North Norfolk Railway Company, who have reopened the line to Weybourne. Two of the last steam engines to be run by British Rail in Norfolk are among their stock. The parish church of St. Aubyn and St. Wadling is not exciting, but the Roman Catholic church designed by Sir Gilbert Scott is well worth a visit.

Whilst we were wandering about the village which, more properly we suppose, should be called a town, we came across Ron, Joyce and Marianne Rose, three very friendly people who run **The Anser Guest House**, which is

Anser Guest House

well known for its welcoming atmosphere. It is just four minutes level walk from the sea at Sheringham. Open all the year round, it has central heating, hot and cold in all bedrooms, plus tea and coffee-making facilities. Guests have access to the house all day and are more than welcome to use the lounge for watching TV or just taking a rest.

The Rose family also run a restaurant and tea gardens, where you can have tea, coffee, light snacks and meals. Also vegan and vegetarian meals are available. Both restaurant and guest house are licensed.

Not content with running two excellent businesses, the Roses also own and run the **Kelling Cake Shop**, which was originally a Victorian dairy, and now sells super home-made cakes, pastries and pies. So you will be well fed in whichever establishment you are in. What is more you will be happy with the Roses we are sure.

If you take the little railway from Sheringham to **Weybourne** or go by car, you must visit **The Swiss Restaurant**. It is a text book example of a Norfolk thatched flint cottage and has been a restaurant for well over forty years. It is one of the best known and longest established restaurants in the region. Its reputation goes far beyond these boundaries. However if you live in the Highlands or deep in the West Country, even in London, Weybourne is not the most well known place, which is why we have included this very special restaurant in this book.

The white interior gives a feeling of a country restaurant with great log fires providing warmth in winter. Scrubbed tables match the wooden floors.

When David and Pam Robertson took over the business two years ago they changed the name omitting 'Gashes' in the title. Apart from that nothing has changed, except for a wider variety on the menu and wine list. Nigel Massingham has been its chef for 31 years, and that says a lot. His standards have always been high, and he has welcomed the arrival of David and Pam, who have allowed him to experiment a little more, but never losing excellence. One innovation has been the addition of an inexpensive and now very popular Cottage Menu from Tuesday to Saturday at lunchtime. For just under £5 you can have a simple, well prepared three course meal. Very good value indeed. In the evenings, again from Tuesday to Friday, there is a slightly more expensive Cottage menu for £9.95. If you want to indulge yourselves, then why not try Aubergine Viennoise followed by Roast Teal or perhaps Sweetbreads a la Creme — delicious!

The Swiss Restaurant

Weybourne is quite an interesting place, for Weybourne Hope, or Hoop as the beach is called, shelves so rapidly that it is possible to bring a large ship within a hundred yards of the shore, hence the local adage:

'He who would Old England Win,
Must At Weybourne Hoop begin.'

This was as true in 1588 as it was in 1914 and 1939. A map dated 1st May 1588 shows 'Waborne Fort' directly opposite Weybourne Hope with a salt marsh between it and the sea, and an earlier historical note credits the village with "possessing four ships and seventeen mariners." Further evidence of military activity in those days comes from an entry in the Holt Parish Register:

> "In this yeare was the town of Waborne fortified with a continuall garrison of men bothe of horse and foote with sconces (earthworks) ordinaunce and all manner of appoyntment to defend (prevent) the Spannyards landing theare. Sir William Xper Heydon (residing at Surlingham and Holt) has prime captaine with many other gent in order came with their companies."

Elaborate plans were drawn up to deter and contain any landing which might be attempted. In the event of local defences being overwhelmed, troops were to fall back to Norwich. A scorched-earth policy was to be implemented and the marshes were to be flooded. These were all measures which were held in reserve between 1939 and 1943, although additional steps were also taken in the Second World War, such as the mining of cliffs, beaches and selected inland sites. A few years before the Second World War the Camp was re-established as a heavy anti-aircraft temporary training site with all personnel accommodated in tents. Tremendous gales in the winter of 1936/37 destroyed much of the tentage (an eye-witness recalls tents and uniforms being blown out to sea) and prefabricated wooden huts, which were assembled on site by the soldiers, made the Camp more of a permanent feature of the landscape. The gunners were joined by RAF personnel who maintained the radio-controlled Tiger Moth targets (the Queen Bees) and girls of the ATS and WAAF manned the Predictors and Range-finders. Life in the Camp was described by some as a mixture of boredom and routine training, although others found it agreeable with social activities, including friendly boxing matches, between personnel and the younger local inhabitants.

The North Norfolk coast endured the frequent passage of enemy aircraft both on their way to and from inland targets, as well as 'tip-and-run' raids on Sheringham and Cromer. Weybourne itself was bombed only once when on 11 July 1940 a stick of five bombs (or was it fifteen?) landed in the main street, badly damaging two cottages, which were later rebuilt to form what is now The Swiss Restaurant.

After the war the Camp became the Anti-Aircraft Permanent Range and Radar Training Wing, providing training for national servicemen. Unfortunately the good relationships with the local people deteriorated and, whilst some were prepared to endure what one local newspaper called "misbehaviour and late night disturbances", others were not so tolerant. In May 1956 Cromer Urban District Council called upon the military authorities to impose a 10.30pm curfew on all troops from the Camp — but without success.

The last gun was fired on 2 October 1958, and the Camp closed in March the following year. The exact number of troops who were trained here is not known, but an educated guess puts the figure between 200,000 and 300,000. Another estimate puts the number of shells fired since 1938 at some one-and-a-half-million.

The future of the Camp was subject to much local speculation: ranging from marina and holiday camp to oil refinery, prison or nuclear power station, views not shared by Norfolk County Council, which insisted that the site be returned to agricultural use; this in fact is what has happened.

But the original NAAFI building remains, to house for posterity **The Muckleburgh Collection**, dedicated to the men and women who served here in all theatres of war, together with their vehicles, supplies and equipment.

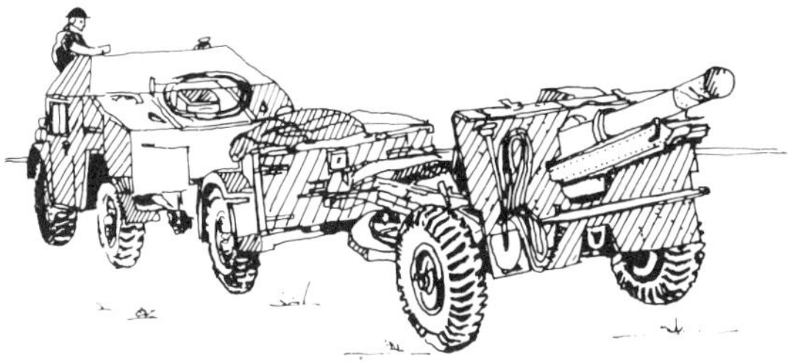

World War II Tank and Gun
The Muckleburgh Collection

The Collection, named after Muckleburgh Hill at the foot of which it stands, has been created by the founders of the Combined Operations Museum at Inverary in Scotland. The success of that project and the experience gained in its establishment, together with the purchase of a Bren-gun Carrier, a six pounder anti-tank gun and some Second World War vehicles from Tom Blyth of Foulsham in 1986, prompted the owner to open it to the public in May 1988. In less than two years the Collection has grown to include many tanks, armoured cars, pieces of artillery and military and 'home-front' artefacts, many of which have required complete restoration. The old NAAFI building itself needed complete restoration. This entailed the reconnection of water, electricity and drainage services, rebuilding the interior and reglazing all of the windows. Care has been taken to preserve original door-signs such as the 'Billiard Room', the 'Reading and Writing Room', the 'NCOs' Lounge', etc., and with its original exterior some of the wartime character is retained.

All of the heavy fighting tanks, armoured cars, and 'soft-skinned' lorries and amphibious vehicles on display are brought up to the highest standard of restoration, and are in complete running order. This work is done mainly on the premises and often entails a complete strip down and total rebuild.

Spare parts and workshop manuals on the vehicles and their engines are essential to success, but some of them are fifty years old. Consequently the search ranges far and wide beyond our coasts: to Holland, Luxembourg, France, Greece, the USA, Norway and even Australia. The vehicles themselves have been brought in from various parts of the United Kingdom, and from Canada, Holland and France; from the Falkland Islands, the Golan Heights and Vietnam and from behind the Iron Curtain. The 7′ 6″ Grizzley Bear mascot in the entrance hall? That came from Alaska over eighty years ago! The great majority of the exhibits are housed under cover approximately named display halls. Even such monsters as the Canadian Sherman, the Russian T34/85 tanks, the 'Honey' Stuart tank, and two French AMX13 need protection from the elements, as do the visitors to the Collection. Can you touch them and examine them at close range? Of course you can, although climbing is discouraged. Remember, they are all 'runners' and accidents must be avoided.

The 'Billiards Room' features a central diorama depicting a typical camp layout, in which several of the model vehicles and armaments are complementary to those in the main collection. A variety of photographs of Weybourne over the centuries, with special reference to the Camp's military role, are displayed also.

Aircraft Exhibit from The Muckleburgh Collection

The record of Weybourne would be incomplete without mention of the Bolding/Monement family who, at the turn of the century, were the largest landowners in the Parish, and whose family home has now become The Maltings Hotel. W. J. J. Bolding was one of Britain's earliest photographers, and examples of his work on village life in the 1880s are on display; probably the only public exhibition of these early photographs. To bring the exhibition up to the present Dr. Moss Taylor, in charge of the private bird sanctuary, displays some of his latest photographs of bird life in the camp and its surrounding area.

Now in its second year The Muckleburgh Collection has greatly extended its display area, with an increased number of exhibits and facilities. With free parking for cars and coaches, a 'NAAFI-type' tea-room with covered and picnic seating, an attractive souvenir shop, and for the energetic youngster an adventure 'assault course', this is a visit for all the family.

The priory of Weybourne was an Augustinian house which was dependant on the bigger priory at Westacre. The Augustinians extended the old Saxon parish church, the tower of which survives to the north of the chancel of the church of All Saints, which is mainly 15th century. It has a beautiful porch and a fine Jacobean pulpit.

Back in Sheringham you will find the delightful Little Theatre, where shows and plays are staged throughout the summer. If you are in Sheringham in August there is a wonderful, traditional fair which comes to Beeston Common. This is something you should not miss.

To the south is **Upper Sheringham**, which used to be a farming village. The 14th century church is quite beautiful. Near to the church is Upper Sheringham Park, an area of outstanding beauty. It is famous for its rhododendrons and fine trees; the former are at their best during late June and early July. The gardens are private but are open to the public on certain days during this period.

Quite by chance we picked up a leaflet that told us about **Cockthorpe Hall** in the small village of Cockthorpe just off the coast road at Stiffkey. Cockthorpe Hall is the home of a wonderful Toy Museum. The Hall is 16th century and charming in its own right. Inside, the cabinets were filled with hundreds of brightly coloured toys of bygone days. There were cars, planes, boats, animals and a whole range of novelty toys. A children's paradise. We loved it.

The village was of interest to us as well because we found it was the birthplace of Admiral Sir Cloudesley Shovel, whose ship sank off the Scillies in 1707, and about which we wrote in our Devon and Cornwall Hidden Places. In the village church of All Saints we found a fine monument to Sir James Calthorpe and his wife Barbara who 'was much comforted by the sight of 193 of her children and their offspring at the age of 86 years'. Imagine buying Christmas presents for that lot!

At the top of Letheringsett Hill near Holt, there is an extraordinary milestone, topped by a pineapple of all things. There seems to be no reason at all for choosing this fruit. We could not find out anything about it, although as usual we were not backward in asking questions! Holt is worth taking a look at. It is an attractive market town with fine Georgian houses, dating from the time that Holt was rebuilt after a fire in 1708. At one end of the pretty main street there is a Methodist Church built in 1862 and, at the other end, the parish church of St. Andrews, which was gutted by the fire of 1708. You can still see traces of that fire in the discolouring of many of the pillars. The church has some very good glass by Kempe in the aisle windows, and by Heasman in the east windows. There is a fine consecration cross in the south aisle.

Between Blakeney and Holt you will find **The Langham Glass House**. It is set in a large, beautiful Norfolk barn, pan-tiled and flint faced. You can watch a team of glassmakers working with molten glass from the furnace, using blowing irons and hand tools, in a way traditional for hundreds of years. There is a viewing area from which the glass-making can be watched at close quarters. The well-stocked shop sells all the glass made and many other good quality gifts. The Tea Room serves home-made food and has a table licence.

Having travelled a little on the **North Norfolk Railway** and enjoyed it very much, we decided it was time to find out a bit more about the company's history and future plans. At one time 64 trains a day used to stop at Sheringham station, but gradually that ceased, and with the closure of the former Midland and Great Northern Joint Railway station in 1967 it seemed to signal the end of a railway era for Sheringham. But much of the character, if not the full glory of the station, has been returned by the effort and enthusiasm of the M & GN Preservation Society, and subsequently the North Norfolk Railway Company. The Society had already bought the section of track from Weybourne, as far as the Sheringham boundary, when the Melton Constable to Sheringham line closed in 1964, and in 1967 it took the opportunity of leasing the now unused station.

The North Norfolk Railway

In 1963, even before the line closed, the Society formed a private company, now the Norfolk Railway Company. This enabled the Society to apply for a Light Railway Order, so allowing fare-paying passengers to travel the railway. In 1973 this order was granted, and the first passengers were carried in 1975.

The company today runs steam locomotives between Sheringham and Weybourne, and diesel railbuses a little further to Kelling Holt. Their ultimate aim is to re-open the station at nearby Holt. The railway opens between May and October, running a regular timetabled service.

They have fun runs too, to celebrate special occasions like Halloween and the Santa Claus Special.

Whether you are railway enthusiasts or not, you will enjoy the collection of railway memorabilia and the souvenir shop at the station. The station master told us that the Company welcome volunteer railway enthusiasts to help restore and maintain the railway and its stock. So now is your chance. Just ring Sheringham 822045 for the details.

For one Sunday afternoon in August each year, Sheringham is invaded by a flotilla of rafts with enthusiastic crews, eager to take part in what is arguably the country's top raft race. If you know of one as good or better, let us know.

The present contest has developed from one of the many activities held during Carnival Week. It normally attracts well over fifty crafts from all over the country.

The sight of Sheringham's West Promenade on Raft Race Day is one not to be missed. The beach is ablaze with colour and awash with activity. The cheerful summer crowds mingle with the crews, many of whom wear elaborate fancy dress. The rafts come in all shapes and sizes. In recent years the beach has played host to paddle steamers, huge floating tyre barrels and even a scale replica of a space shuttle.

As well as trophies for the class winners, prizes are awarded for the best dressed crews and most original craft.

Various entries ready on the morning of the Raft Race

One of the finest acquisitions ever made by the National Trust was **Sheringham Hall** in 1986. It is an elegant early nineteenth century villa built by Humphrie Repton. On his own admission Sheringham Hall is his masterpiece. In the Red Book (Repton's original book of plans and drawings of the Hall) he states that Sheringham Hall is "such a specimen of my art as I never had before the opportunity of displaying". He goes on to say, "This may be considered my most favourite therefore I may say of it 'exeg monumentum' ". Since their design the Hall and the Park have not been significantly altered, therefore they demonstrate what Humphrey Repton, one of this country's greatest ever building and landscape architects, considered to be the ideal country estate.

Its purchase by the National Trust has ensured that it will remain as an example of classic British architecture for future generations. The Trust aims to replant dying trees in the park, following the plans contained in the Red Book, so retaining its original character. An appeal has been launched to finance projects on the estate. The Trust plan to build a boarded walkway for those in wheelchairs; something we applaud. They also want to build viewing platforms, as recommended by Repton, to enable visitors to enjoy the spectacular views.

The park is open from sunrise to sunset with limited parking for cars near the south entrance off the main Cromer/Holt road. The Hall is open by appointment only.

Further information concerning the future of Sheringham Hall can be obtained from the East Anglia Regional Office of the National Trust at Blickling, Norwich, telephone Aylsham (0263) 733471. Donations to this appeal, which will be much appreciated, can also be sent to the above address.

Sheringham Hall

For sixty-eight years Sheringham was one of the few coastal towns in Britain that could boast two lifeboats: one private boat, and one sponsored by the R.N.L.I.

Today she still houses two lifeboats. The R.N.L.I.'s *Manchester Unity of Oddfellows* stands ready to rescue any unfortunate fishermen or sailors in difficulty off the Norfolk Coast. The other, the *Henry Ramey Upcher,* lies safe in her boathouse, lovingly preserved as a reminder of Sheringham's long seafaring history. The *Henry Ramey Upcher* patrolled the waters off Sheringham from 1894 until 1935, saving over 200 lives without the loss of a single lifeboatman. A fine record.

Sheringham has a motto on its coat of arms. What it says is true. 'MARE DITAT PINUSQUE DECORAT' — The sea enriches and the pine adorns.

Having spent so much time west of Cromer now let us take you to the east.

First however let us introduce you to a rare treat, a visit to **The Dolphin Free House and Restaurant** just opposite the pier at Jetty Cliff. There is no other way of describing The Dolphin except to say that it is delightful. This 17th century building has been skillfully modernised without losing its charm. It has eight marvellous bay windows, which look over the sea and the pier from which the village gets its name.

At Jetty Pier you can have that rare and magical experience of watching the sun rise and set over the sea. If this is something you have never experienced come to The Dolphin and watch. It is an awe-inspiring sight.

Apart from being an extremely good pub, Ron and Margaret Cooke run a first class restaurant. It has a full a la carte menu, but in this area it would be very foolish not to cash in on the fruits of the sea! The fish is superb, in fact all the seafood is, and the dish of the day is always the fisherman's catch. The restaurant will seat 120 people comfortably. Choose your starter from king prawns or whitebait, paté or Cromer crab, amongst other dishes. Your main course could be a Shellfish Platter of scampi, langoustines, crab claws, and half a crawfish tail, served in either garlic and parsley or herb butter. We had one of the best grilled Dover soles we had ever tasted, with parsley butter. Sometimes there is turbot on the menu or fresh lobster. Whatever you choose it will be served with a fresh vegetable of the day, saute potatoes and a crisp, seasonal salad.

It is not cheap but it is worth every penny you choose to spend. The wine list is well chosen and will not hurt your pocket.

Dolphin Free House and Restaurant

Walks in the area are plentiful but we particularly enjoyed one over the cliffs to Overstrand, and then on to Sidestrand. There are also walks to the lighthouse and the Roman camp that are thoroughly enjoyable.

Felbrigg Hall, just south of Cromer is a pleasant outing. It has a beautiful park, possibly landscaped by Repton, which is overlooked by the south front of the Hall. 1620 is approximately the date of the Hall but a western wing was added in 1686, the work of William Samwell, an architect from Watton who also built a house for Charles II at Newmarket. The estate was left to the National Trust in 1969. There is a fine collection of pictures and original 18th century furniture. Outside the traditional walled garden is a gem, complimented by the orangery with camellias. The park has a lake and there are a number of woodland walks.

Felbrigg Hall

Further down the road is Blickling Hall, a magnificent Jacobean red brick mansion. Its most special room is the 123ft Long Gallery, which now houses a library of over 12,000 volumes. The garden is especially beautiful with colour in every season of the year.

On our last evening in Cromer we went to the little village of **Sea Pelling** which has a 17th century pub, **The Hall Inn**, which originally was the village hall. It was converted some years ago into this very charming pub complete with oak beams. There are two marvellous inglenooks, and super open fires which burn those large logs that throw out warmth, and lend an atmosphere to the inn. There is something very welcoming and homely about the whole place.

The Hall Inn

The restaurant serves a wide range of dishes at very realistic prices from steaks to roast duck and local fish. There are six letting rooms with plans to convert them to en-suite, if you would like to stay in this quiet and peaceful place which is not in the least commercialised. The beer garden is a pleasure to sit in, and you need have no fear of difficulty in parking; the car park is large.

Mr. and Mrs. Baldwin run the Hall Inn. Mrs. Baldwin does the cooking herself and Mr. Baldwin looks after the beer! Both do their jobs admirably.

The Baldwins have one permanent guest, a ghost known as the Grey Lady. They believe she was a resident many years ago. We asked why she does not go away and the Baldwins said they thought it was because she did not approve of the change, but we are not so sure; The Hall Inn is a very nice place to be, and maybe she would rather stay for that reason.

We left Cromer to stay in **Southrepps** just off the A149. If you want a good guest house to stay in this area then you will find, as we did, that **Church Farm Guest House** at 20 Church Street is comfortable and very good value. Bed, breakfast and an excellent evening meal will cost just £14 per night. Apart from the warm welcome you will get from Mr. and Mrs. Codling, you will find this listed building has comfortable bedrooms, all

Church Farm Guest House

with hot and cold water, electric blankets and tea and coffee making facilities. Children are very welcome and you can have a special high tea for them if you wish. The food, as you might suppose from a farm house, is home cooked and fresh garden produce is a speciality.

The Codlings also have three self-catering cottages with the delightful names of Rose, Lilac and Honeysuckle.

Lilac and Honeysuckle cottage are both just across the road from Church Farm Guest House and sleep six to ten people respectively, whilst Rose Cottage, which is in the grounds of Church Farm, sleeps seven and is especially suitable for the physically handicapped, with a ramp for wheelchairs. They are all nicely furnished and offer every facility including automatic washing machines. Each cottage has access to the children's play area with its climbing frame, swing, slide and trampoline. There is plenty of parking space. At certain times of the year fresh garden produce and 'pick your own fruit' are available for sale. Just ring Mr. or Mrs. Codling on (0263) 79248 if you think one of these cottages would suit you.

In addition to the guest house and the cottages, the Codlings have a small 'Hideaway' caravan and camping site with just simple facilities like toilets and a tap.

We found that whatever is your choice you will be well catered for.

It is only about four miles from Southrepps to **Mundesley**, with its superb sandy beach. It is a quiet, friendly place, ideal for a family holiday. It is totally unspoilt but it is not lacking in facilities. There is excellent provision for campers and caravanners. The nine hole golf course gives visitors a lot of enjoyment. You can go bowling or fishing, and enjoy the safe bathing for all the family. The ebbing tide leaves lots of shallow pools which the children will love. These pools are known locally as 'lowies', a term we had not heard before. Keen fishermen use the beach between Mundesley and Trimingham to catch cod, Dover soles, eels or skate.

The beaches seem endless, to the north lies Trimingham and just beyond that is the solitude of Sidestrand. The tiny resort of Overstrand is always a delight to visitors seeing it for the first time.

To the south lies Bacton and Happisburgh, pronounced 'Hayzbrough', a marvellous place for beachcombing. Even in the height of the season you can frequently find stretches of almost deserted sand.

We found **North Walsham** an easy run from Southrepps. Although not strictly part of Broadlands, the towns of Aylsham and North Walsham lie on its northern borders and have some connection with it. The River Bure passes through Aylsham, and at one time there was traffic by river to and from the dock on the Banningham Road. North Walsham used to be connected with Barton Broad by the North Walsham and Dilham Canal, but the canal has been derelict for some years although there are plans to restore it for pleasure traffic, something that seems to be happening in canals and waterways throughout Great Britain, thank goodness. We recently enjoyed talking to the Kennet and Avon Canal Trust who operate the Canal from Bristol to Reading. The canals are so enjoyable, either for water travel or for wandering along the tow paths watching the wildlife. We hope very much that this trend will continue, and that when we write about Norfolk again in two years' time this canal will be in full use.

North Walsham is the market town for Mundesley, Bacton and Happisburgh and the northern part of the broads. It is the centre of the Norfolk reed thatching industry, and skilled thatchers with lorries piled high with bundles of reeds often travel for hundreds of miles to thatch houses. Norfolk reed is the most durable material for the purpose. Norfolk thatching is not so decorative as, say, the straw thatching of Wiltshire, but it lasts a great deal longer. The reeds also used to be laid under the tiles of houses in East Anglia as a form of insulation. You learn something new all the time, do you not?

St. Nicholas in Market Street has a craggy ruined tower, which forms a picturesque accompaniment to the lofty, restored mediæval church. The 14th century porch is decorated with fine flushwork panelling and shields.

Sir William Paston, a member of the family from which the famous Paston Letters issued, figures on a spectacular monument of his own design. He is propped up on an elbow looking out. A pelican presides over the tall, perpendicular font cover. The Communion table is one of the most curious we have ever seen. At the back of the church, houses and gardens snuggle up to its walls. Close by is the market place which on Thursdays is absolutely teeming with people. In the market place there is an interesting cross built of timber, with a lead covered domed roof and lantern which dates from 1602. Horatio Nelson was a pupil at the Paston Grammar School. The school has a building which dates from 1765.

St. Nicholas' Church

There is a pretty road from North Walsham to Norwich which passes through Westwick Park with its lake and masses of rhododendrons. Not much further along, a turning leads to **Worstead**, which gave its name to the renowned worsted cloth. It is little more than a village today, with a square flanked by Georgian and Queen Anne houses.

In Mediæval times it was a bustling industrial town. The former prosperity is reflected in the beautiful church of St. Mary, which was built sometime between 1379 and 1450. The chancel screen has a dado which is remarkable, with the paintings of 16 saints, and in front there is a brass to John Alblastyr, who donated the screen before his death in 1520. There is a fine hammerbeam roof. Box pews with intricate carvings and a traceried font made this church very worthwhile visiting.

The brilliant colours of the flowers in the hanging baskets outside **The Weavers Arms** at **Swanton Abbott**, a very pretty pub, attracted us. It is run by Carol and Gary Smith who told us something of the pub's long history. It was built in the 17th century as a social club for Dutch weavers, hence its name. It has been used for many purposes in its lifetime and you can see some of its history about the pub now. There are some splendid stone fireplaces. There are strong oak beams, and lots of old farm implements hanging on the walls and in the alcoves.

Garry Smith pulls a fine pint of real ale, whilst Carol produces delicious home-cooked dishes in the restaurant. The a la carte menu is not extensive but well selected, and vegetarians are well catered for. Seasonal specials are very popular with the locals and visitors alike! Sunday lunches are good traditional fare and very popular. There is also a take-away food service.

Children are not forgotten. There is a children's room and in good weather there is a safe enclosed play area. A children's menu is also provided. It was nice to see that mothers with small babies were given thought: a baby changing facility is available; quite a rarity in pubs.

Families are obviously very welcome here and whether you go inside the pub or sit in the beer garden watching farm animals, and birds in the aviary, you cannot fail to enjoy yourselves. The pub is open from 11 am – 11 pm so there is no rush.

As we left we were amused to see there were special horse stops, something town dwellers like ourselves seldom see.

It was time for us to leave this part of Norfolk, but we wanted to tell you a bit about the incredible feeling you get as you travel the coastline in the northern part of the county. Our first introduction to the North Norfolk coast was on a dark night. The headlights of the car lit up the quiet village streets as we passed through. It was eerie, yet we woke to a county of great beauty, bustling with life both human and wild! We woke to the strangeness of towns like Wells-next-the-sea, whose name is a complete misnomer. Its harbour is over a mile from the coast at high tide and a good deal more than twice the distance from the sea when the tide is low. We woke to the complete silence of Sidestrand. We saw where Overstrand is fighting a losing battle with the sea; one by one its houses fall over the tall cliff. We woke to the sounds of some of the finest bird sanctuaries in the world. It is lovely, it is wild, it is mysterious and magical, and we would come back time and time again and always find more to delight us.

The Weavers Arms

King's Lynn & West Norfolk

Customs House, King's Lynn

Area covered in Chapter 3

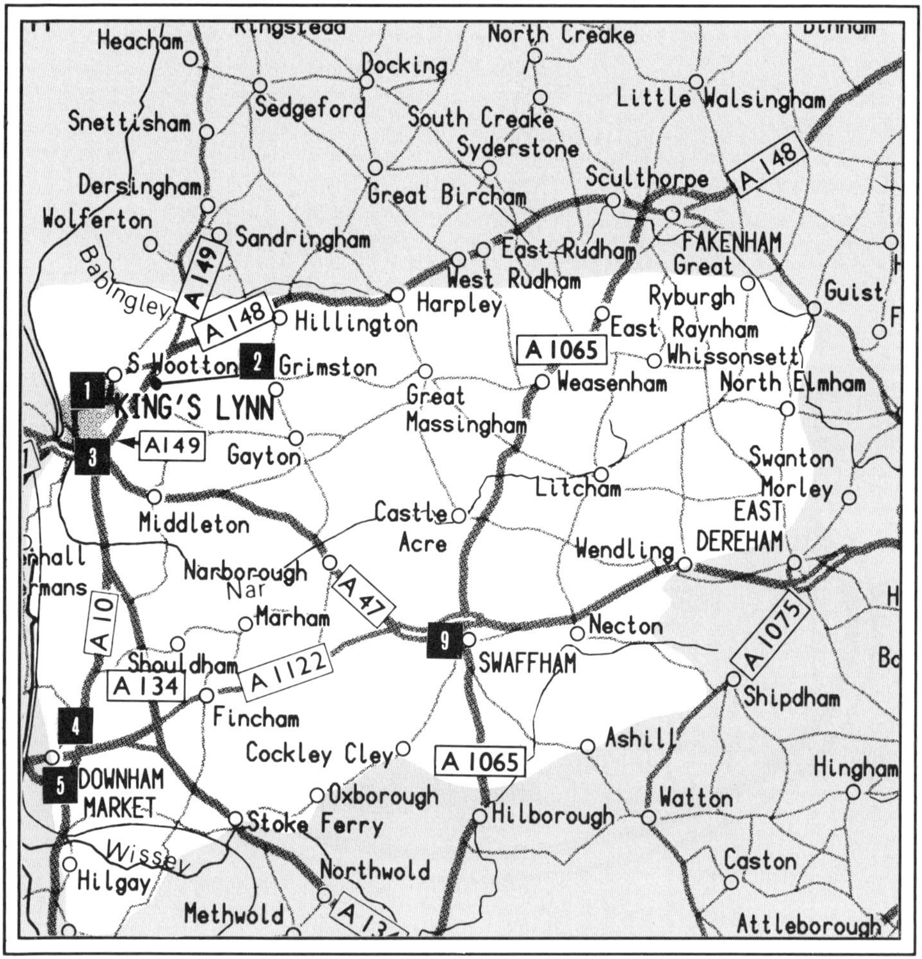

1 The Bankhouse *(King's Lynn)*
2 The Ship Inn *(Gaywood)*
3 The Bear Restaurant *(King's Lynn)*
4 The Chequers *(Wimbotsham)*
5 The Crown Hotel *(Downham Market)*
5 The Rose and Crown *(Downham Market)*
5 Daymond Services *(Downham Market)*
5 Dial House *(Downham Market)*
9 The Norfolk Hero *(Swaffham)*

CHAPTER 3

King's Lynn and West Norfolk

King's Lynn, at the southern end of The Wash, is the third largest town in Norfolk and, after Norwich, has to be the fastest growing. It is an interesting and attractive place, full of contrasts. The passing motorist tends to believe it has nothing to offer but industrial estates, cemeteries and factories. For that is what you see if approached from the A10 or the A47. Do not be put off, you will find it delightful.

This ancient town and sea port is the natural centre for the western half of Norfolk and the Marshland, and for centuries was the gateway to the Midlands for commerce with the Continent.

Once King's Lynn was known as Lynn Episcopi: Bishop's Lynn, but under a charter granted by Henry VIII the name was changed to King's Lynn. King John had granted the town an earlier charter when he visited the town in 1205. He stayed again in 1216, before his journey to Newark where he died. It was on this journey that he lost his baggage in The Wash. Treasure hunters have been searching for it ever since.

We had not booked in at an hotel for our visit here. Unusual for us, but it turned out successfully. In King Staithe Square we discovered **The Bankhouse**.

"Welcome to the Bankhouse" were the first words we heard as we entered this entrancing restaurant. Fred and Jenny Hackworth told us about themselves over a drink, and offered us a bedroom in the limited but very pleasant accommodation available, which we readily accepted. Fred and Jenny are newcomers to The Bankhouse, having acquired it in 1988, although it has been a restaurant for ten years. It is an independently-run establishment, which they operate with a philosophy that good food, drink and accommodation should be offered at prices that do not require a second mortgage. They believe that service should be informal and friendly, and that you, the customer, are there to enjoy yourself. A philosophy that quite obviously works. The atmosphere is marvellous and the food excellent. Fresh food is bought locally and delivered daily. The fish, which was particularly good, comes from Albert Balls (what a wonderful name). Succulent steaks are purchased from Sawyers in St. James Street. Fruit and vegetables come from E. C. Cook at Terrington St. John.

All the dishes are prepared on the premises and every member of staff, from the most junior to the Hackworths themselves, works to ensure you enjoy your meal and come back again.

In addition to the restaurant, we found that The Bankhouse was a Free House serving Real Ales. They have a pleasant beer garden, which on a warm day is a very attractive place to have a drink and a bar snack, if you feel so inclined. Children are made welcome and the ones we saw seemed to enjoy themselves.

We were taken on a conducted tour of this old building. It was originally a Bank, hence its name. Built for Messrs. Guerney and Creswell in 1782, you can see a statue of the reigning monarch of that time, George III, up above the window over the front door. It later became Barclays. The house that was attached to the Bank was built in several stages, and was at one time two residences. The restaurant was originally the old kitchen, hence the large old cooking range that remains there. The cellars beneath, which were originally used for wine storage, are even older than the Bank, going back five hundred years. You are welcome to explore them after your meal.

One of the Cresswells of Guerney and Cresswell was the explorer, Samuel Guerney Cresswell, who was the first man to bring England the news of the discovery of the North West Passage.

We stayed several days and loved it. Do visit The Bankhouse yourselves. We promise you will enjoy the experience.

The Bankhouse

If you hear or read about King's Lynn, you will get conflicting views. We read that King's Lynn is not a pretty town; on all but the sunniest of days much of its brickwork is sombre, and too many of its streets are disfigured by shabby and neglected buildings and patches of derelict land. We would say to you that beauty is in the eye of the beholder and, thanks to the exertions of the King's Lynn Preservation Trust, many of the buildings of the town have been saved. We believe this lovely Georgian brick town rewards exploration. Be sure you see the 17th century Customs House on the banks of the Purfleet. It was built in 1683 as an Exchange by the Lynn merchant Henry Bell, who was twice mayor and an architect of some note. He seems to have played a major part in the building of Northampton after the fire of 1675, and in Lynn he was responsible for The Duke's Head Hotel, and the now vanished market cross of which prints can be seen in the town's museum.

The chequered patterned Guildhall built in 1421 is still much used. It is a fine sight to see the light shining out of the huge 15th century windows at night, when there is a civic function. Inside, the stone 15th century hall leads to the Georgian Assembly Rooms and Card Room. The mediæval undercroft has a display of regalia and plate, which includes the exquisite King John Cup decorated with lords and ladies engaged in courtly pursuits. Next to the Guildhall is the former goal, with festooned chains over the door, built by William Tuck of Lynn in 1784. Mediæval St. George's Guildhall in King Street, once a theatre where Shakespeare is said to have acted, became a warehouse for many years but, thanks to the vision and generosity of the late Alec Penrose, it is a theatre again, and the centre of the King's Lynn Festival. Warehouses behind have been skilfully converted into galleries and a restaurant overlooking the river. Next door a fine stone-fronted house is used as a museum of social history.

The church of St. Nicholas in St. Anne Street was built at the beginning of the 15th century. The long perpendicular church has a 13th century tower, with a charming Victorian lead spira. The south porch is superb. It is like a magnificent stone fanfare of niches and panelling, taken up in wood in the nave's angel roof. We found Robinson Crusoe's grave there.

Have we done enough to persuade you that King's Lynn is more than worthy of a visit? Good. Then you can reward yourselves by calling in at **The Ship Inn, Gaywood**.

When the circus comes to town at King's Lynn, its home is the five acres of land alongside The Ship Inn, which is a busy, happy pub. Sometimes you will find fairs there as well and, in between, the pleasant rural sight of horses and cattle grazing.

The Ship Inn

No one seems to know quite how old the pub is but, as the locals told us, it has been a pub for as long as anyone can remember. There is a large bar and a pool room, laid out to give the effect of having three levels. You can get very good bar food, with delicious baked potatoes from 75p and other dishes like gammon steaks for as little as £3.00.

The pub has its own bowling green, and the locals are very keen on sports of all kinds. They play regularly against other pubs at cricket, pool, crib and bowls of course.

On a nice day you can sit outside and enjoy the aviary, with ducks, canaries, budgies and finches. The children always love this, but if the weather is not good enough they are allowed in the top deck area of the pub.

Mr. and Mrs. Reynolds, mine hosts, told us the pub has no claim to fame, but we felt the warmth and fun the pub generated was a claim to fame in its own right.

A visit to the **Caithness Crystal Factory** is informative, and a pleasant way of spending an afternoon. There are conducted tours which allow you to view glassmaking at close quarters. You will find a display of glass-making tools and moulds, and each step of the way the trained guides will give you introductory talks on each process. There is a resident engraver who will personalize any piece of glass you choose to buy. A friendly tea room serves home-made scones, cakes, sandwiches, cream teas, tea, coffee and soft drinks.

In the factory shop you will frequently find some super bargains. The Caithness Factory is on the Hardwick Industrial Estate, on the southern outskirts of the town, and has ample parking space.

Forty years ago the King's Lynn Festival was founded by The Princess of Wales' grandmother Ruth, Lady Fermoy. Sadly this excellent festival lost her services last year, after some unpleasant arguments which left much bitterness. At the same time she asked for her name to be removed from The Fermoy Centre, in King Street, the home of music, theatre, dance and much more. This centre nonetheless continues, and brings the town continuous entertainment. The Fermoy Centre has the Crofters Coffee House and Theatre Bar for coffee time, lunch and tea, a pre-performance drink or snack, and of course an interval drink. The Riverside Rooms provide special pre-theatre suppers at reasonable prices.

If you are interested in joining the ranks of the Friends of the Fermoy, which will entitle you to many discounts and privileges, do write to the Membership Secretary at the centre, who will be delighted to give you the information you seek.

We were glad to read in the *Sunday Express* that Lady Fermoy has decided not to deprive Norfolk of her energies in the field of music. This charismatic lady who is a Woman of the Bedchamber to the Queen Mother has quietly, over the last six months, raised support for a new arts festival 'Music in Country Churches', using artists of international renown. It will be launched in late May at the church of St. Peter and St. Paul at Salle, near Reepham. Prince Charles has agreed to become patron, and also to grace in person the second concert, at which the famous Sixteen Choir and Orchestra will perform.

How lovely to listen to music in some of Norfolk's lovely churches. **Salle**, where the first concert is to be held, is ten miles north east of East Dereham, off the B1145. The church is marvellous. It was built on a grand scale in the 15th century by local magnates, including the Boleyns. Rich ornamentation adorns the tower. There are fine turreted two-storey porches, an angel-studded nave roof and bosses with Biblical scenes on the boarded chancel roof. There is wonderful carving everywhere: on the stalls, faces and flowers on the misericords, poppy heads on the bench ends. The church still has mediæval stained glass. The Seven Sacraments font has an amazing 12ft. cover complete with pulley.

There is a perpendicular pulpit, with Jacobean extensions. The 15th century brasses are superb. Can you visualise what a perfect setting this will be for a concert?

Now for something quite different. **The African Violet Centre** at **Terrington St. Clement**, just 3½ miles out of King's Lynn on the A17. It is a nursery unique in Britain, specialising solely in the production of African violets. Its half acre of greenhouses contain a colourful and extensive collection of the most popular houseplants. The centre was founded in 1970

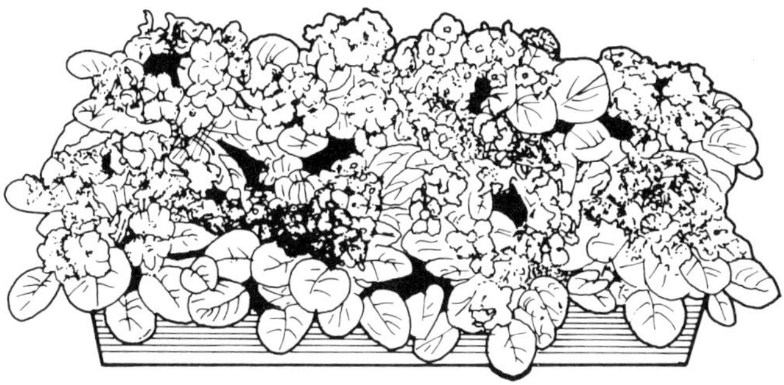

Some of the 5,000 plants to be seen at the African Violet Centre!

by author and broadcaster, the Reverend Tony Clements. A Chelsea Flower Show exhibitor since 1979, he was awarded the coveted Gold Medal of the Royal Horticultural Society in 1987.

Each year some quarter of a million African violets are grown at the Centre, in a wide range of colour and type. In addition to singles and doubles, bi-colours and frillies, there are tiny micro miniatures, and trailing violets for hanging baskets. The plant breeding programme ensures a constant stream of new varieties. These may be seen, and purchased, at Terrington, and also at the principal flower shows throughout Britain, from the Royal Cornwall Show in the far south west to the Highland Show in Edinburgh.

In the Show House, selected plants are prepared for exhibitions at flower shows throughout the summer season. During 1987 Tony Clements received 20 Gold Medal awards. In the Show House you can see a preview of this year's display and make your own judgement on their medal prospects!

Also set for your interest and information are demonstrations of seed sowing, micro propagation and leaf propagation. So that visitors may appreciate the wide range of African violets available, there is a selected display across the entire range of named varieties. This includes original wild violets from Tanzania in East Africa.

The Propagation House has 100,000 plants in all stages of growth: tiny plantlets from sterile tubs being weaned from agar to compost under polythene covers; sturdy young plants ready for potting-on and, in the final stages, healthy violets coming into bud and bloom.

In the Finishing House there are 5,000 African violets in the final stages of growth, coming into bud and bloom. You can choose you own plants from here, but if you are in any way like us you will not know what to choose, the colours and the choice are bewitching. Any one will bring colour and beauty into your home, and be a source of delight and pleasure.

You can see this colourful spectacle from 9.00 am – 4.30 pm Monday to Friday and 11.00 am – 5.00 pm on Saturdays, Sundays or Bank Holidays.

For those of you who love shopping you will find the pedestrianised centre excellent. There are some fine shops and of course the weekly markets. See if you can find a local delicacy called samphire in one of the many restaurants. It is a seaweed boiled and served like asparagus.

To go to King's Lynn without looking at **St. Margaret's Church** would be sad. It dated back in part to the 12th century. The lower parts of the western towers date back to that century. It was founded by Bishop Herbert de Losinga, the first Bishop of Norwich. The remainder of the building belongs to different periods; the strange impression given by the interior of the nave is due to the fact that the gothic arcades were built in 1745–6. The church has two of the largest and most famous brasses in England, both of Flemish workmanship. One dedicated to Adam de Walsokene and his wife is dated 1349. It has a scene at the bottom showing corn being carried to a post mill. The other commemorates Robert Braunch who died in 1364.

Marks left by flood water show on the lower part of the west towers. The most recent inundation was in 1953, when the whole of the east coast was affected. A tremendous gale coincided with a high tide and raised the level of water in the North Sea to an abnormal height. It was horrendous, and damage was done from Yorkshire right down to the mouth of the Thames. It proves how tough buildings were in the 12th century, for it is the lower part of the 12th century towers that show the flood marks of 1953 and those of previous notable floods.

Doctor Charles Burey was at one time the organist at St. Margaret's. The organ he played, built by Snetzler in 1754, is still in use. He had six clever children, one of whom was James, who was third in command of the Resolution when Captain Cook was murdered by natives and his second command died, leaving James to bring the Resolution back to England. One of his daughters, Fanny, is famous as the first really notable English woman novelist. Her novel Evelina is a classic, and her diary tells much of life at court in the reign of George III, when Fanny was keeper of the Robes to Queen Charlotte. There is a poignant description of the King during his dreadful illness. Fanny Burney married a French emigre, General D'Arblay, and the diary continues in a French setting, and includes a description of Brussels during the battle of Waterloo.

It is interesting to note that George Vancouver, another King's Lynn man, who gave his name to the city in British Colombia, was a midshipman in the Resolution when Captain Burney brought her back to England.

King's Lynn was the only town to be besieged in the Civil War, which might surprise you, but in view of its strategic position it makes sense. It is the gateway to Norfolk from the north and the west, as well as from the sea.

After a day spent sightseeing we decided that a visit to **The Bear Restaurant** would be a means of recharging our batteries before we set off for Sandringham the next day.

The Bear, in Norfolk Street, is one of those restaurants where you can dine at leisure. No one is going to ask you to leave as soon as you have finished eating. Just the place to be after an exhausting day. It is quite a small restaurant, with covers for a maximum of 54. There are candles on the tables, and some gentle piano playing in the background.

The Bear Restaurant

The menu is extensive from traditional English to gourmet French. They specialise in local fish and shellfish, which you can have simply served or with delicate, delicious sauces. If you have a vegetarian with you it would be advisable to say so when you book your table, to make sure that a suitable menu is produced. While you are booking ask if they are having a special evening. Normally once a week there is either cabaret, jazz or country and western music.

If you enjoy wine, you will be delighted with the care that has been taken in selecting a sizeable wine list. They have a very good St. Joseph 1986 at £11.00, and a 1985 merlot at £9.95. The house wine at £6.50 a carafe is excellent value.

The Bear was once a chapel, and was converted some four years ago into this intimate restaurant. It is family run and, perhaps in keeping with the chapel image, it is run on very high standards.

At lunch-time you can just pop in for a quick snack or take time over a leisurely lunch. In the evening there is only one sitting. Lunch is from 11.30 am – 2.00 pm Monday to Saturday and Dinner 7.30 pm – 10.00 pm from Tuesday to Saturday.

Sandringham is just eight miles from King's Lynn, and no one could come to this part of Norfolk without taking a look at one of the Royal Family's favourite homes. It has been the private residence of the Monarch since the estate was bought by King Edward VII when he was Prince of Wales. With a front that is 150 yards long, the house replaces an older building that burned down. The present house was built in 1869–71 and stands on a 20,000 acre estate that takes in seven villages.

Kings have died here. Princess Diana was born on the estate when her father, Earl Spencer, was an equerry. Sandringham is open from April to September, when the Royal Family are not in residence.

Sandringham

"Dear old Sandringham, the place that I love better than anywhere else in the world", wrote King George V who had known it for as long as he could remember and for whom it was above all home. King George VI's affection for it was no less keen. "I have always been so happy here", he wrote to Queen Mary. King Edward VII, its first royal occupant, made it a glittering centre of society during the forty-nine years he owned it, and transformed the shooting into some of the finest in the country.

The grounds of Sandringham are entered by an oak door set in the perimeter wall, and the recommended route follows the gravel path which leads to the shrubberies. Most of the plants and shrubs are named, and bear the date of planting. Opposite the heather bed by the wall are the camellias, and this area also contains a variety of other shrubs such as cornus, hydrangea, sorbus, cotoneaster and philadelphus. After the lavender bed comes the delightful woodland glade, which has been planted with countless specimens of azaleas and rhododendrons. In early summer the polyanthus are outstanding and there is colour all through the summer. Especially remarkable is the polar bear rhododendron, which flowers in July. The scent of the lilies in July and August fills the air. Just before you reach the drive leading to the Norwich Gates you will see on the left a fine specimen of the handkerchief Tree.

Sandringham has a museum full of royal possessions which will delight you. You can see Royal Vintage Motor Cars and a fine collection of Royal Photographs. A cafeteria will provide for your hunger and thirst.

The lovely little church at the corner of the park was old four hundred years ago, and King Edward, voluptuary and bon viveur notwithstanding, was a regular worshipper for 47 years.

There are reminders of the royal family here, memorial brasses are among them, and the graves of two little princes in the churchyard. Many of the church's rich sittings are the gift of a wealthy American as a tribute to the King who was known as Edward the Peacemaker.

The Kaiser, the Tsar and numerous members of other royal families have stayed at Sandringham. They would arrive at Wolverton Station, which is now a fascinating museum in its own right, filled with royal memorabilia. Here they would be received by their hosts and the station today is much as it was in its hey day, a very grand place indeed for such a tiny halt.

Edward's eldest son, the Duke of Clarence, celebrated his 21st birthday at Sandringham with a command performance by an entire circus. The Duke died and his brother, George, married his dead brother's fiancee, who became Queen Mary. One of the brasses in the church 'To my darling Eddy' is a touching tribute from his mother, the beautiful Queen Alexandra, to the dead Duke.

The present Queen's father and her three uncles and aunt were born there but Edward VIII, who abdicated, disliked the place so much that he only spent one night in the house.

Some of Sandringham's 365 rooms were demolished by the Queen fifteen years ago on economy grounds. The estate has always been well farmed and the 'Big House' dominates the economy of the surrounding countryside.

Another Princess once lived just up the road at **Heacham**. She was a Red Indian princess, Pocohontas, who had saved the life of the King's Lynn born Captain John Smith, one of the founding fathers of Virginia.

John Rolfe, whose family were lords of the manor at Heacham, went out to the colony to become the first Englishman to grow tobacco there and, after his first wife died, he fell in love with the chieftain's daughter, married her and brought her back to England in the year that Shakespeare died.

She was received by Queen Elizabeth I, lived at the Hall at Heacham in great happiness, and bore a son. Sadly, as she was about to return to her old home, she died of consumption at Gravesend in Kent. She was only twenty-two and it was the end of a remarkable love story.

But from this union, through their son, sprung some of the best known families in the United States. You will find her commemorated in the parish church.

On the way back from Sandringham to King's Lynn, we drove to **Castle Rising Castle**. It stands within some of the most impressive earthworks in England. It was built in 1138 by William d'Albini, later Earl of Sussex, after he married the widow of Henry I, and it became the seat of the Earls of Sussex. The castle has had a long and distinguished history. Several Kings of England have stayed here. In 1331 it became the chief residence of Queen Isabella, wife of the murdered Edward II, who was in disgrace for her liaison with Roger Mortimer and her part in the fall of the King. She was visited here by her son Edward III and grandson, the Black Prince. From 1544 until 1693 the castle belonged to the Dukes of Norfolk, and it has remained in the Howard family to this day. The castle has a massive oval bank and ditch crossed by a brick bridge with a gatehouse. A handsome decorated doorway leads to the two storey keep.

There are several events held at the castle during the year including mediæval tournaments. The castle is open daily except Mondays and Tuesdays in winter.

Castle Rising

To the west and south west of King's Lynn there is an irregular triangle that runs about fourteen miles from north to south, and seven miles from east to west. It contains within its boundaries some of the finest villages and churches in Norfolk. The names themselves roll around the tongue. Terrington St. Clement we have already talked about as the home of the African Violet Centre and then there is Terrington St. John, Tilney All Saints and Tilney St. Lawrence. **Walpole St. Peter** is a village with a marvellous church, glory in the beauty of it and don't miss the sentry-like box that is a moveable shelter for the vicar to protect him at wet funerals! Walpole St. Andrew, Walsoken and West Walton; and then the four Wiggins come next — Wiggenhall St. Germans, Wiggenhall St. Mary Magdalen, Wiggenhall St. Mary the Virgin and Wiggenhall St. Peter. By the end of the day looking at all this beauty you will be suffering from sore feet and mental indigestion, but it will have been worthwhile. Before you go and try, find time to read Dorothy L. Sayers' fine detective story, 'The Nine Tailors'. She invented a village, Fenchurch St. Paul, and her description of it will describe much of what you will see.

Walpole St. Peter

Just before you come to Downham Market from King's Lynn you will find the village of **Wimbotsham**, just off the A10, and opposite the picturesque village green you will find **The Chequers**. Sometimes looks are deceptive, and this was the case when we arrived here. This Greene King Pub is much larger than you would imagine. The setting has to be what anyone would imagine an English pub to be. There is certainly a traditional welcome waiting for you inside. The brewery refurbished this pub completely in 1986, and had the good sense to keep its image in keeping with the age of the building. It is comfortable and attractive. Some years back the next-door

The Chequers

cottage was incorporated into The Chequers, which accounts for its spaciousness inside today. Hosts Neale and Anne Wolder have very high standards, and they try their best to meet customers' requirements.

Anne Wolder looks after the catering, and you will always find good home-made steak and kidney pies and casseroles on the menu, but that does not mean to say you cannot have anything from Tagliatelle to Tacos if that is what you wish. However hungry you are The Chequers can provide just what you want. We thought Anne's home-made soup was delicious. She herself is a vegetarian, so you can imagine that fellow vegetarians are more than well catered for.

Traditional Sunday lunch is served in the function room, which is also available for private parties and meetings.

It was good to see that in addition to the Real Ales, Abbot and IPA, Neale and Anne carry a wide range of low-alcoholic and non-alcoholic drinks. Good thinking for drivers!

Downham Market, once famous for its horse fairs, is very conveniently situated in north west Norfolk, and makes a good centre for touring an interesting part of Norfolk as well as North Cambridgeshire. It lies on the edge of what was once wild fen country, which is still remote in many places, and is in easy reach of King's Lynn, with its Hanseatic buildings; and Ely, with its famous Cathedral and waterfront. Nearby is the north Norfolk coast, with its fine natural coastline and nature reserves, the Norfolk lavender fields, Holkham Hall and many other stately homes, and of course the Royal Sandringham Estate.

Downham Market

Downham Market itself can lay modest claim to fame, having helped to educate the youngster who was later to be known as Lord Nelson. Captain Manby, who invented the life saving shore-to-ship rocket line, also lived here, and nearby in Denver Sluice, which controls most of the major waterways and rivers of the fens, the king pin of the drainage and flood protection of the low-lying land.

The Crown Hotel, in the centre of the town adjoining the market square, is thought to have been first built on the site of a mediæval monks' hospice. Some of the cellars are still remaining and since then its progress has been closely linked with that of the town of Downham Market. An inn later occupied the site, but it was extended with the main part built as a coaching inn in the early 17th century. It retains this character today: 'timber, brick, flint and slated, colour washed, sashes, projecting eaves and dormers', is the official description according to the Department of the Environment's list of 'Buildings of Historic and Architectural Interest'. The main high-arch entrance still stands, as does the stone mounting block.

It was still advertised simply as an inn in 1796, but about town it was also considered important enough to be the headquarters of the Downham Yeoman Cavalry.

As a coaching inn it lay on the stage routs from King's Lynn to London, and Peterborough to Norwich. In the 1820s, according to the local directory, The Crown was a posting house where the mail had to arrive by 11.00 am for sorting after the mail coach to London was despatched at 3.45 pm.

The Crown Hotel

The aftermath of the Napoleonic Wars, however, brought hard times to the area. In 1816, Monday May 20th, The Crown became the focus of Bread Riots by local people, as the magistrates and overseers were holding their monthly meeting there, but it was broken up by the Yeoman Cavalry. At least one of the ringleaders was hanged for his part in the uprising.

By 1912 the hotel had moved into the 20th century and was boasting a motor garage, earning AA and RAC recommendations as early as 1916. In 1922 it had the telephone installed.

The bar still remains much as it has been for the last century or so; wood-panelled and oak-beamed, with brick hearths and log fires. The bar counter is made from old sherry casks, from which a selection of real ales is served, amongst other drinks. During the last war the famous Pathfinder Squadron was based nearby and used this fine old bar as their 'local'.

The hotel was again extended during recent years, and the buildings which comprise the former Yeoman Cavalry barracks and stables were converted into the Stables Restaurant, the walls still being of the old original brick, with seats and table built in each former loose-box. Here visitors can choose their own steaks to be cooked on the griddle, and also from a selection of home-made gateaux, fruit pies, and other puddings.

Breakfasts are served in the lovely old oak beamed Fox Room, named thus because the West Norfolk Hunt once ran their quarry to earth in this room, which has been described as Dickensian in character. Adjoining this room is the famous Jacobean staircase which has remained unaltered from the day it was built.

The accommodation has been tastefully modernised. All rooms have central heating, telephone and complimentary refreshment trays, and most have a bath/shower room en-suite and television.

The hotel is run by the resident proprietor, Mr. Champion, together with some of his family and a cheerful staff who are always ready to help guests enjoy their visits.

We like people who enjoy life and have a sense of humour. Steven Geary, the landlord of **The Rose and Crown**, Bridge Street, Hilgay, **Downham Market**, is just such a man. We thoroughly enjoyed our visit there. The pub is close by the river bridge, and whether you are boating or driving in the area you will find The Rose and Crown a good port of call. There are moorings available and the river is non-tidal, so you can come and go at any time. Steven Geary describes The Rose and Crown as a traditional village pub, offering modern entertainments and amenities. It is much more interesting than that. The front of the building we would guess is early 19th century, and the back mid-Victorian. When alterations were being carried out, they discovered bread ovens which are now in the inglenooks. In 1837 the pub was a coach stop on the main road to London, and the horses were changed in the yard.

The Rose & Crown

We stayed there for a few days, and found the rooms comfortable, the food good and the company excellent. Our fellow guests were fishermen enjoying the river, but it is equally good for bird watchers and those wishing to explore the East Anglian countryside.

Dial House in Railway Road, **Downham Market**, was built in the late 1600s. It is covered in that lovely Carr Stone — iron stone to the uninitiated. All the old houses used to have this covering, and it is creeping back in again with some of the new ones. It is very much a feature of the local area.

Dial House is in a quiet and peaceful area. Ann and David Murray, who run this friendly house, say that their guests always tell them they have slept well, we certainly did, the beds were comfortable, fitted with electric blankets, and the rooms were warm and delightfully furnished to go with the style of the house.

The house has two en-suite bedrooms (one double and one twin), and a very large family room with plenty of space, even though it has two beds beside the double bed. There are televisions in all the rooms.

Ann produces a first class breakfast making sure that food is grilled, not fried. For your evening meal you can have almost anything you want. Ann knows a lot about health foods and will cater happily for people who need special diets. You will find her to be a very nice lady, nothing is too much trouble. Tea and coffee are available at any time with hot drinks at night at no extra charge.

Dial House

The large lounge is very comfortable and warm, heated by a solid fuel fire. Very sensibly it is the only room where smoking is permitted.

Dial House makes a good base from which to visit a lot of the National Trust Houses in Norfolk, and we had the super experience of going to the Welney Wildlife Trust and seeing the birds feeding under floodlights. A very dramatic sight. We have to say this only happens in winter, but what a good excuse to take a winter break and stay at Dial House.

No more enjoyable times can you have than messing about in boats on the beautiful waters around **Denver Sluice**. Heather and Frank Daymond of **Daymond Services** will give you this opportunity by hiring you one of their three 'Nipper' boats, which are very easy to use and great for a trip down the river. Life jackets, which are compulsory, are provided and there are certain rules and regulations for safety reasons, but the emphasis is on enjoyment. Children can steer the boats too.

It was only in 1986 that Frank and Heather Daymond started their business, which took off almost immediately, and they have seen a steady increase in demand ever since. The boats are available for hire up until an hour before dusk, and they are fully equipped with necessary items for pleasure and safety.

Hiring boats from Daymond Services appeals to all sorts of people, from visitors like ourselves to locals, and townsfolk anxious to see the lovely countryside and the wildlife. You can see swans, ducks and geese amongst the many birds. There are masses of flora and fauna to see, and the Daymonds are aware of the need for conservation of all this natural beauty in the area. The engines used in their boats are designed to keep pollution to a minimum.

Boats for hire from Daymond Services

You can take a boat out for an hour, which would give you time to go from Denver to Ten Mile Bridge and back, or you can go for as much as six hours. This will allow you to go as far as Ely and spend an hour ashore looking at the magnificent Cathedral there before you come back to base.

Full instructions for the use of the boats are given to you by Heather and Frank Daymond, and if there should be some delay in your return to the moorings next to the Jennys Arms at Denver Sluice, they will come looking for you. It is great fun, and a wonderful way to look at the countryside.

South Runcton and **Runcton Holme** are two charming unspoilt little villages just north of Downham Market; both have attractive churches and are worth while taking time out to see. Just a little further east along some lanes you will come to Shouldham Thorpe and then **Shouldham** — everything seems to go in pairs in this part of Norfolk. Shouldham once had a Gilbertine priory, a large grammar school and a famous spring called the Silver Well. It was a busy market town with two annual fairs. All that has gone and now it is a pleasant, quiet place with old houses, some thatched, some with red and others with blue pantiles, grouped round a green. Above the village on a hill stands the big flint church of All Saints with embattled tower and a roof with carved hammer beams. From records and excavations it would seem likely that Shouldham has been inhabited for about two thousand years.

At **Marham**, a little further down the lane to the east, Trinity Church has a good perpendicular tower which was given as a bequest in 1450, and a rare tympanum to the Norman north door. We did not know what a tympanum was until it was explained to us. It is a lozenge motif. The church has a lovely hexagonal tiled floor, and best of all we found some good bench ends there.

We drove on aiming for the A47 and our destination, **Swaffham**, but we stopped where the little B-road joined the main road at **Narborough**. The great antiquarian, Sir Henry Spelman, author of the History of Sacrilege, lived here at Narborough Hall. All Saints church contains wonderful monuments and brasses, mostly to the Spelman family. One of them is to Sir John and his lady, dated 1607 with a little kneeling daughter and a baby in swaddling clothes. Such brasses always make us sad.

We soon cheered up when we walked into **The Ship Inn**. Barges on the River Nar used to take refreshments at this 17th century inn, and the landlord took river and road tolls. The river is no longer navigable, but still produced some of the best trout in the region, which is a particular speciality of the kitchen. Jenny and Frank White run The Ship Inn and are especially proud of the reputation The Ship Inn has for good food. Everything is fresh where possible and home cooked. The blackboard menu in the stately oak-panelled bar changes daily, or for a little more formality you can try the delightfully quaint 24-seater restaurant. We came across the game petanque again here if you want to play, or if you wish Frank and Jenny will help you arrange fishing or shooting parties.

The Ship Inn

Swaffham is a very busy market town on a main road. In recent years it has steadily been growing in stature. The very large market place is triangular rather than square, with roads branching out of each corner. There are some good-looking Georgian houses around it as well as the grammar school, and the headmaster's house, which bears the date 1736. The elegant Market Cross was erected by the Earl of Orford in 1783. It is round, actually, with a lead-covered dome and a statue of Ceres on the top. Markets seem to develop, and what were originally stalls become shops developing into permanent buildings. This has happened here in Swaffham. The shops are grouped together in a higgledy-piggledy fashion towards the north side of the Market Place. The Assembly Rooms and the Corn Exchange also form part of the group.

A little lane on the east end leads to the very fine parish church standing at the end of a beautiful avenue of tall trees. It is a 15th century church built mainly of Barnack stone, which is unusual in Norfolk. There is a tower which was built in 1507–10 with a fine Georgian spire. It was the angel roof and the soaring perpendicular arcade of the nave which impressed us most. Here we found some carved bench ends which depicted a little man and a dog on a chain. It reminded us of the tale of the Swaffham Pedlar who is incorporated in the town's coat of arms. Have you heard the story? John Chapman, the legendary pedlar of Swaffham, is reputed to have travelled to London, and there dreamed of finding gold in his garden at home. A hasty return and much digging revealed two pots of gold! Some of this wealth was used in paying for the north aisle of the church.

In Swaffham there are several old pubs, but one in particular took our fancy, **The Norfolk Hero**. This simple name is dedicated to Nelson who was born close by, and was known as the Norfolk Hero. It was the name that attracted us to the pub, and we found the building was well over two hundred years old. It is a homely place, nothing pretentious, with fine exposed old beams and an open fireplace. The O'Brien family run the pub, and there is always one of them about to make you feel welcome. There is a comprehensive bar menu, real ale and, on Sunday, a good traditional lunch. On a nice day you can sit outside and watch the world go by. The Norfolk Hero stays open all day, which is very useful for visitors, and did not seem such a bad idea to the locals either.

The Norfolk Hero

Castle Rising Church

There is plenty of shooting around Swaffham. Pheasants abound, and you come across high hedges that have been grown to provide cover for the 'guns'. There are pretty villages too, with equally pretty names such as Cockley Cley — the Cley is pronounced 'sky'. St. Mary's church here has been restored. It is believed to have been built about AD 628, making it one of the oldest churches in the country. Take a look at the village and also at the site of an Iceni village. In 1971 a replica of what the village must have looked like was built and provides a vivid lesson in history.

Norfolk continually surprises us, and no doubt it will not change as we continue on our travels. We are off to Norwich next.

Norwich to East Dereham

Walpole St. Peter's Church

Area covered in Chapter 4

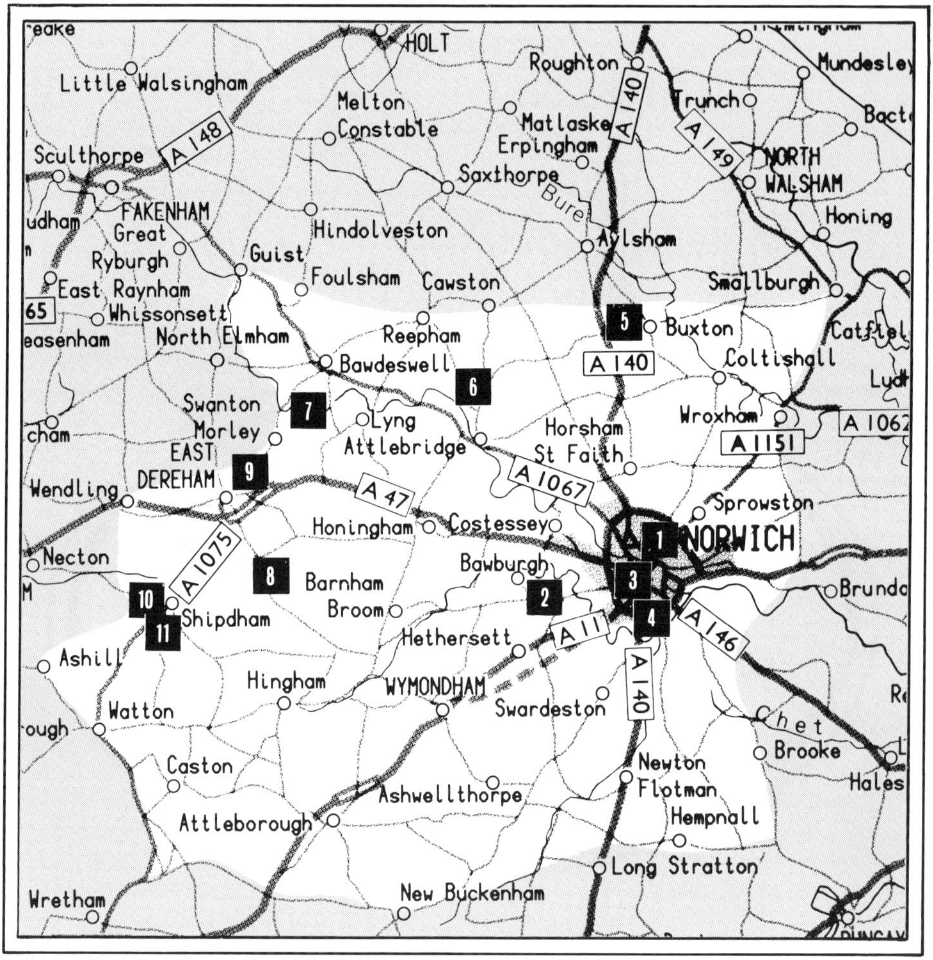

1 The Station Hotel *(Norwich)*
2 Bangkok Restaurant *(Bawburgh)*
3 Chiltern House *(Norwich)*
4 The Prince of India *(Norwich)*
5 Buxton Mill Tavern & Free House *(Buxton)*
6 Swannington Hall *(Swannington)*
7 Church Farm Motel *(Elsing)*
8 The Kings Arms *(Garveston)*
9 Nelson House Restaurant *(North Elmham)*
10 King Row Farm *(Shipdham)*
11 The Kings Head *(Shipdham)*

CHAPTER 4

Norwich to East Dereham

Norwich is the most surprising place. You might be surprised to learn that Norwich was the first British city to be mentioned in the E.E.C's recent league-table of Europe's 'most habitable' cities. It was Britain's 'second' city throughout the Middle Ages, right up to the 18th century, and it has more pre-Reformation churches than London, York and Bristol put together. Also, except for the Three Choirs of Gloucester, Hereford and Worcester, it hosts the oldest festival in the country, the Norfolk and Norwich Triennial, founded in 1824.

Having given you all that information, we can tell you that only touches the tip of the iceberg. It will not be possible to do full justice to this exciting city.

First of all we found an ideal place to stay, **Skeet's Station Hotel**, at Riverside Road, Norwich. City centres conjure up images of high rise office blocks, endless traffic noise and general mayhem; not so where the Station Hotel is situated. It is in an area that is quaint and picturesque, right on the bank of the River Wesum. With its slow-running waters and river boats, nothing could be less hurried. The relaxing atmosphere is rarely found in the heart of a city. It all belies the activity just a few streets away.

The Station Hotel

The Station Hotel maintains a high standard. Most of the bedrooms are en-suite, all with colour TV, coffee making facilities, central heating plus direct dial telephones. Even when it's chilly outside you will find your room warm and comfortable. The restaurant overlooks the river, and as the yacht station is opposite there are always boats coming and going. It is nice to have something to watch while you are enjoying your meal, and very good for your digestion. There are two menus, each offering a great variety and using local produce. We found the food delicious.

With so much to see on our itinerary it was a bonus having a hotel so close to all the action.

If you stayed a month in Norwich exploring it carefully you would still not have seen everything. In fact you would only just be discovering your way around, for the city is a network of narrow streets and passages. You will need to be guided to discover the charms, for it is not just the county town of Norfolk but a regional capital and centre. This does not go down too well with Ipswich but it is fact.

The real focal point is Tombland, the old Saxon market place. The seventeen roads which lead to Norwich from every point of the compass once met there. Strangely the **Cathedral**, which has one of the highest spires in the country, is not the guiding point as one would expect. It is so low-lying that it cannot be seen from many of the streets.

Before you enter the doors of the Cathedral you will find yourself embraced in the almost mediæval arms of the Cathedral Close, which is like a village of those times; a very private world. The Bishop's Gate from Palace Street, the Erpingham Gate and St. Ethelbert's Gate from Tombland admit us to this wonderful scene. There is Upper Close and the Lower Close, there is Green Yard and Almery Green, the buildings of Norwich School, larger grander houses in the Upper Close and smaller houses, side by side with cottages, in Hook's Walk. Whichever way you go there are always more alleyways and more unexpected corners to turn. We found it a place of enchantment. Lovely gardens and gables delight the eye, and the sun sparkling on the mullioned windows can make you believe you are in fairyland. You must walk round and absorb the outside of the Cathedral: the immensely long nave, the shorter chancel, the traceried windows, flying buttresses and the long arms of the transepts. The 15th century spire crowns the Norman central tower.

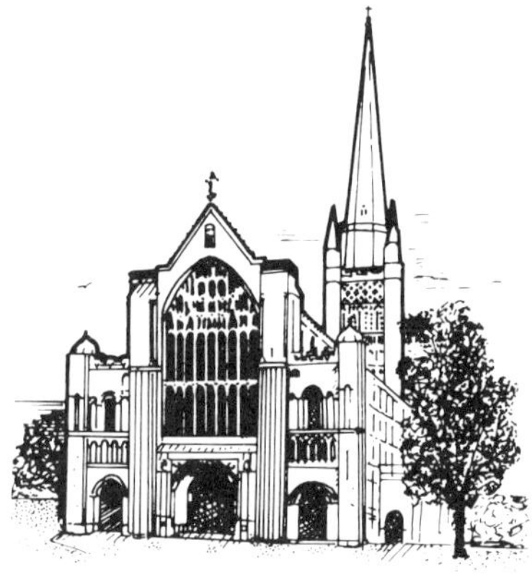

Norwich Cathedral

The present Cathedral was begun in 1096 by Bishop Herbert de Losinga, and the main church was completed in the middle of the 12th century. In 1362 tremendous damage was done when the spire fell, which, strangely, was no bad thing, for the opportunity was taken to rebuild the east end in its present dramatic form. A fire in 1463 destroyed the original timber roof. The

15th century vault was constructed then, Norwich's crowning glory.

If , before you start your journey of awesome wonder inside this superb building, you wish to read a fine, informative description, Henry Thorold's book on Cathedrals, Abbeys and Priories of England and Wales, published by Collins, is for you. The book includes some wonderful pictures by Peter Burton, which give you visual proof of what there is to see, and afterwards will be a constant reminder of a day of spiritual and artistic contentment.

The Cathedral, unlike its neighbours Ely and Peterborough, has not been altered much; all three are Norman of course. In Norwich you can see its plan, as it was intended in the first place. The round apse, which was the fashion in buildings of its period has, in its centre, facing west, a Saxon bishop's throne, the only one of its kind remaining in Europe. There is a wonderful rhythm of Norman arcades which in spite of the size, and they are massive, do not detract from the light, airy feeling that fills the Cathedral. Above the clerestory is the chief addition to the original nave; the glorious stone vaulting added nearly 400 years later, with its hundreds of coloured and gilded bosses. There are 2,000 in all, and if you want to study them closely you will find those in the cloisters of great interest and easy to study.

There are small chapels which surround the apse, the Cathedral St. Andrew's Chapel, the Jesus Chapel, St. Luke's Chapel and the Chapel of Our Lady of Pity. They are quite delightfully furnished, and give you a sense of intimacy and peace. Here there is a wonderful display of mediæval painted panels. The reredos in the Lady Chapel, and the Despencer reredos in St. Luke's, are outstanding work, rare surviving examples of the work of the 14th–15th century Norwich school of painters.

The cloisters are among the finest in England and, although they were built over a long period, great harmony was achieved.

At the end of your visit, preferably in the evening when the Close is at its best, walk gently through to Pull's Ferry and see the Cathedral from the river.

After a day of visual delight spent in Norwich Cathedral we decided to change the scene entirely for our evening out. In Plymouth, just next to our offices on the harbour, there is a Thai Coffee House, where we were taught that Thai restaurants are very special. It was because of Rori and Supin Smith who own this Thai Coffee House, that we ventured into the attractive **Bangkok Restaurant** at Lodge House, New Road, Bawburgh in Norwich. To our delight we found it was owned by an equally charming and knowledgeable couple, Roger Smith and his Thai wife Sommai. The Bangkok was once two 19th century cottages, which later were tastefully converted into a single dwelling house. It was in the spring of 1987 that it became the Bangkok Restaurant. Roger and Sommai (who is responsible for the cooking, of course!) moved from a very well known Thai restaurant of the same name in Little Walsingham — perhaps you have been there? It was the first East Anglian Thai restaurant.

A Thai restaurant is not the place to go if you want a meal in a hurry.

Everything is individually prepared with loving care, and cannot be hurried.

For those of you who have never eaten Thai food it comes somewhere in between Indian and Chinese, with its own special character but without the currys. It is subtle, tantalising and delicious, the best Oriental food, basically. The Bangkok has all the best ingredients of the Orient, both in hospitality and cuisine.

The restaurant itself is relaxed and friendly, with a warm welcome from the traditionally-dressed waitresses. Roger, who serves in the bar, makes sure you feel at ease the moment you arrive. It's fun, and we know you will enjoy the unusual and spicy foods.

Car parking facilities are there, which are invaluable, and they open from 7 pm until midnight. Last orders are taken at 10 pm Tuesday to Sunday. It is best to book.

Bangkok Restaurant

On February 15th 1823, Jeremiah Colman took his nephew James into partnership, and created the famous firm of J. & J. Colman.

To mark the anniversary of this event, Colmans opened a Mustard Shop, the only one of its kind in Britain, in 1973. The shop can be found in 18th century quarters in Bridewell Alley, one of the attractive little alleyways in the old centre of Norwich which are wonderful to explore.

The shop has now become a major tourist attraction for both overseas and British tourists visiting East Anglia. Its fame and popularity has become worldwide.

The premises have been extensively restored and decorated in late 19th century style. The shop houses a mustard museum, which takes the form of a series of displays illustrating the history of Colman's mustard from the early years to the present day. Many of the articles offered for sale are based on old designs taken from the company's archives, and are unique to the shop.

To those unable to visit the shop personally, they offer a comprehensive mail order scheme for all their items. All you have to do is send for their catalogue, or you can telephone if you would rather. The number is (0603) 627889.

We spent a wonderful afternoon discovering the second great historic building in Norwich, the **Castle**.

The Castle dominates the city, and the streets go round it. After all, it was built in the time of William the Conqueror, and placed where it would block the main road! It was built by one Roger Bigod in the 12th century, and is surrounded by 19th century buildings, which strangely do not seem out of place. Until 1887 the Castle was used as a county gaol. It is now a museum, and one of the very best provincial museums in the kingdom. The collection of birds is superb.

You can see the last bustards, shot at Lexham in 1838. The Norwich School of painters produced some wonderful works, and many of these famous paintings are there for you to see. Local antiquities figure largely here, and are uncommonly good. There are fine manuscripts, one of which is an early fourteenth century Book of Hours.

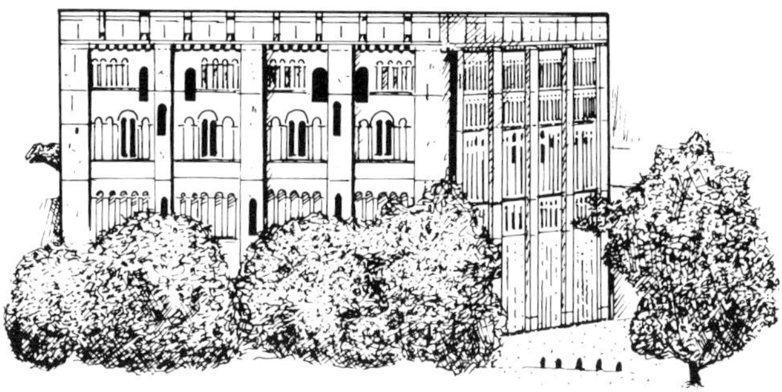

Norwich Castle

Too much history or sightseeing of any kind can become a bore to one or more members of a family, so we have looked for other things to do. The theatre is almost universally loved, and so may we suggest you visit the **Theatre Royal**, next to the Assembly House? It is the third building of its name to stand on the site. In the 18th century the first theatre stood opposite the west front of St. Peter Mancroft Church; don't worry, we are not going to talk about Norwich's plethora of churches now. It was built by Ivory in 1757, but was burned down and replaced by another building in 1826. This in turn was destroyed by fire, and the present building was erected in 1936 and extensively altered in 1970. Today it is one of the leading theatres in the provinces. First class productions are shown here, and there is a constantly changing programme.

Another theatre, the **Maddermarket Theatre**, was converted into an Elizabethan-type theatre in 1926. Here plays dating from every period and country are produced each month by the Norwich Players; mainly amateur, but with a professional producer and designer. It has been a highly successful venture, both from a cultural and entertainment point of view.

The Maddermarket Theatre

Adjoining the Maddermarket Theatre is the Strangers' Hall Museum. It was the home of prosperous citizens from the Middle Ages to within living memory, and the rooms are furnished in the styles of various periods from the 16th century onwards. It is a bit of a shock to see how the ideas of comfort have varied over the centuries. It is open every day except Sunday from 10 am – 5 pm.

One of the painless ways to see and learn about Norwich is from boat trips, which you can take from the heart of the city. There is a commentary given about the past, and the future, as your boat floats past the historic buildings. We were lucky enough to have a commentator who not only knew Norwich and its history very well, but also had a keen sense of humour, which lightened the trip.

For those of you who love to dawdle and window shop, Norwich is the regional shopping centre. All the major national stores are represented, but you can see them almost anywhere. It is the multitude of boutiques, antique and craft shops that delighted us.

If, after you have been shopping, you are overcome with a need for alcoholic beverages, then it has been said that there are three hundred and sixty five pubs in Norwich, one for every day of the year, so you should not have too far to go to quench your thirst! There are still some fine coaching inns, which you find if you stroll along the 18th century walk. The Maid's Head Hotel, built in the 16th century, from which the city's first stage coach, 'The Norwich Machine' left in 1762, is a fascinating hostelry. It is only a short distance from **Elm Hill**, where the quiet cobbled streets have houses and shops of all periods rising from them. The elm tree, which gives it its name, stands at the top near the thatched Briton's Arms, the only house in the street to survive the disastrous fire of 1507. There are other super houses to see here as well, the 16th century timbered Stranger's Club, the 17th

Elm Hill

century Flint House and the 15th century church of St. Simon and St. Jude.

The beauty of Elm Hill for us was that it was full of shops that were carrying on trade to harmonise with their setting. Not some contrived, staged piece of history, but a live street capable of attracting customers in its own right.

Talking of St. Simon's and St. Jude's church on Elm Hill brings us to the enormous responsibility Norwich has, with no less than 32 mediæval churches and two old non-conformist churches to deal with. They are no doubt one of Norwich's greatest assets, but also a great liability. Some of them have been put to secular uses. St. Peter Hungate, for example, is a museum of ecclesiastical art. Nearby all the churches are from the 15th century and very fine. The best in our view is **St. Peter Mancroft**, standing on the south side of the market place. It is one of the great examples of the Perpendicular style. The substantial tower is arched over the street and is lavishly panelled. It is crowned with nice turrets and a charming Victorian Gothic spirelet, which seems to be slightly out of place amongst such grandeur. The clerestory forms a magnificent wall of light in the lofty interior, where it meets the superb boss-studded roof which has hammerbeams covered by coving. The 15th century stained glass that fills the east window will leave you breathless. It shimmers with its beauty. Take time to see the impressive font canopy and the brasses and monuments. The Mancroft Heritage Exhibition is housed in the church, and is worth sparing time to see.

St. Peter Mancroft

It is open from 10 am – 5 pm Monday, Tuesday, Thursday and Saturday, and from 7 am – 5 pm on Wednesdays. Sundays it is slightly different, to conform with the services no doubt. It is open from 8 am – 7.30 pm. The services are always very well attended, surprisingly enough, for the parish has few inhabitants. At the opposite end of Bethal Street is St. Giles Church, the lofty tower of which once sported a beacon. In St. Benedict's Street, just north of St. Giles, there is a whole row of ancient churches. St. Benedict's was destroyed by fire and bombing in the last war, and has never been rebuilt, but within a few hundred yards you will find St. Swithin's, St. Lawrence's and St. Gregory's. A large painting of St. George and the Dragon graces one of the west walls of St. Gregory's, making it by far and away the most interesting of that little group. But we are not done yet; proceeding eastwards St. John Maddermarket, St. Andrew's and St. Michael's at Plea follow in quick succession. St. Andrew's is the most important of these. It is one of the major churches in Norwich with a wealth of monuments.

In amongst the industrial buildings north of the River Wensum there are several buildings of interest, well hidden. Colegate for example has a number of fine houses, and the oldest Congregational Chapel in the country; it was built in 1693. A few doors away is the Octagon Chapel, designed by Thomas Ivory, who also designed the Assembly House. Much worn-out property has been swept away round here, and a modern shopping centre has taken its place, but it has not affected a charming group of Tudor cottages, which face St. Augustine's Church, and are known as Gildencroft.

Somebody once said to us that Norwich is not a university city, but a city with a university. We did not quite understand what they meant until we saw it. It is so out of keeping with one's visual idea of what a university in Norwich would be.

The University of East Anglia came into being in 1963, and we cannot believe it is quite what the people of East Anglia expected when they so generously gave large sums of money for its creation. The site is magnificent, but the buildings give the impression of being a factory, albeit in this case a factory for turning out students. We could say that it has taken hundreds of years for the Cathedral to be taken to the heart of the city, so maybe the university is just going to need patience; we have to say that we were disappointed.

The disappointment was forgotten when we watched Norwich City play at home. This team has become the pride of Norwich in this season of 1989. They have every chance of winning the First Division title. Secretly we hope they will not, for we are dedicated Liverpool fans!

Two of the chief reasons which draw people from every part of the county to Norwich are the Cathedral, where representatives from the 600 parishes in the Diocese meet on several occasions in the year, and Norwich City Football Club, which draws crowds which other league clubs envy. When the Cathedral team and Norwich are playing at home at the same time there is chaos in the streets!

Norwich is a city of which the residents should rightly be proud. For visitors like ourselves it is a place that no matter how many times you came to it, there would always be more to see.

Having been so uncomplimentary about the university we hope we will be forgiven. The students are a marvellous bunch, and whilst we were exploring the city we twice met parents of those who had successfully come through to graduation and were filling the city with proud fathers and mothers. One couple told us of a very good guest house. We took careful note of their remarks so that we could pass the information on to you.

Chiltern House in Trafford Road is run by Celia and Ken Harrison and, knowing how difficult it is in a busy city like Norwich, to find somewhere to stay that is comfortable, friendly and within a few minutes walk of the city centre and bus station, was a bonus. The prices also fit comfortably into most people's budget.

It is open all the year round, has colour TV, telephone and radio in all the bedrooms. Baby-sitting is available if you need it, and you will be very well fed! There are no irritating restrictions in this friendly house, except that pets are not permitted. Very obligingly there is one of Norwich's three hundred and sixty-five pubs situated across the road; not the most exciting one that we have ever visited, but it was a friendly place and the beer was good. Give Celia or Ken a ring before you go to the Chiltern to make sure of a bed — their number is (0603) 663033.

Chiltern House

Walking along Price of Wales Road we were assailed by the tantalising aroma of curry. We were right outside **The Prince of India**, which lives up to its regal name without losing any of its Eastern promise. In addition to the delicious smells that made our nostrils twitch, the tinkling sound of authentic Indian music excites your imagination and creates the desire to taste the dishes of the Orient.

It goes without saying that to go to an Indian restaurant it is because you enjoy Indian food. The careful preparation of the spices and the quality of the ingredients used make a meal at the Prince of India special. The range includes the speciality of the house, Mughlai Murgi, which is a whole chicken, Moghul style, served with special rice and a vegetable curry. It was memorable, but you do need to give them 24 hours notice for Mughlai Dishes.

For those of you enjoying self-catering holidays, do make use of the excellent and very competitively price take-away service the Prince of India offers.

The Prince of India

There are many places you can visit easily from Norwich. Just 10 miles south of the city off the B1113 is **Forncett St. Mary**. The village is tiny, but it has the **Forncett Industrial Steam Museum**. This museum houses an unusual collection of large stationary steam engines, including one of the pumping engines previously used to open Tower Bridge in London. There are 28 different engines, seven of which can be seen running on Steam Days; the 1st Sunday each month from May to October and also the 3rd Sunday in each month in July, August, September; Spring and August Bank Holiday Sunday and Monday from 2 pm – 6 pm. There are static opening days too; Sundays from May to the end of September 2 pm – 5 pm. Apart from the most famous exhibit that we have already talked about, the most powerful is a 200 hp Robey Tandem Compound from Sleaford Maltings. The largest is an 85 ton Worthington Simpson Triple Expansion Vertical engine from Dover Water Works.

The oldest is an 1873 Hick Hargreaves Corliss engine from a Nottingham lace factory. The longest-serving is a 9 hp Jessop and Appleby from Sarsons Malt Vinegar Works, and the newest is an 1891 beam engine from a Yorkshire water works.

Until we went there we had no interest in anything like steam engines, but how could you not be fascinated by the reminder of how stationary steam engines supplied power to drive factories, water works, dairies, laundries, breweries, maltings and a host of other applications, from the middle of the 19th century until recent times.

Researching and writing these books has given us an insight into so many spheres that otherwise we might never have seen.

In addition to all this power, the museum provides an excellent home-made tea. It was good fun and extremely informative.

Another day saw us heading up the A140 towards Buxton where for centuries the Mill was the scene of much activity with the great wheels grinding the flour from Norfolk wheat, and is mentioned in many books, in particular the Domesday Book — more famous than this one is yet! We refer obviously to the present building, though this was built during the 18th century.

Buxton Mill Tavern Free House at **Buxton Mill** is rather like a huge superstore, it offers customers everything from carpets to antiques, with craftsmen displaying their skills. So fascinating is this to watch that it makes you want to have a go yourself.

The ground floor is entirely given over to the restaurant and free house. The bar, which overlooks the river, offers real ales and bar snacks, whilst the oak-beamed restaurant, renowned for its good food and service, provides a relaxing atmosphere in which to watch the river activities (novice rowers can be hilarious). Ducks are adept at dodging the boats fortunately.

Cream teas taken outside on fine days are great for families. The children can play happily without too much restraint. It was a good day out, with plenty to see and do.

Buxton Mill Tavern Free House

Along the Reepham Road from Norwich we turned right to Swannington, and there we discovered **Swannington Hall**, an Elizabethan manor house with a fascinating tale to tell. Today it is a free house and restaurant, offering good food and an excellent range of real ales. The main bar has a magnificent Tudor beamed ceiling, and an original open fireplace with log fires.

The candlelit restaurant is delightful and has a super menu, but you can find yourelf equally well fed with one of the very good bar meals. A beef and stout pie took our fancy, although the steak and kidney pie looked just as good. On Saturday night and Sunday lunchtime you can enjoy the fun of a barbecue, and perhaps take a gentle walk round the 5½ acres of lovely, mature gardens.

It is the history of Swannington Hall that we enjoyed hearing about. Apparently the manor and its land was gifted by William the Conquerer to his cousin Walter Giffard, who fought alongside him at Hastings. The Giffard family died out in the male line and, in the reign of Richard the Lionheart, the manor was owned by Richard De Clere, Earl of Hertford.

A moat surrounds most of the Hall, and is most likely to have been excavated between 1250 and 1350. The oldest section of the present house is the south wing, which may date back to the 15th century wars of the roses.

It was to this house that the leader of the 1549 rebellion, Robert Kett, was brought following his capture in a nearby barn. Kett was on the run after the defeat of his forces by the Earl of Warwick, at Dussins Dale on the outskirts of Norwich. After he was captured by the Warwick's men he was hung in chains from Norwich castle battlements; very unpleasant! Such memories, however, do nothing to detract from the pleasure of visiting Swannington Hall today, and it can be truly described as a fine hostelry.

Swannington Hall

Close by to Swannington Hall are **Swannington Manor Gardens**. A lovely, peaceful and romantic four acre garden surrounding a 17th century house, which sadly is not open to the public. There is a 300 year-old yew box hedge. With fine herbaceous borders, a stream, knot and herb garden as well as orchids and greenhouses, you can spend several contented hours here. There is a restaurant and an exciting presents shop. There were some very unusual plants, and box topiary. It is only open from April to September.

If you like gardens then **Rainthorpe Hall Gardens** at Tasburgh, which is eight miles south of Norwich on the A140, will give you enjoyment also. They are the large gardens of the Elizabethan manor house, which is open by appointment. We have never been inside, so we cannot tell you much about it. The gardens however have fine trees of botanical interest and a collection of bamboos.

Something totally different is the **Norfolk Wildlife Park**, which has one of the largest collections of European mammals and birds in the world, exhibited under near natural conditions in 40 acres of beautiful parkland. Take a look at their breeding groups of Barbary apes, European bison, boar, lynx, otters, seals, six different kinds of deer and lots of other mammals, not to mention a wide range of birds, including waterfowl. Wander round the acres of mown grassland, picnic where you like while the children run about and enjoy themselves in this fairyland of wildlife.

Parents can take tea and relax on the terrace, outside the tearoom, and let their children feed the waterfowl and peacocks nearby. You will find this exciting place on the A1067, 12 miles north west of Norwich at Great Witchingham. It is open from 10.30 am – 6 pm every day of the year.

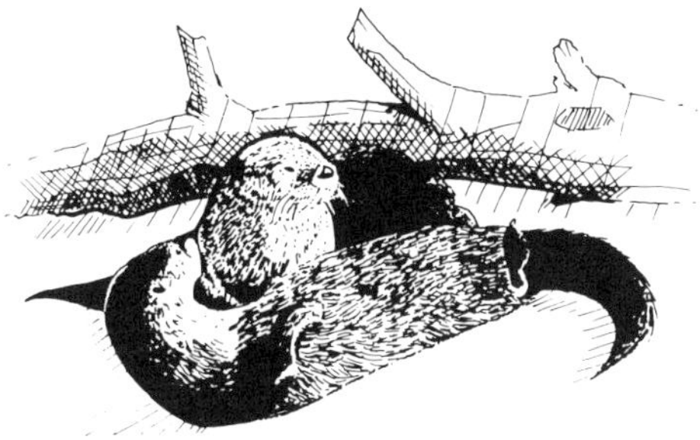

Otters, at the Norfolk Wildlife Park

We left the Station Hotel in Norwich to take up residence at the **Church Farm Motel** at **Elsing**, in the heart of Breckland, not too far from Norwich but closer to East Dereham, off the A47. It certainly offered us a chance of a peaceful retreat from which to enjoy the Anglian atmosphere. The Motel is hidden away, but there is nothing remote about the welcome that Roy, Pat and Roy will give you. Do not be confused; there are two Roys!

The Motel has luxury en-suite studio apartments, some of which overlook the meadow and the ponds, offering privacy and tranquillity. Each apartment is tastefully furnished and has colour TV, hairdryer, trouser press and tea making facilities. For a very special occasion, a honeymoon perhaps, Studio Four comes complete with king size four poster bed.

Meals are taken in the fully-licensed restaurant, which has a good varied menu. There are never less than seven starters; Brie Almondine is one of them, crispy fried wedges of brie coated with ribbed almonds served with hot bread and cranberry sauce. Devilled Whitebait is another. For your main course try Elsing pie or Russian fish pie; flaky pastry envelopes filled with a mixture of salmon, fish, prawns and mushrooms, bound with a creamy white wine and parsley sauce. Does it make you feel hungry? A delicious meal like this with three courses will only cost you £9.95.

On Sunday you can still tuck into a traditional three course lunch with a starter followed by roast beef, pork or perhaps chicken, all served with a selection of fresh vegetables and roast or boiled potatoes. If you can find room after that there are various sweets available. Coffee afterwards is included, and all that for just £5.95. We thought it was excellent value. The wine list amused us; the choice was limited but well selected, but no matter what you choose the price is always £4.50 per bottle!

If you come to Norwich bus or train station either Pat or one of the Roys will pick you up and make you feel very welcome from the moment you arrive.

It is so easy to reach many of the finest places in Norfolk and Suffolk or Cambridgeshire from here. There is horse riding, coarse and fly fishing, nature reserves and a wildlife park all within three miles, and Norwich is only 12 miles away.

Church Farm Motel

Garvestone is on the B1135 out of **East Dereham**. On the outskirts of the village, perched on top of the hill. **The Kings Arms** looks out over rolling countryside on three sides, and the village church on the fourth.

However good the beer is, or how attractive the building, the enjoyment is marred if the publican is dreary, and they do exist, sadly! Rodney Parker, mine host of the Kings Arms, is anything but dreary. A larger than life character, he was Barmaster of the Year in 1981 and has qualified in bartending training, so he knows how to pull a good pint! He is a super storyteller, and when you are sitting comfortably round the open fires with a drink in your hand he will tell you how the pub started life as a cottage in 1580, with barns and stables and a piggery, as part of a small-holding. Most of the building disappeared over the years, and became today's car park. What remained and is part of the Kings Arms today became a single-roomed ale house for centuries, until it reverted to a private dwelling whose last occupant, in spirit, still resides in the pub! Rodney will tell you this story with great zeal. Apparently strange happenings and apparitions occur round about Christmas time in the private part of the pub. It's not just Rodney who has seen this female ghost; his son has had visits as well. She's a friendly soul, not at all harmful and quite possibly the great aunt of a customer. However we will take an even bet that you will suffer from goose pimples while he is telling this story — we did!

In the 1940s two extensions were built to the cottage, and now the pub has two bars as well as private accommodation. Some of the old beams are still to be seen but sadly many have been hidden behind new plaster.

The Kings Arms

East Dereham is in the geographical centre of Norfolk, and is the fourth largest town in the county. It has a long history, dating back to AD 650, when Withburga, a daughter of Anna, King of East Anglia founded a nunnery here. She was canonised after her death in AD 654 and buried in the churchyard, where the well named after her can still be seen.

The church stands on a sloping site, and is interesting. It has several monuments, amongst them one by Flaxman to the poet William Cowper, who lived and died at Dereham. At the corner of the churchyard are some pargetted cottages, very rare we understand in Norfolk. One is named Bishop Bonner's Cottage, and is enchanting. The tower of the church is detached, and stands at a short distance from the east end. This tower was used to house French prisoners of war during the Napoleonic Wars.

Today East Dereham is no longer the pretty place it was in bygone years, because it has become a manufacturing town. Because Norfolk is such a large county, Dereham has become almost a parting of the ways between east and west. You would be quite surprised to find how many people there are to the west of Dereham who have never visited Norwich in their lives.

There is a super village to the north east of Dereham called Swanton Morley, which was the home of the ancestors of President Abraham Lincoln. The Angel Inn there incorporates part of the house in which they lived in the early 17th century. The church at Swanton Morley is well worth a visit. It was probably built about 1360, and completed after Sir William Morley left money in his will towards the building of the church 'now begun'. It was consecrated in 1440 according to the records. The church is full of light, with the Perpendicular arcades soaring towards the heavens.

Going further north on the B1110 you will come to **North Elmham**, which straggles along for nearly a mile through the village before it comes to the church. An extensive Saxon settlement was unearthed here on the site of the vineyard to the west of the church. To the north of the church the remains of a Saxon Cathedral have been accessible for many years. Although the remains of the Cathedral are very interesting, do not let it stop you from looking at the parish church. Strangely, upon entering the church you go down a flight of steps to the nave, with its 13th century round and octagonal piers. There appears to be some evidence of Norman work as well, though from the outside the church seems to belong mainly to the Decorated and Perpendicular periods.

Having had our fill of sightseeing, we went to Janet and John Tunney's excellent **Nelson House Restaurant** in the High Street. It is a lovely 17th century building with much to tell in historical terms, but even more as a restaurant offering unusual dishes, some of them for two to share; excellent for a romantic evening out.

Nelson House Restaurant

The Tunneys told us that they believed it to have been a coaching house; the main road runs along the whole frontage of Nelson House. You can imagine the horses being reined to an abrupt halt, quickly unharnessed and just as speedily replaced by a fresh team before galloping on their way again, no doubt shaking the bones of the unfortunate occupants. The frontage shows that the original oak beams are still supportive of the structure, with roof beams visible as well.

At some later date, we could not discover quite when, the use was changed to a drapery, which was bought in 1778 by Nelson's younger brother. He stayed there for many years, and today the counter is still in use with a later Victorian top added for use as a bar.

Janet and John Tunney have the fortunate knack of making everyone welcome, and you will thoroughly enjoy a meal there. If you cannot tear yourselves away, then accommodation is available.

Coming back to our base at Elsing, let us tell you something of Breckland before we up sticks and make for Shipdham.

Breckland is a highly distinctive region in the south east of Norfolk covering some 400 square miles, about one third of which lie in Suffolk. In Norfolk the western boundary runs in a fairly straight line from Mildenhall and Lakenheath to Castle Acre, following the edge of the chalk which underlies most of Norfolk. What makes Breckland so distinctive is that the chalk is over laid by a layer of windblown sand, which in time past has made it almost barren. Where cultivation has taken place the ground is covered by inumerable flints, turned up by the plough. This is the broken land which gives the name 'breck' to the area. It is of great interest to naturalists. Basically it is a part of the countryside unique in England.

The flora and fauna have been left undisturbed, and there are mysterious meres and lakes which have a reputation for appearing and disappearing as a result of changes in the level of the water table in the soil. For this information, which is so well put, we are indebted to Bernard Dorman whose book, simply entitled 'Norfolk', is a joy. We enjoyed staying at Elsing, and touching on the Breckland.

Shipdham is south of Dereham, on the A1075 towards Watton. We were heading there to stay at **King Row Farm**. Shipdham is well-known locally for parish walks, a good golf course and a splendid church. It is also within easy reach of many Norfolk towns and villages, which makes it ideal for a

King Row Farm

holiday centre. It is two and a half miles from the village off the main road, and approached by a single-track lane. King Row Farm stands in almost three acres of open farmland. Guest accommodation is offered in this interesting house, part of which is believed to date back 400 years. Old ships' timbers are embodied in the construction. There are two luxurious and generously-sized bedrooms, one twin and one double, each with tea and coffee making facilities and private bathroom. One bedroom has ample room for a cot, or a child's bed if it is needed. Dinner is optional, and prepared by the owner Mrs. Lilford. Her menu features a choice of unusual starters, followed by a traditional main course and a tempting dessert. The dining room is attractive, and the inviting lounge is an excellent place to take your after-dinner coffee and watch the news on the colour TV. For those energetic folks, a hard tennis court is freely available.

King Row Farm is open all year except Christmas. There is full central heating and double glazing to keep you warm, but the most welcoming sight in winter is the open log fire.

When we walked into Shipdham village we were intrigued by the village sign on the green which depicts **'Drynkkings'**. Apparently 'drynkkings' were social gatherings of the parish around the 16th century, and correspond to our present day garden fêtes or tea parties. They were also known as 'Church Ales', and usually held in the Church House, which in those days stood in the parish churchyard. We were told that Shipdham once boasted 27 public houses and inns, and four bakeries.

The parish church was originally built during the Norman period and, after being destroyed, was rebuilt in the 15th century. It still retains some of its Norman features, but the pride of the church is the wooden lectern of that period, around 1500, which is one of the finest of its kind in all England. Another very distinctive feature of the church is the two-tier lantern on top of the tower, which forms a landmark for the centre of the village. This lantern is comparable with the one on St. Peter Mancroft church in Norwich.

The church has eight bells: the clock bell, the sanctus bell and the six ringing bells. The sanctus bell is reported in the contemporary church warden's accounts as having been purchased in Norwich in 1525.

A war memorial to the fallen of two wars stands in the churchyard, and nearby is a commemorative plaque in honour of the American airmen of the 44th Bomber group, 'The Flying Eightballs', who arrived at Shipdham in 1942, and had such an illustrious and poignant wartime history.

These aircraft and their famous crews were involved in some of the most intensive and bloody air battles in the history of aerial warfare, and in their 343 missions the group lost 153 aircraft. With ten men on each aircraft, fatalities were very high. The Flying Eightballs flew numerous sorties over Europe, and their final mission from Shipdham was on 25th April, 1945.

September 3rd, 1983 saw the return of some of these veteran 'Flying Eightballs' to Shipdham. They came, some with their families, from many corners of the United States, to dedicate a plaque in memory and in honour of their fallen comrades. The plaque stands in the churchyard, and has a Liberator aircraft engraved above the triangle of runways, and also the motif of the 8th U.S. Airforce. These men made an indelible impression on the life of Shipdham, and are remembered with pride and affection.

Many of these American airmen used **The Kings Head**, where we met Mark and Sue Elvin who run the pub. We asked them what their aim was for the pub. The answer was simple, "We want to attract families and give them quality and value for money". We found they were already achieving that aim.

The pub was rebuilt in 1928, after a fire virtually destroyed it. It is a one-bar house, with an L-shaped bar. There is a pool and darts area, and French doors open onto a small patio and beer garden. There is a large car park at the side, which gives easy access.

During world War II, when the Americans were stationed at Shipdham, the Kings Head was their local, and it was the start of a growing collection of photographs of people and events of those days which still continues. Many of the American servicemen who were based at the airfield come to England and visit their old haunts, not forgetting the Kings Head. Mark and Sue told us several amusing tales of under-the-counter black market dealings that were carried on in the pub. We kept expecting Arthur Daley to pop up!

The Kings Head

And so to **Wymondham**, a busy market town with much to see. On a fateful Sunday in June 1615, while most of the inhabitants were in church, a fire destroyed more than 300 houses, and much has been rebuilt since that date. It was at this time that the picturesque Market Cross was rebuilt. It is octagonal and timber framed. There is a room on the first floor which is reached by an outside stair, while the ground floor is open on all sides. It is crowned by a pyramid roof. The emblems of the town, a wooden spoon and a spigot crossed, appear in the wood carving round the building.

It is the Abbey that dominates the town however. The magnificent, formerly monastic, mediæval church has two proud towers. The monks and the townspeople were always at odds, and the church was virtually divided in half. There is a superbly adorned 15th century north porch. Above the Norman nave the hammerbeam roof is gloriously arrayed with angels and starry bosses. There is a wonderful font on which lions, wild men and angels figure. On the south side of the altar an arch is filled up with a terracotta erection of the early 16th century, which is very unusual and beautiful with its delicate Renaissance detail. It is in the form of a sedilia, and it is described as the monument to the last abbot. A most rare treasure is the 13th century Corporas Case. The church is open daily from 10.00 am to 6.00 pm Easter to October, and in winter from 11.00 am to 3.00 pm.

There is a Bridewell in Wymondham, with the cell windows still barred, built in 1787, and the Public Library is housed in the 14th century chapel of St. Thomas a Becket, which for many years was a part of the grammar school, which sadly is no more. Next to the library is the half-timbered Green Dragon, one of the oldest inns in England, and a marvellous place to end this chapter.

Wymondham Market Cross

Great Yarmouth & The East Norfolk Coast

Beeston Hall

Area covered in Chapter 5

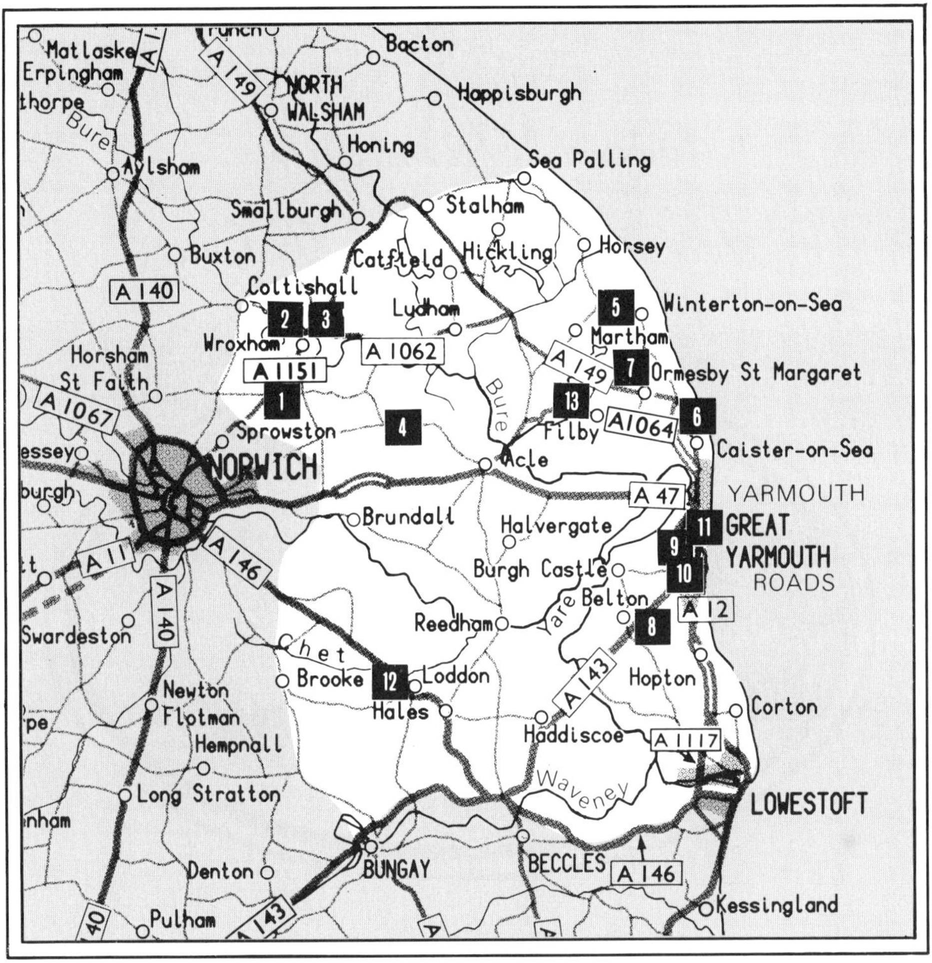

1 Barton Angler Country Inn *(Neatishead)*
2 Geo. Smith & Sons *(Wroxham)*
3 La Carozza *(Wroxham)*
4 Fairhaven Garden Trust *(South Walsham)*
5 The Fisherman's Return *(Winterton-on-Sea)*
6 The Lantern Restaurant *(Caister-on-Sea)*
7 Scratby Hall Caravan Park *(Scratby)*
8 Norfolk Barn & Old Forge Restaurant *(Belton)*
9 The Coachmakers Arms *(Great Yarmouth)*
10 The Crossford Hotel *(Great Yarmouth)*
11 El Santo *(Great Yarmouth)*
12 Stubbs House Hotel *(Loddon)*
13 Hillcrest Riding School *(Filby)*

CHAPTER 5

Great Yarmouth and the North East Coast

Wroxham with **Hoveton** is the undisputed capital of the Broadland, so it is here we decided to base ourselves whilst we became familiar with the delights of the Broads. We chose to stay at Neatishead, a few miles south of Wroxham, just off the A1151. We had been recommended to the **Barton Angler Country Inn**, originally a rectory of Georgian elegance and Victorian architecture. It is very pleasing to look at from the outside, and the visitor is not disappointed when they go through the doors. Mr. and Mrs. King, the owners, are clearly perfectionists in every department. The bedrooms are beautifully furnished, as one would expect. There are four-posters in the double rooms, and lovingly polished antiques everywhere.

In the winter the hotel is ablaze with log fires, and in summer you can wander through the four acres of landscaped gardens down to the moorings for boats. There is availability to hire a motor launch if you wish or, if you are feeling energetic, there are rowing boats. Having used all this energy, you may find that the proprietors have put on an excellent barbecue for you. Indoors, preparations are made for you to have a delicious dinner. The menu is not extensive, but the dishes available are mouth-watering.

The Barton Angler Country Inn

Begin with a selection of fresh fish from Lowestoft market, lightly bound in a fish veloute and placed into a parsley and lemon pancake, served with a sauce made from whole langoustine and fennel. Follow that with a pork cutlet, using just the eye of the meat, wrapped round a smoked chicken mouseline, with chopped fresh apricots and spinach leaves. This is then served upon a sauce made from reduced chicken stock, small pieces of dairy butter and parsley.

If, like us, you enjoy a good wine, you can indulge your palate with a fine Edesheimer Rosengarten Ortega, Auslese 1986, or a Mersault le Cru, Limosins. More modestly, the house wine is very acceptable. After dinner the bar entices you to relax with coffee and liqueurs. On Saturday evenings a pianist plays gently in the background, complementing your feeling of well-being.

The twin villages of Wroxham and Hoveton are linked together by a hump-backed bridge over the river Bure. The banks are alive with boatyards, and the water is usually crowded with boats. Naturally there are many boat hire and provisioning facilities, so we set out to find one that would deal competently with novices like ourselves. We found there is nowhere better to go than to **Geo. Smith and Sons** of Riverside Road, **Wroxham**. Here you will be sure of a warm friendly welcome from this family-owned boatyard. They willingly answered all our questions, some of which, we have to admit, must have sounded pretty dumb!

You can have the choice of hiring a small motor launch for up to six or seven persons for approximately £40.00 per day, or indulge in one of their new, own design picnic boats, for up to ten persons, with cooking facilities, heaters and a toilet. This will cost you about £60.00 per day. These boats will also convert into a mini-break cruiser for two, for that long weekend or a few days mid-week break. On all these craft you will be given a helpful suggested route by Duncan, the owner, or one of his sons, and full instructions on the control of the boat.

If you prefer to be taken on a trip around the Broads, this yard also runs the *Broadland Explorer*, a passenger craft for two hour or three hour trips, or all day excursions. They include free refreshments of tea or coffee, and home-made cakes served personally by friendly stewardesses. One of the special aspects of the *Broadland Explorer* are the facilities, thought of by Duncan and his wife Jenny, for the disabled or elderly passenger, with access made easy by a hydraulic lift at the stern for wheelchairs. There are two toilets on board, one especially wide enough for a wheelchair and a helper, if necessary. Together with a shore-linked telephone and a medication sick bay area, everything has been done to make the Broads accessible to people with disabilities, who may not have previously thought it possible to go on a river trip.

Behind the hustle of this small yard, surprisingly, many other projects are flourishing. Geo. Smith and Sons specialise in the refurbishment and repair of the traditional wooden Broad cruisers. They also produce luxury small cruisers, from drawing-board to the full fitted boat, for the private market, or indeed to go into the hire fleets of other boatyards.

The boatyard is open all the year, and boats are available to hire from approximately Easter to the end of October, depending on the weather. A telephone call is all that is needed to reserve a boat, or to enquire about the availability throughout the year.

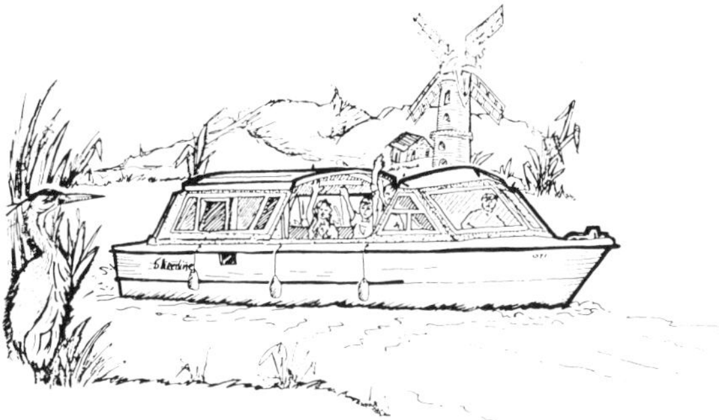

One of the boats from Geo. Smith and Sons' boatyard

Wroxham church has a very fine Norman doorway. Hoveton church stands about a mile away, on the road to Horning, where hotels, shops and boathouses line the village street, which runs along the north bank of the River Bure. Ludham is not far away; it is a pretty village but, like its neighbours Catfield, it does not stand on a river bank. They are each about a mile from the water. All these little villages are great for wandering about. We found that there is a public car park enclosure on the wooded shores of Wroxham Road, which was excellent for watching all the boating activity.

We dined in Wroxham at a remarkable place called **La Carozza**, meaning 'carriage'. This place originally belonged to British Rail, and was the Hoveton and Wroxham railway station. It is an experience; Mr. Nando Sappia, the proprietor, has done most of the conversion himself. It is 102 ft. long and 12 ft. wide, and was the ticket office, waiting rooms and store rooms of the old station. The Cromer to Norwich line still runs close by.

La Carozza

The concept of the internal design came from a brochure on the Orient Express, which Mr. Sappia was glancing through. Inside, the restaurant is exactly the same as a railway carriage, even down to a replica of British Rail windows! On the walls are pictures of London, Paris, the Swiss Alps, the Italian Lakes and Venice; the five stopping-points on the Orient Express journey to Venice.

The menu consists of mainly Italian dishes, using beef, chicken, veal and fish with a variety of Italian sauces. Pastas are also prominent on the menu. The spices and herbs which go into the sauces are imported from Italy, and all the dishes are complemented by an extensive range of Italian wines. Nando claims that his chef, Tony Zavanaiu from Sardinia, is the finest Italian chef in the country. The meal we had was superb, so he may well be right. The prices range from £10.00 to £15.00 per head.

We paid a visit to **Ranworth**, which is just south east of Wroxham and nine miles north east of Norwich. The parish church of St. Helen is a great attraction, because its tower commands a wonderful view across the Bure valley Broads. It is a fine Perpendicular church, and the gracefully soaring tower arch heads the nave, at the end of which there is a glowing testimony to the craftmanship of mediæval times in the superb 15th century rood screen. It is carved with delicate cusps, and opulently gilded and painted with apostles and saints, wearing the most wonderfully coloured robes. On either side of the church are fine altars, divided from the rood screen by painted projecting wings, which are joined to the posts by ethereal flying buttresses.

One of the great treasures of this lovely church is the cantor's desk, with a plainsong Gloria painted on the front, and an eagle, with the opening words of St. John's Gospel on the back. Also in the church's possession is an exquisite mediæval illuminated Antiphone. The church is open daily from 9.00 am until one hour before dusk. We were saddened to see some visitors merely using the tower to gaze at the view, and not taking the time to absorb the richness of the church and our history.

Beeston Hall is only a little way north of Wroxham. From Neatishead, where we were staying, it was almost next door. The Hall is a charming 18th century flint faced castle-like 'Gothick mansion with typical Georgian interiors'. The house and its contents reflect the lifestyle over several generations of the Prestons, the Norfolk family who built it and still live there. There is always something special about houses one visits in which the families still live, and this is one of them. Having whiled away an afternoon very pleasantly we had tea in the orangery.

While you are in the village, the church of Beeston St. Lawrence has an interesting Gothic interior, put in around 1803. There are also some stylish wall monuments here, to the Preston family.

At **South Walsham**, on the B1140 from Norwich, or southerly through the winding lanes that are so much a feature of this part of Norfolk, you will find that the well-tended churchyard shelters not one but two churches. St.

Mary's, which is the 14th century parish church, has some interesting features; the other is the derelict church of St. Laurence. It was not to see the churches that we came to South Walsham, but to visit the **Fairhaven Garden Trust.**

There are few places in England where at all times of the year you can find an innate beauty and tranquillity, which forms an idyllic escape from the hustle and bustle of daily life. To find one, just travel along the road into South Walsham and the Fairhaven Garden Trust. Be prepared to spend many happy hours there.

The village was first recorded in history during the reign of King Harold. After the battle of Hastings, William the Conqueror took over the land, and gave the manor of South Walsham to the Earl of Norfolk, later to become the Duke of Norfolk. There is much of interest to see, and we should have drawn your attention in the beginning to the 15th century rood screen and carved poppy heads on the pews in St. Mary's church. The fine 18th century organ in the church was originally built for the Assembly House, Norwich, but was donated to St. Mary's by the late Lord Fairhaven.

About a mile to the north lies Malthouse Broad, leading to Ranworth Broad and its Nature Reserve. To the north east there is road access to the public South Walsham Outer Broad: this leads through a narrow channel called 'The Wells' into the private Inner Broad, which forms part of the Fairhaven Garden Trust.

Fairhaven Garden Trust

Lord Fairhaven was not only a gardener, but also a naturalist. He purchased the South Walsham Estate in 1947, and the whole garden was a wilderness. The dykes of the present garden existed, but the whole area presented an inpenetrable jungle of fallen trees, brambles and nettles. Inspired by his friend, Sir Eric Savill, creator of one of the first woodland gardens in the world, Lord Fairhaven conceived the idea of a woodland garden in Norfolk. The jungle was slowly cleared, and as each new area was conquered, shade and water-loving plants were introduced: primulas by the thousand; Lysichitum Americanum, which now grows in almost wild profusion; camellias and rhododendrons were just a few of the plants chosen.

What you see today took fifteen years to create, and Lord Fairhaven achieved it with the help of a single woodman, Jack Debbage. Since then there have always been Debbages at Fairhaven. The head gardener and resident warden is now George Debbage.

The Fairhaven Garden Trust property covers about 170 acres including the Inner Broad, and a further 60 acres comprising the bird sanctuary to the west of Ranworth Road. There have been 92 varieties of birds in the woods around South Walsham, and the bird sanctuary may be visited by prior arrangement with the warden. So much more could be written about the Fairhaven Garden Trust, but seeing is better than reading, so do go and experiece this enchantment for yourselves.

From Wroxham it is not too great a distance to visit **Winterton-on-Sea**. If you are looking for a traditional Norfolk pub, then you have found it at **The Fisherman's Return**. It is about 300 years old, and is built of brick and flint, with super wood panelling. There is good ale and good food, either in the bar or the dining room. The garden room has been especially furnished to make it attractive to families, and on fine days the children can play in the large enclosed garden.

John and Kate Findley are just the right kind of people to run this sort of business. You will see the warmth of their personalities, not only in the pub, but in the cosy old-style accommodation, if you choose to stay there. They have three double rooms and one single. The pub has been in the Egon Ronay Good Food Guide since 1980, and we believe the standard has got better every year. You will enjoy the Fisherman's Return; we did.

The Fisherman's Return

Winterton-on-Sea is a very pleasant place to spend a holiday, especially if you have children who love to play on the beach. The beach here is very wide and sandy; at low tide there are innumerable little pools which delight children. Behind the beach there are extensive sand dunes, which can give some protection, and have masses of coastal plants and considerable bird life. There are many delightful places around Winterton-on-Sea, which makes it good sense to stay at the Fisherman's Return and make the most of the area. Sailing, of course, is right on your doorstep here anyway, as are many other fine pursuits, including some fine walks.

Martham is only a few miles inland, and it has a wealth of Georgian houses and cottages, the best of which are to be found around the well-kept green. The church is unusual inasmuch as it has a fine 15th century tower, with an exceptionally well constructed modern hammerbeam roof. There is a fine sculptured 15th century font, and the Victorian chancel gives pleasure to the eyes. Just north is **Somerton Staithe**, which is a charming unspoilt spot at the end of a navigable channel up through Martham Broad, with grassy banks, a few houses and a fine view westwards over the marshes. From here you are only about two miles from Winterton.

At Horsey, midway between Winterton and Sea Palling (don't forget **The Hall Inn** at Sea Palling if you want a pleasant pub), the minute village is about a mile from the sea, but with another splendid old in, The Nelson Head. There is a lovely thatched church too, if you can find it beneath the overgrown churchyard.

Horsey Mill stands at the head of a staithe linked to Horsey Mere. There is a fine drainage windmill here, in brick, with a wooden capping and well-restored sails. It is owned by the National Trust now, and opens throughout the holiday period. Just below Sea Palling is **Waxham**, a strange place. There is a farm within the walls of the long vanished mansion, Waxham Hall, built in the 15th century; it is reputed to be haunted.

Turning our backs on all this peacefulness, we made tracks for **Great Yarmouth**, which is an entirely different sort of place. It is a curious mixture; the old town was once an important sea port and, until recent years, one of the great fishing ports in the country. There is also the holiday resort which thrives on visitors, and somehow does not seem in keeping with the Norfolk we have seen so far. We have to admit to preferring the part which is not holiday resort orientated. However Great Yarmouth gives enormous pleasure to thousands of visitors every year, and so it must be the right place for them. Strangely **Caister-on-Sea**, which is virtually a suburb of Great Yarmouth, is different again.

Caister was originally a Roman settlement, and some of the excavations can be seen here. It is advertised as the remains of an important Roman port, and you can take a look at the excavations. While you are in Caister, take a look at the famous lifeboat as well. We always get a thrill when we see a lifeboat. You realise that the comparatively small vessel, together with its incredibly brave crew, have pitted their wits against the elements time and time again to save lives. So many people from all over the world are indebted to the lifeboat service.

When we had seen the Roman port and lifeboat, we went looking for somewhere to eat. In Yarmouth Road, we found **The Lantern Restaurant**. We love Chinese food, and this proved to be a good choice. Cantonese is our favourite, and Mr. Tai specialises in this. The food was well presented; you can be brave and use chopsticks or stay British and settle for cutlery. Somehow Chinese food improves with chopsticks and we are always willing to use them, even if not very skillfully.

The Lantern Restaurant

The restaurant opened in 1978, but Mr. Tai has only been there six years. In that time he has refurbished the place very attractively, although in an English style rather than Chinese. The restaurant is fully licensed, and opens from Sunday to Thursday 5.00 pm to 12.00 midnight, and on Friday and Saturday he opens for lunch as well, from 12.00 midday to 2.00 pm.

We forgot to talk about **Scratby** on our way down the coast to Great Yarmouth, possibly because Great Yarmouth is the nearest town. At Scratby there is **Scratby Hall Caravan Park**, with five acres of lovely ground for touring caravans and tents. It is just three-quarters of a mile from the sea, and is a marvellous place for a caravan site. It is well sheltered, and is an ideal place for a family holiday. The site has a launderette,

Scratby Hall Caravan Park

excellent showers and toilets, electric hook-ups, a hairdressing salon, games room and a very useful 'Take One Leave One' library. The shop is well stocked with everything you need, including home-grown produce.

There is something different you can do or see every day you are there. There is a golf course nearby, and a dog track too, if that is your sport. You can also go stock car racing, fishing or sailing. Take air trips, or join the 'Drinking Trough' club; clamber around Caister Castle, or just lie on the beach. If you want to explore Norwich, then you will have to drive twenty miles, but with so much happening within five miles of Scratby Hall Caravan Park that you will probably be too busy to go further afield.

Now we really are going to tell you more about **Great Yarmouth**. Our problem is that these places are all so close together. In fact there have been, in the main unwelcome, suggestions that Great Yarmouth should be linked to Lowestoft to form one large city, even though Lowestoft is in Suffolk. In the eyes of the church, Lowestoft is already linked with Great Yarmouth, because ecclesiastical boundaries have made it so.

Charles Dickens stayed at Yarmouth, at the Royal Hotel, and there is a tablet on the wall to commemorate this fact. Charles Dickens, you may remember, wrote of Blundeston, which is to the south of Yarmouth. His famous character David Copperfield, was born there. The road from Blundeston to Yarmouth has changed very much since Barkis drove his carrier's cart there. You will not find the site of Peggoty's home either.

In summer the long sandy beach is full of happy holiday-makers, enjoying all that the resort has to offer them, and it has a lot. Marine Parade has lovely colourful gardens, countless attractions and amenities; there are two piers, which give endless fun. There are also boat trips, fishing, sailing, wind-surfing and everything that an active holiday-maker could desire. If you wish to explore outside Great Yarmouth, then many places are within easy reach.

At **Belton**, a village only a few miles away, you will find **The Norfolk Barn and Old Forge Restaurants**. The original farm buildings were probably erected in the late 1700s. From the existing old accounts book, we

The Norfolk Barn and Old Forge Restaurants

know that Elmgrove Estate, as it was known then, was the property of Ted Bland, a rare and talented character who, with his wife and six children, embarked on what was to be an extraordinary career. With the barn as his engine room, he masterminded a kaleidoscope of business activities: master builder, contractor, coffin cart and barrow maker, carpenter, joiner, wheelwright and blacksmith.

The last survivor of the Bland family died in 1968, leaving Elmgrove Estate neglected and dilapidated. Fortunately restoration began in 1970, using the original sound timbers, and The Norfolk Barn Restaurant opened its door in 1976. The 'Old Forge', with its original blacksmith's forge in good working order, was renovated in 1982 to cater for parties, functions and barbecues. Both restaurants are brimming with character, and with treasures from bygone ages. The a la carte menu is full of delicious, mouthwatering dishes, offering beef, poultry, game, fish and shellfish, and is changed periodically. We are sure you will enjoy the excellent food and wine in the atmosphere of days gone by.

Market days in Great Yarmouth on Wednesdays, Fridays and Saturdays are fun. It's all hustle and bustle, mingled with interesting and enticing smells. When you have had enough of wandering through the colourful stalls and you are hungry and thirsty, just make your way to **The Coachmaker's Arms** on the corner of the market. It is set amongst historical old buildings, dating back to the 16th century, Anna Sewell, author of 'Black Beauty', lived here, and further along Miles Corbett, reputedly one of the signatories to the death warrant of Charles I, occupied one of the houses. Incidentally he became Great Yarmouth's first Recorder and Registrar in 1625.

The Coachmaker's Arms

There are times when I am writing about all these interesting, but sometimes quite useless pieces of information that bring Michael Caine to mind, with his fascinating book 'Not Many People Knew That'! Perhaps you would like to be enrolled in the U.I.S. of which I am life-long Vice President (U.I.S. stands for Useless Information Society). It would be nice to hear from readers with useless information about any county. We in return will reward you with a complimentary copy of any one of the other county books we are writing.

More importantly, going back to the market place and the historical buildings, the most picturesque are the fishermen's houses, originally designed as a hospital to look after the crews of the herring boats, but now dedicated to retired seafarers. All these houses have plaques on the walls, which will give more information.

Finally to the Coachmaker's Arms! It is a building totally in keeping with the rest of the market place. As you enter the portals you feel as though you are stepping back a century or two. The beams and the brasses are old, but the ales and the food are certainly up to date. Although Janice and Cozy have been at the inn for a short time, their friendly approach has already made a mark on the place. What is more, they are knowledgeable about this historical corner of Norfolk, and will enjoy telling you many interesting stories.

Peter and Olga Brown run the friendly **Crossford Hotel** at 15/16 Nelson Road North. It would be difficult not to be happy here. There are 14 well-furnished letting rooms, five of which are en-suite with tea making facilities. The hotel is licensed, and does both bed and breakfast and evening meals. The food is good, well presented, English traditional fare.

Crossford Hotel

It is not so long ago that the hotel was refurbished, and very well done, we thought. Peter and Olga managed to keep the best of the Edwardian features of the hotel, whilst modernising it sufficiently to make it more comfortable. If you stay here in winter you will appreciate this, because it is now centrally heated throughout. Children are very welcome, and there is a baby listening service.

The hotel is near the sea, the market and the theatre; you can go to the racecourse, or watch stock car racing. The Crossford Hotel, at £15.00 per head, is very good value indeed.

We were asked by friends of ours to find a riding school where children could have a holiday with horses. We enquired where in Norfolk such a holiday could be found, and where, if so wished, the parents could ride as well.

We struck lucky! **Hillcrest Riding School** at **Filby Heath**, near Great Yarmouth, proved to have all we needed. It is situated approximately four miles from Great Yarmouth on the A1064, between Caister and Acle. The riding school is both A.B.R.S. and B.H.S. approved. One hour rides, and lessons for both beginners and more advanced, including jumping and dressage, take place every day (except Mondays). Two hour beach rides in the evening are great fun, and take place most evenings, except during the winter, and start at 6.00 pm.

Safety standards are very high; all rides are escorted, and hard hats, to the B.H.S. recommended safety standard, are available for hire at 50p. The riding school (which is open all year except Christmas Day and Mondays) has ten horses and nine ponies, suitable for both the novice and the more experienced rider.

Accommodation is available for children from 7 to 16 years old to enjoy a holiday with horses. Each child chooses their own pony or horse that they wish to look after for the week, naturally with guidance in their choice. The children come down to the riding school each morning and join in with all the stable duties. During the morning they have riding lessons, giving them a healthy appetite for their lunch. The afternoons are taken up with one or two hour rides, and then it is back to the stable to finish off, groom, feed, clean the tack, etc. By the end of the week they are all ready for the gymkhana, and the award ceremony. The youngsters wear their rosettes with pride.

The evenings are catered for as well. Great Yarmouth is a lovely seaside town, and there are many attractions for which some pocket money is needed. We thought it was a super place for children to stay; the riding school is very efficient and well organised, and has a happy and relaxed atmosphere.

Hillcrest Riding School

What makes people return to a guest house time and time again? Is it the situation? The food? Maybe, but the most superbly sited building, with comfort and good food, can still not be right unless guests feel happy and relaxed.

Kath and Mick Prestedge at the **El Santo, North Denes**, have discovered the formula for this successful approach. It is only 300 yards from the sea, and is open all the year round. Even if the sea is pounding against the quay, and the wind is howling, El Santo maintains its aura of warm, friendly hospitality. It is licensed, and has a large dining room and private car park. The breakfast is more than ample to set you up for the day, and the evening meal offers you good, traditional English cooking. The 15 bedrooms have all been refurbished, and have colour TV and tea making facilities. The prices are very competitive as well, from just £9.50 per head.

El Santo Guest House

The race course, dog track and speedway are all nearby. We have already told you about the market days, and to add to all this, the shopping centre is excellent. There are tennis courts, a boating lake, a bowling green and the waterways as well. It has to be a marvellous place for a holiday, doesn't it?

Before we leave this part of Norfolk, we wanted to take a look at **Loddon**, where some friends of ours stayed. Loddon is a busy little market town, with many attractive 17th and 18th century houses, shops and inns. We stayed at **Stubbs House Hotel**. Somewhere that has a reputation which induces local people must be a recommendation, and indeed a percentage of Stubbs House Hotel's clientele come from the surrounding area.

Stubbs House Hotel

A typical Broadland scene

Georgian architecture was very grand, and is reflected to this day in the style and comfort within. There are original marble fireplaces in the style of Adam, decorative alcoves, and a grand restaurant with two menus which can seat up to 50 people. The building was a farmhouse, which would account for the Victorian tiled floor, laid possibly for ease of cleaning.

There are nine bedrooms, all en-suite and furnished to a high standard. We stayed here eventually for six weeks during our research of the area, and the treatment we received was friendly and co-operative. The proprietor, Mr. Constantine, is continuously improving his hotel, adding many facilities for the comfort of his guests, but he never loses sight of its Georgian origins.

During our stay at Loddon we visited many places, like **Ellingham**, a delightful riverside spot, complete with white weather-boarded mill, a little Gothic miller's house and a square-towered church, in which there are some box pews and a 16th century wall monument; not one of Norfolk's most exciting churches. **Kirby Cane** was much more to our liking. The church here has an Anglo-Saxon round tower, and an interesting Norman south doorway. Inside there is a 14th century octagonal font, a 16th century tomb chest and an early Jacobean pulpit. Our final excursion, which should by rights go into the Suffolk part of the book, was to **Somerleyton Hall**, and whether you are staying in Norfolk or Suffolk this must be on your list. We came back to it time and time again; we hope you will too.

Somerleyton Hall and gardens, with its famous maze, is worthy of much more space than we can give in this book. We will just wet your appetite for this beautiful family home, and it is a family home in the true sense of the word. Lord and Lady Somerleyton live there with their five children. They are very proud of their heritage, and their ambition is to conserve it, not just for themselves and their children, but also for the many visitors who come each year to enjoy the house, and particularly the garden, which is ever-changing.

The story of the house and family is recorded in an excellent guide, available when you visit the house. Each room has its own particular attraction. For example, the Oak Room is representative of the 17th century; here the panelling is from the original Jacobean house, and was made from oaks grown within Somerleyton's extensive parklands. The carvings on the chimney breasts are partly by the hand of Grinling Gibbons.

Between the windows of the northern wall of the Oak Parlour hangs an exquisite silver and gilt moulded mirror, which was originally made for the private apartments of the Doge's palace in Venice, and at one time was owned by Queen Anne. That is a brief description of just one room! Each room you come to has paintings, silver Meissen and superb antiques. It is a delightful way to spend an afternoon, and that is simply talking about the house!

The gardens and grounds have long been considered of first rate importance. Twelve acres of garden surround the Hall. One of the most popular features has always been the maze, one of the finest in Britain. There is a profusion of colour from the plants and shrubs, and as you wander through the gardens you constantly come to arches and statues, and a very special pergola which is 300 ft. long. A miniature railway was opened in 1972, and gives hours of pleasure to children and adults alike. Those taking a ride are able to have a different view of the house and park, and also various breeds of cattle, sheep and ponies.

Somerleyton Hall

Three miles from Somerleyton is **Fritton Lake and Country Park**. It is another part of the Estate activity which is open to the public. The two and a quarter mile long lake is one of the most beautiful expanses of water in East Anglia, and attracts many visitors each year, who enjoy fishing, boating, playing pitch and putt, windsurfing, looking at wildfowl, or simply relaxing in this beautiful setting. Children spend much of their time in the adventure play area, or having pony rides. Somerleyton Hall is open to the public from Easter to the end of September. Please phone (0502) 730224 for details.

We have talked about the Broads rather generally in this chapter, assuming you know about them. This assumption is probably half true, for like us you will have heard of the Broads. Some people will ask, "What are the Broads?" So we will try to tell you simply from what we have gathered. They are about 200 miles of interconnecting waterways; partly lakes, partly rivers, which lie between Norwich, Beccles, Lowestoft, Great Yarmouth and North Walsham. The whole area gives delight to many people and, for those of you who take to the water in boats and travel these waterways, you will have unsurpassed beauty wherever you go. The wildlife, and the flora and fauna are incredible. There will be more about the Broads and the villages in Chapter 8.

Thetford to Mildenhall

Norfolk Broads

Area covered in Chapter 6

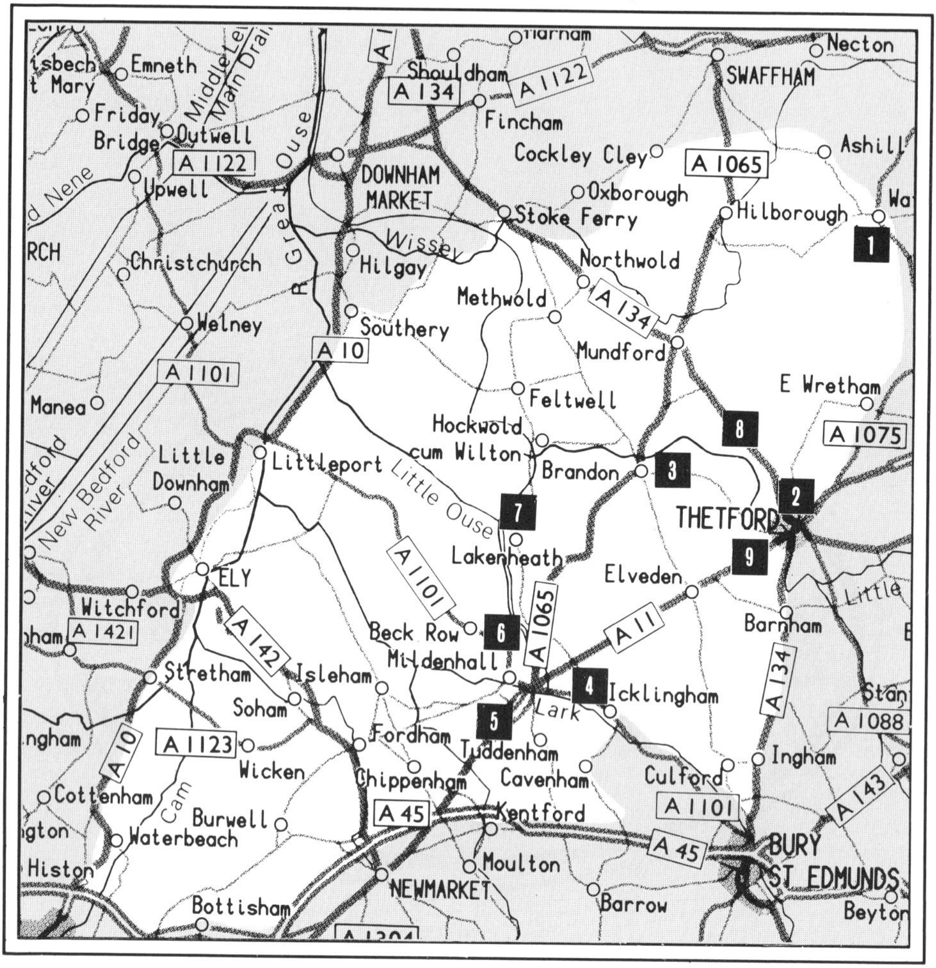

1. Griston Hall *(Griston)*
2. The Kings Arms *(Thetford)*
3. Brandon Lodge Motel *(Brandon)*
4. The Plough Inn *(Icklingham)*
5. Worlington Hall Country House Hotel *(Worlington)*
6. The White House *(Holywell Row)*
7. The Bull Inn *(Lakenheath)*
8. Grimes Graves
9. Kilverstone Park *(Thetford)*

CHAPTER 6

Thetford to Mildenhall

There is a 'Once upon a time' story about **Watton**, just on the eastern boundary of Breckland. Just a little further north is Wayland Wood, which is reputed to be the scene of the famous pantomime tale of 'Babes in the Wood'. Certainly the ballad from which the nursery story is taken tells that Norfolk was the setting. The locals told us that Wayland is a corruption of 'wailing', which is associated with the unhappy story of the babes. Also, Griston Hall nearby was the reputed home of the 'Wicked Uncle'.

Griston Hall is a Grade II listed ancient manor house, standing half a mile south of Wayland Wood and one mile from Watton, on the A1075. It became identified with the 'Babes in the Wood' in 1595, when the story was published by Thomas Millington.

The Hall was rebuilt in 1597, following a fire in the north east end of the house. Mediæval carved beams have been retained by splicing them to the newer oak beams. Above the porch is a tablet recording the rebuilding, with the words 'Thomas May 1597', and engraved around the edge of the plaque 'God Save the Queen'. There is also a Norwich Insurance Fire plaque, few of which are still in position today. Griston Hall is the central feature of Hall Farm, which extends to 400 acres of arable and livestock farming.

There are two miles of footpaths, which the bed and breakfast guests are encouraged to use. Nearby Wayland, belonging to the Norfolk Naturalist Trust, is recorded in the Domesday Book as one of the oldest woods in England, containing over 200 various species of plants. The Peddars Way long distance footpath, which stretches over 90 miles from Knedishall in Suffolk to Hunstanton, on the North Norfolk coast, passes two miles to the west of Griston Hall, through the village of Thompson. A few miles away is the village of Santon Downham, which is the centre of Thetford Forest; here there are nature trails and fitness courses.

Thompson Watering offers facilities for coarse fishing while, 15 miles away, at Narborough, trout fishing is available. Thetford, Dereham and Wotton Sports Centres offer swimming and indoor sports. Griston Hall is central for touring East Anglia, with day trips to Cambridge, Ely, Newmarket, Bury St. Edmunds, King's Lynn, Norwich, the Norfolk Broads and the seaside resorts; an excellent base for visitors.

The local market towns of Watton, Swaffham and East Dereham do brisk trade on market days, although the livestock sales have finished, except for poultry sales at Swaffham on a Saturday. The house is open all year round for guests, offering two family rooms and one double room, all with en-suite toilet and shower, colour TV, and tea and coffee making facilities.

The dining room is small, with a low ceiling divided by oak beams, and has a small inglenook fireplace. Traditional farmhouse cooked breakfast is normally served, although continental breakfast can be requested. Evening meals are catered for locally in the two village pubs, or there are first class restaurants in Watton.

Griston Hall

Going south on the A1075 from Watton, we came to **Thetford**. It is hard to imagine today what this town was like many moons ago, but for a long time it was a quiet oasis, dreaming about its greatness in Saxon times. It awoke from its dreams to find industry of all kinds had come its way and, if that was not enough, the U.S. Air Force had established two big bases at Mildenhall and Lakenheath, with the R.A.F. not far away at Marham and Watton.

Thetford once had a castle, which was demolished in 1173, but it has left a huge, impressive mound rising from a dry moat. These earthworks dominate the place where the Ickneild Way crosses the rivers Thet and Little Ouse. Even the buildings in Thetford are not typical of Norfolk. Many of the old buildings are of a hard chalk, though occasionally you will come across half-timbered structures like the Bell Inn, but it was not the Bell Inn we were looking for.

If an inn that is immaculately kept takes your fancy, then it must be **The Kings Arms**. On the corner overlooking the market square, this 300 year old pub has a landlord to be proud of. Local man Brian Worby is not only a Town Councillor, but he also has merit awards for Innkeeper of the Year. Real ale buffs are sure to enjoy their beer, as are those of you with healthy appetites. The food is good pub grub, and there is plenty of room in the restaurant for you to enjoy it. The inn is kept in old world style, with oak beams and comfortable seating. Why not, like us, bide your time and enjoy the view, in an atmosphere of warmth and friendliness, and watch the world go on its busy way.

The Kings Arms

In the **Ancient House Museum**, in White Hart Street, which is a fine restored early Tudor house with splendid oak ceilings, you can take a look at various displays of local history, archæology, natural history and, of course, flint. It also acts as the local Tourist Information Centre. They open daily from 10.00 am to 5.00 pm, except Sundays, when the museum is closed in the winter, and in summer it only opens from 2.00 pm to 5.00 pm.

One mile from Thetford on the A11 is **Kilverstone Park**. Lord and Lady Fisher have been building up this wildlife park since 1973. It is a super place, set in the beautiful valley of the River Thet. It provides an area of recreation and interest, where old and young can enjoy a day in the country.

The Latin American Zoo creates great interest. It is composed of animals and birds that are rarely seen in this country, and seldom anywhere in such variety. Amongst the 650 animals and birds are eight species of South American cats, from the giant jaguar down to the little Geoffroys cats from Argentina. There are also eighteen species of monkeys, marmosets and tamarins, and the very rare maned wolves.

Adjoining the zoo area, situated behind the station, is the Adventure Play Area and Ridearound. This area is devoted to amusements and coin-operated rides, with mini motorbikes, bumper boats, and a tiny tots' merry-go-round. There is a 'Patting Area', where children can safely meet and pet a variety of tame animals. The magnificent miniature railway runs near the lake.

Kilverstone Stud of Senor Julio Cesar Falabella's Miniature Horses surrounds the house, and these little horses may be seen in their stables, or out at exercise in the paddocks. The original animals were personally selected by Lord and Lady Fisher, under the watchful eye of Senor Falabella himself, when they were taken to his ranch in Argentina.

The ever-talkative parrots are scattered throughout the park, and the South American ducks, flamingos and penguins are kept near the great figurehead of H.M.S. *Calcutta*. The guanacos, alpacas, llamas, bison, deer , rheas, peccaries, capybaras and tapirs live in the paddocks outside the walled garden which is the main area.

The park is open every day of the year, from 10.00 am to 6.30 pm, but closes at dusk in winter. The cafeteria provides hot and cold snacks and drinks from Easter to October. On Sundays in winter you can get a cup of tea in the gift shop.

Miniature Horses at Kilverstone Park

Not far from Thetford is one of the most exciting and interesting places in Breckland, possibly in the whole of Norfolk. **Grimes Graves**, 'Grime' being the local name for the devil, is quite extraordinary. The 'Graves' are a large number of depressions in the ground, and have absolutely nothing to do with burial. They are Neolithic flint mines 4,000 years old. They were first excavated in 1870, and are an intricate network of over 300 pits and shafts.

One pit, 30ft deep, with seven radiating galleries, is open to the public. You will reach this unique place on the B1108, one and a half miles north of Brandon. To find out details of the opening times, contact Mr. D. Moore, The English Heritage, Government Buildings, Cambridge. Tel: (0223) 358911. It would be sad to miss out this fascinating experience.

Even today you will find that flint miners are still at work. The men of Brandon and Santon Downham work very much in the age-old method, but using slightly more modern tools! These present-day miners can produce implements similar to the ones of prehistoric times. If, God forbid, civilisation as we know it was destroyed, what better place to start all over again, and make tools from the natural material which, presumably, would still be there.

The term 'flint knapping' intrigued us; what was it, and how was it done? 'Knapping' is the art of striking a piece of flintstone in exactly the right spot, so that each stone divides into flakes or pieces. The pieces are used to repair the beautiful flushwork patterns you see on the walls of many ancient churches in Norfolk. They have many other uses, of course, and the flakes once were used for flint lock guns. Trade boomed in the Napoleonic wars, when large quantities of gun flints were required.

Weeting is only a flintstone's throw away from Grimes Graves. William the Conqueror encamped here, whilst he was rooting out the last of the Saxons, under Hereward the Wake. Detective work was alive and flourishing even then; Hereward tried to creep into the camp disguised as a potter. His cover was blown rapidly. He had the misfortune to have one brown and one blue eye, and was recognised almost immediately! We wondered who had known that, and where they kept the record!

Weeting Heath is a wonderful place for bird watchers, although you are only allowed to watch from the hides on this lovely stretch of Breckland. You will find a vast variety of birds, and the area is famous for its flora and

Weeting Heath Birdlife

fauna. You will need to get a permit from the warden on site; the months in which this is possible are April to August. To get to it, take the Weeting Road towards Thetford.

We did not like Weeting itself at all, so we quickly went on to **Brandon**, which is just over the county borderline into Suffolk. In the centre of Brandon we were very surprised to discover a modern purpose-built motel. **Brandon Lodge Motel** was built four years ago by Mr. Guthrie, a Scottish gentleman who loves people! It is well-designed, and offers excellent single, double and two-bedroomed apartments, which are supplied with everything you could possible need, including microwaves.

The Brandon Lodge Motel

It is an excellent place to make your base for a holiday in this part of East Anglia. Thetford, Norwich, Bury St. Edmunds, Cambridge and Ipswich are all within easy reach or, if you would prefer to stay in Brandon, all you have to do is walk outside the door of your apartment, and you are immediately in the centre of Brandon.

There is a restaurant attached to the building, which is partially licensed. It specialises in American and Italian fast foods, so much loved by children, and a Godsend to anyone in a hurry, or who finds it difficult to entertain children whilst trying to enjoy a more leisurely meal.

We think you will find **Santon Downham**, set in the forest on the bank of the Little Ouse, a lovely village; we did. The village was built on the shifting sands of the Breckland, and it was buried, almost, in the 17th century, when the sand covered most of the surrounding countryside. Today the man-made forest has done much to bind, and to control, the land. The pretty village has become the headquarters of the Forestry Commission in the area. The Commission provides much employment for the people of Santon, Downham and Brandon.

The Norman church has two Saxon doorways, and it stands in one of the most beautiful churchyards in the county. If you wander through the churchyard, and then take a footpath which runs behind, you will walk through an archway of fine old linden trees, leading you to the river.

Thetford Chase is the state-owned forest we are talking about, and over the years it has become the home of much wildlife. It is a designated nature reserve. The light sandy soil, which caused so much havoc in the 17th century, provides the ideal ground for coniferous trees, such as pines, firs and larches. Whilst in the area, where the soil is more fertile, we found glorious beeches and oaks.

If you sit quietly, you are more likely to see Muntjac deer or red squirrel, and if you are very lucky you will see badgers and otters. The birds love the area, and we saw goldcrests, crossbills, goss hawks and red-backed shrikes. Plant life abounds; you will find gentians, militiary orchids and maiden pinks, and a host of other flora.

Just down the A11 from Thetford, or the B1106 from Brandon, we came to **Elvedon**, almost surrounded by heaths and warrens. The church is quite remarkable, and worth visiting, but it was the strangeness of Elvedon Hall which wetted our interest. The Hall was once a modest Georgian residence, but the Maharaja Duleep Singh acquired the house, and transformed it into an Oriental palace. He had been banished from his court at Lahore, and from India, by Queen Victoria, so he concentrated all his wealth and efforts on Elvedon.

There were copper domes, masses of Italian carved marble, and the most ornate decor you could imagine; totally out of keeping with this peaceful part of the world. On his death, the palace was bought by Lord Iveagh, of the Guinness family, who added even more lavish adornments and Baroque work.

Mildenhall Market Cross

While we were in this part of the county, we took a quick look at three other villages, all in a little triangle, just south of Barton Mills. **Icklingham** was the first; it stands on the north bank of the River Lark, in the centre of many interesting relics. The remains of Saxons, Romans and Britons have been found here. There are two churches, but the church of St. James and All Saints is lovely. It has a thatched roof, and very beautiful east windows in the south aisle.

If you are a CAMRA enthusiast, then please do not miss out on the superb real ale you will get at **The Plough Inn**, Icklingham, on the A1101, about five miles north of Bury St. Edmunds. Mr. and Mrs. Brueton keep some of the best ale we have ever tasted.

The pub is about 200 years old, or at least the building is. It was originally farm cottages, and became a pub in the late 1880s. When we were there we

The Plough Inn, Icklingham

were made very welcome, even though they were extremely busy with refurbishing and building on a large additional public bar. The lounge bar is part of the original building, and has super open fires.

There is a wide selection of bar meals; we counted a choice of 30 different dishs the day we were there, from sandwiches, which are freshly made, to a first class shepherd's pie. The home-made steak and kidney pie looked particularly good.

We had read about them in the Good Beer Guide, and we can confirm that they certainly deserved their mention in there. Even if the beer is good and the food delicious, a pub is not right in our minds unless the atmosphere is good, and the welcome friendly. Here you can final all the ingredients that make for a first-class watering hole.

Tuddenham St. Mary is only three miles away from Icklingham, just south west of Mildenhall. The pretty village green and the outstanding 14th century church made it a very worthwhile stop for us. Even amongst East Anglia's many fine historic buildings, we were enchanted by **Tuddenham Mill**, and even more delighted to discover it was a first class restaurant. The Domesday Book records it as a working mill. The interior of this 300 year old building has been totally refurbished in the most elegant manner.

The waterwheel itself is a feature of the reception lounge; we were shown into the spacious beamed restaurant, which overlooks the river, and presented with a first class menu. On offer that particular evening, amongst many dishes, was a delicately poached salmon, with the crispest vegetables. The sweet trolley made choice impossible, so we were beguiled by a charming waitress to try a little of everything. Apparently, this is a regular happening, and if you dine there often you would ask simply for the 'Grand Dessert'. The wine list carries some 130 wines for you to choose from, including some very good vintages.

It would be a great place for conferences, or a private party. It rained the night we were there, otherwise we could have dined on the lawn, by the river, which we could imagine to be a very pleasant way to have such a good meal.

Finally, in that same day we took a look at **Cavenham**, which is bordered on the north by the River Lark. The river winds its way from Bury St. Edmunds through Mildenhall, until it joins the River Ouse, near Littleport. The famous prehistoric Icknield Way runs diagonally through here; strange to think that it led deep into the land of the Iceni tribe, and Queen Boedica.

Wondering where to stay for three or four days, we came across **Worlington Hall Country House Hotel**, not far from **Mildenhall**. We were offered a bargain break for either two, three or four nights, at a price ranging from £45.00 for two nights to £90.00 for four nights (per person of course). We were very taken by this elegant 16th century former manor house, set in five acres of grounds. The original house was built in 1570, and added to in the 18th century. Having become a hotel has done nothing to detract from its original elegance. We discovered it was a listed building, because of its historical interest. We also found that it was exceedingly comfortable.

We were welcomed into our room with a complimentary decanter of sherry; there were fresh flowers and fruit too. These are always touches which enhance a stay anywhere. There are eight individually designed rooms, most of which have toilet and bath, or shower, en-suite. All the rooms are equipped with tea and coffee making facilities, remote control colour televisions, direct dial telephones, radio and alarm clock, trouser press, hairdryer and a fully-stocked mini bar. Each room is named; we stayed in 'Kingfisher', but it could have been the 'Robin' room, or the 'Lark' room.

Before dinner, we went to the lounge bar for a drink, and found it a beautifully panelled room, dating back to the 16th century. There was a blazing log fire, and it really set the scene for a memorable meal in the charming surroundings of the restaurant. If we had wanted to give a private dinner party, we could have used the 'Alcove Room', which is also available for business meetings and working lunches. It is also used for breakfast.

Worlington Hall offers facilities for business and private meetings, both large and small. Weddings, christenings and dinner dances are catered for as well. The 'Garden Suite' has its own entrance from the car park, and is perfect for weddings, dinner dances and conferences. Up to 150 guests can be accommodated in comfort, with room for entertainment and dancing.

From Worlington there are a wealth of places you can visit. For golfers, the Royal Worlington and Newmarket golf course is an excellent choice. Newmarket Races is always a good outing, taking a visit to the Horse Racing Museum and National Stud at the same time. Cambridge, with all its beauty, Grimes Graves Flint Workings, the majesty of Ely Cathedral, historic Bury St. Edmunds, or the Duxford Imperial War Museum; certainly no lack of variety. We have to confess that we just took the chance to relax in the comfort of this first class well run hotel.

Worlington Hall Country House Hotel

Mildenhall was our next port of call. The town centres around the market place and the church, St. Mary's, is widely considered to be the finest church in western Suffolk. We found it superb, but more of St. Mary's in a minute. We were to stay at **Holywell Row**, a small community surrounded by farmland, and very close to the U.S. Air Force base. Holywell Row, together with West Row and Beck Row, are known collectively as 'The Rows'.

Our first introduction to the fun of staying at **The White House, Holywell Row**, was the lively welcome from Joe-Joe the parrot, who was a constant source of entertainment. The second welcome we received was from the master of the household, Doug Mantripp, and his wife Jackie, who assured us that they would do their best to make our stay enjoyable. From then on, we do not have to tell you that we have seldom been so cared for in a guest house.

This former farmhouse has been converted into a comfortable and tastefully decorated dwelling. The Mantripps make sure you are well fed in the traditional English manner, and we would suggest that, apart from people like us touring the area, the White House would make a good base for business people working in this part of Suffolk.

The White House

The parish of Mildenhall is apparently the largest in Suffolk, covering some 14,000 acres. The town has a good shopping centre, and is blessed with much open space, including the Jubilee playing fields and riverside walks, which run along the banks of the River Lark. There is a swimming pool and a good sports centre; however for us St. Mary's was the jewel. It stands impressively in the High Street, and has been a landmark across the fens for hundreds of years. Pinnacles climb out of shafted buttresses, and make their way up the tower, though there are none on the top.

Fine panelled battlements crown the elaborate north porch, which has niches in its buttresses, and a vault inside, studded with carved bosses. During the Puritan ravages, the church was attacked, but the roof escaped the worst of it, because of its great height; sadly the angels in the north aisle roof were defaced. There is a fine 13th century chancel arch, and in the east window the tracery is equisite. The church is open daily from 9.00 am to 4.30 pm.

Mildenhall has a museum, which you will enjoy. It is not vast, but it houses many fascinating exhibits, reflecting the history of the town as far back as the Neolithic and Bronze ages. You can see that, with Mildenhall so close by, and also with Newmarket, Bury St. Edmunds, Ely and Cambridge fairly near, the White House is not only fun, but also well placed.

Wherever we go in the parish of **Lakenheath**, we have a mixture of fenland and Breckland heathland. The village is a very large one, with the boundary adjoining the counties of Norfolk and Cambridgeshire. It is arrived at by the B112, if you are coming by road, but if it is by train, do please note that Lakenheath station, on the Ely to Norwich line, is over two miles from the centre of the village.

The village is a curious collection of houses, built in flint, brick, chalk, 'clunch', carr stone and limestone, giving it a well lived-in appearance. We liked the church very much, especially when we found a wonderful set of 15th century carved benches. The cambered tie-beam roof almost gave us a crick in the neck, because we spent so long in admiration, looking up at it.

The 13th century font is what most people like best, and indeed we can understand why; it is considered to be the best of its kind in the county. The ancestors of Lord Kitchener are buried in the churchyard. For those of you too young to remember anything about him, he is remembered not only as a famous general, but also for the World War I posters, on which he was drawn pointing a finger at every man, saying "Your Country needs YOU".

We talked to the locals in **The Bull Inn**, at Lakenheath, and learned something of fenland, a world of mystery to those of us who do not live anywhere near it. No other area of rural Britain can have changed so much as the fens in the 900 years since Hereward the Wake. What he would have recognised as fen and marsh for fishing and fowling has been transformed by massive drainage programmes, to form some of the most fertile land in Britain. Using Dutch experience and ingenuity, and generally, from what we were told, much against the wishes of those who lived in this area, the fens have been drained. Waters pumped by wind and steam, dykes and drains carved through the landscape and sea, and flood waters held at bay, all served to create something that, you have to admit, is in total contrast to the typical English countryside.

The Bull Inn

Whilst most of this fen country is not Suffolk, folk living in Lakenheath are right on the edge of it. We were glad that we called into the Bull Inn; Marcia and Malcolm Bucknell have made it a true family pub, a place where you know that the children will be welcome, and you will not have to be constantly worrying that they might be doing something wrong.

Malcolm and Marcia are well-known in the area for the wide range of whiskies they stock in the bar. We had no idea there were so many varieties, until we started talking to them about it; they pride themselves too on the quality of their real ales. Malcolm deals with the food, and produces super home-made dishes, together with succulent steaks and a variety of seafoods. You can have meals served in the front bar, or in the garden, which is particularly popular with children, because there is a pets' corner. If you are a pool player, beware of the natives! The Bull has several good players. Malcolm told us that at the weekend there is invariably live entertainment.

We read an article called 'The Village Pub' not so long ago, and it gave us a great deal of food for thought. It quite rightly said that the personality of the publican and his wife is of the essence; that the dreadful cliché 'mine host' really does precisely define the role. The hosts have to direct the continual 'party' that goes on in the pub, and do it without showing any sign of boredom. They have to be sympathetic listeners, no matter how dull or repetitive is the tale being told. They should be good entertainers in their own right, and never show impatience or favouritism, and certainly not air any troubles of their own. They must be able to control the over-enthusiastic drinker, and sometimes encourage those who are shy. They must suffer fools gladly, and finally they must like people.

When you read that list, you wonder how anyone ever tackles the task. We are lucky enough to have met several of these super-human people on our travels, and would certainly include Malcolm and Marcia in that number. It was a happy chance that took us to the Bull.

Attleborough to Eye

Village of Eye

Area covered in Chapter 7

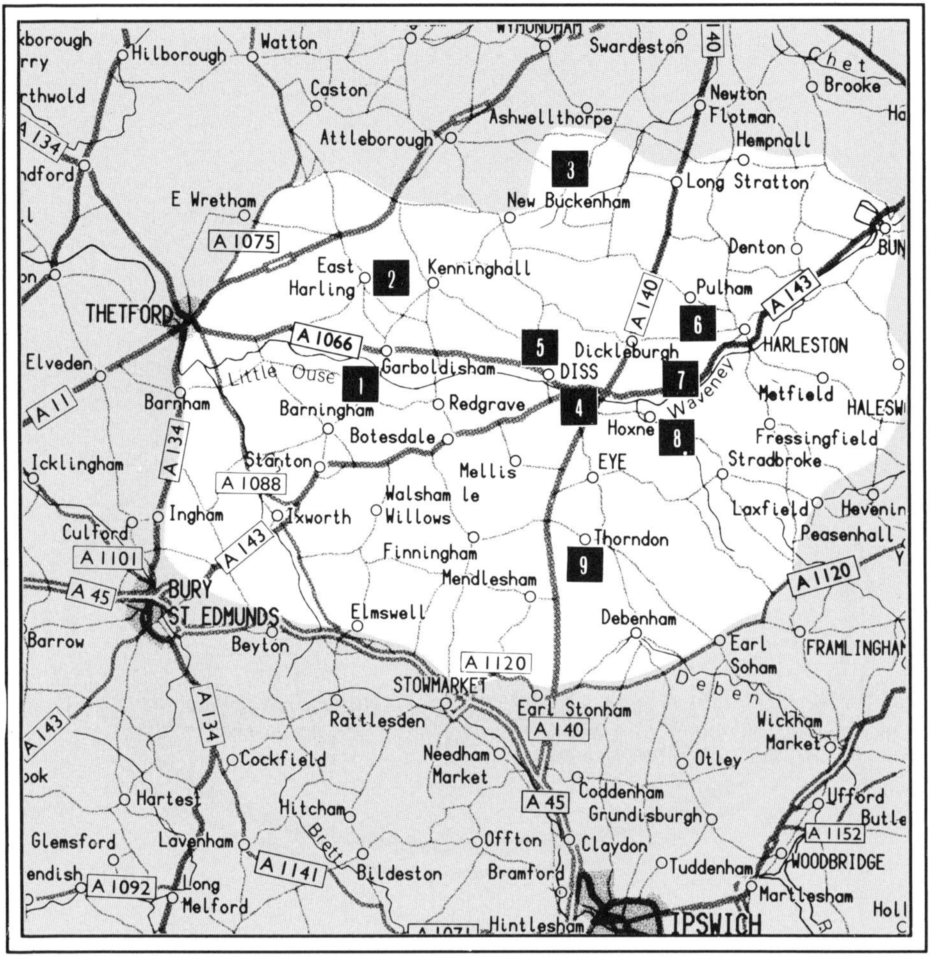

1 The Vine *(Hopton)*
2 The Swan Inn *(East Harling)*
3 Bunwell Manor Hotel *(Bunwell)*
4 The White Lodge Guest House *(Scole)*
5 Flax Farm *(Scole)*
6 The Kings Head *(Pulham St. Mary)*
7 Ye Old Kings Head *(Brockdish)*
8 The Grapes *(Hoxne)*
9 The Black Horse Inn & Stables Restaurant *(Thorndon)*

CHAPTER 7

Attleborough to Eye

The road from Thetford to Diss is a pretty one, and it encouraged us to stop several times to sightsee. We left the main road, the A1066, taking a right turn onto the B1111, at the signpost for **Hopton**. It is only a few miles from Diss, but has a nice community spirit about it. After having a good look round, we were thirsty and hungry, and we were not amiss to calling in at **The Vine**. The pub was built in the middle of the 19th century, we think. It has a lot of original oak beams, and some fine woodwork. The big stone fireplace, with a glowing fire, was a welcome sight, because the morning was decidedly chilly.

We are always nosey about pictures, and anything adorning walls. The Vine has old implements hanging from every wall, some of them very old, telling something of what farming was like in times gone by. We ordered real ale, and a glass of very good cider, to go with our lunch. The food was served in a dining area that was attractively laid out, and our meal was good.

In the summer, we were told, they have a very good salad bar, which is popular with locals and visitors. Another tradition at the Vine is the Sunday lunch, when you will get a very generous helping of the day's speciality, with fresh seasonal vegetables. We took a peep at the wine list which, whilst not extensive, was well chosen, and the prices very fair.

The Vine, Hopton

Children can play in a room specially set aside for them, and in good weather they can go outside to the play area, where there are swings and frames to delight them. The Vine has a large function room, which Mr. Bradley, mine host, says is used for weddings, birthday parties and other occasions which, we can believe, would be very well done. We enjoyed meeting Mr. Bradley, and we are sure you will.

Rejoining the main road, we crossed immediately over and took the B1111, going north this time, which took us to **East Harling**. The church has a marvellous spire, which is thought to have been the inspiration for the somewhat similar one added to St. Peter Mancroft, at Norwich, in the 19th century. Like St. Peter Mancroft, East Harling has some beautiful stained glass. East Harling has grown enormously in the last few years, but it still has the air of a market town.

You will think we have an obsession with pubs, but it would be wrong not to introduce **The Swan Inn**, which started its life almost 500 years ago as the home of a rich wool merchant. Sometime later it was sold, and became 'The Grapes', the largest coaching inn in the whole of Norfolk. You can imagine the post horn raising the inn, and the sound of the coach and horses approaching; their weary travellers just longing to alight and refresh themselves.

A change of name to the Swan Inn has made no difference to the welcome travellers receive, except that, whilst retaining all the character of this fine old building, Dick and Sally Conway have brought 20th century comforts to the bedrooms, with four double rooms, all en-suite. The restaurant has a good traditional family atmosphere, but offers an a la carte menu as well. There is an attractive beer garden for sunny days, and a bowling green; with a safe children's play area, and a genuine welcome to pets. The Swan Inn is a good place to be.

The Swan Inn

While you are in this area **Kenninghall**, just three miles to the east, is worth a mention. It was once a place of great importance, with a palace. The Dukes of Norfolk owned Kenninghall Palace, but it was taken from them by Henry VIII, and given to his daughter, Lady Mary; who was so briefly a Queen. It is claimed also that Queen Boedica lived at Candle Yards, near

Kenninghall Palace. If that is so, then the enclosed rectangular earth bank is the remains of Candle Yards.

You can meander along lanes through many villages: Banham, with a square green, and some picturesque shops and houses; New Buckenham, which has a strange history, and worth a visit, but the countryside becomes rather tame until you come to **Bunwell**. It was here we found **Bunwell Manor**, a perfect place for touring the nearby villages, and also the surrounding counties. Both coasts are within easy reach of this attractive country house with marvellous gardens, dating from the 16th century, and although it is very much a 'hidden place', which is one of its charms, it is easily accessible. If you are on holiday, then Norwich, Bury St. Edmunds, Ely, Cambridge, King's Lynn and the Broads are nearby.

If it is business that brings you to Norwich, or elsewhere, what could be better than staying in this quiet, lovely place, after the grind and stress of a working day. The nice thing about Bob and Maggie Nylk, who own Bunwell Manor, is that they will cater for everyone's various needs. You can be pampered with breakfast in your comfortable en-suite room, have an excellent dinner in the restaurant, or a meal which answers dietary requirements. If the mood takes you, and you decide to spend the day relaxing in the garden, they will serve you with a delicious light snack, while you watch fellow guests play croquet!

What a wonderful place it would be for a wedding reception, or for a small business seminar. It is open all the year round, Christmas as well; we loved it, and we think you will too.

Bunwell Manor

Bunwell is a pretty place in its own right; there are attractive groups of thatched cottages in Bunwell Street, and an old mill at the bottom. The parish church of St. Michael has an impressive tower, for which money was left in 1499 to 1508. The big Perpendicular windows in the nave and chancel strike you immediately you enter the church. You can see the Royal arms of Queen Anne, and a very impressive high altar. An east window, designed by those fine stained glass artists, Hardman and Powell, in 1914, is very beautiful.

One morning we decided to go back down the road to look at **Carleton Rode**, where the village is lucky enough to have All Saints' church, with its squat 18th century tower. It had to be rebuilt then, for the former one, which was built around the 13th century, collapsed. There is still a fine 13th century chancel, a very graceful double piscina, a screen base, with the twelve apostles, and some excellent consecration crosses.

We had only given **Old Buckenham** a cursory look on our way to Bunwell, which is why we retracted our steps. If you are a keen cricketer, then you may know that the famous Jack Hobbs rated the pitch at Old Buckenham Hall, with its imported Australian turf, the finest in all England; probably deadly boring to the non cricket lovers, but we would defy you not to be satisfied with the village.

Old Buckenham has all the ingredients; a thatched church, of All Saints, has Norman work in the north doorway, and the carr stone of the west wall, while the polygonal tower, nave and chancel, are in the Dec style. With its thatched roof, white walls and a churchyard full of roses, what more can you ask for? There is more; the green is enormous, and has straggling clusters of cottages round it, with the enchanting names of 'Cake Street', 'Hog's Snout', 'Puddledock' and 'Los Wroo'. There is also a windmill, and the remains of a castle.

New Buckenham is a different kettle of fish. The demolished castle is of considerable historical interest, as the first English example of a round keep. Also of interest is the layout of the village which, unlike Old Buckenham, with its haphazard planning, is a rare example of a planned mediæval settlement, with a grid-iron street pattern.

In the remains of the old market place, you will find the polygonal Market House, built in the 17th century. Tuscan columns support the upper floor, and the middle column was once a whipping post. Look for the carving on the boards, and you will find angels, harts, a gatehouse and heraldic shields.

Now back to Bunwell Manor, for a game of croquet, and the knowledge that, after a pre-dinner drink, we will have a super meal. It was worth the very few miles down the little lanes to discover so much delight.

While we were in the Swaffham area, we did not have time to do justice to **Oxburgh Hall**, which is a short journey away from Bunwell, but definitely worth taking the time to see. You will find it seven miles south west of Swaffham, or two miles north east of Stoke Ferry, off the A134. It is not the easiest place to find, but do search diligently, as it is worth it. The first view of this moated, fortified manor house, home to the Bedingfield family for over 500 years, will be reward enough.

Sir Edmund obtained a licence, from Edward IV in 1482, to build walls, towers and battlements; and the Charter, complete with massive seal, is in the Hall today. His direct descendant, Henry, lives in the south west tower, although the National Trust took over the Hall in 1952. A strongly royalist and Catholic family, they have not always had good times. In the mighty gate tower, there is a cunning little hiding hole, used for priests in about

1578. Try to get into it; you will see just how tight the squeeze is. Imagine hiding there!

In 1497 King Henry VII and his Queen, Elizabeth of York, spent two nights there, and used the same circular brick staircase that links all the rooms in the gate tower. There is a very elaborate tapestry map of 1647 hanging now in the room the Queen used. It depicts all the towns and villages in Oxfordshire and the surrounding counties. The room in which the King slept has a fine portrait of Sir Henry, Governor of the Tower of London when Elizabeth was incarcerated there.

In one of the rooms, protected against strong light, there are some superb green velvet embroidered panels, the work of Mary, Queen of Scots, and Elizabeth, Countess of Shrewsbury, in about 1569. Oxburgh has several different architectural styles, and you can best see them by climbing up to the roof of the gate tower; it is a wonderful sight. You will also see the chapel in the grounds, which has a superb Bruges triptych behind the altar.

Oxburgh Hall

Between New Buckenham and Kenninghall is **Banham Zoo and Monkey Sanctuary**. A spacious meadow adjoining the zoo has been set aside for touring caravans, which we thought was an excellent idea. The grassed, level site also provides full facilities, including showers, toilets and laundry facilities, to ensure a comfortable stay. There are all sorts of amenities, such as the Grove Farm Barn Shop, which will provide you with all your groceries and provisions, plus fresh produce too, including fresh free range eggs and Banham cider.

There is an amusement arcade, which we generally hate, but it is of the family kind, rather than ones where vast sums of money get swallowed up very rapidly. The 18-hole putting green seemed to be very popular, and a nearby garden centre had a wide selection of plants, shrubs and garden sundries.

Every Sunday morning, there is the biggest and best regular car boot sale in Norfolk, if not East Anglia. There are dozens of stalls, offering thousands of bargains, in the main car park. Even if it is raining, it is fun browsing through books and bric-a-brac, clothes and clobber, tools and toys, handicrafts and hobbies.

Now for the zoo itself. It is well laid out, with animals of all kinds. Snow leopards, zebras, camels, sea-lions and otters. There are owls, flamingos, wallabies, racoons, llamas, emus and maned wolves.

We had a special interest in the Monkey sanctuary, to see how it compared with the sanctuary at Looe, in Cornwall, as we thought that this one had not yet been equalled. Apart from anything else, it would be hard to compete with the superb setting, overlooking the sea! However this one was full of happy, chattering monkeys, some of them rare, and living in colonies and groups. There were chimpanzees, tamarins, lemurs, langurs, spider monkeys, sakis and many more. There are special walks, for example the woodland walk, with flamingoes. If you like reptiles and insects, you will enjoy their house. Children will enjoy the Pets' Corner, and the Farmyard Corner. We could imagine that while parents were staying in the caravans they would be pestered by their children for a daily visit!

Monkeys at Banham Zoo

The turbulent history of England is concealed behind the neo-classical facade of **Wingfield College**, seven miles east of Diss, on the B1118. Together with the fine church of St. Andrew that overlooks it, the buildings have seen much. Sir John de Wingfield, a close friend of the Black Prince, distinguished himself at the battle of Poitiers, and determined to found a college with the ransom money he got from the French. Sadly, he was struck down by the Black Death in 1361, and it was his wife who was left to seal the college Charter a year later. The college flourished, until it was surrendered to Henry VIII in 1542.

The de Wingfield daughter married the grandson of William atte Pool (to become de la Pole), who founded the town of Kingston-upon-Hull. It was their grandson who became the first Duke of Suffolk, and married the grand daughter of Geoffrey Chaucer. You may remember from Shakespeare's Henry VI that he was beheaded over the gunwale of a boat, after being caught while fleeing to France. Shakespeare does have his uses in reminding us of historical happenings.

The college was built on the site of an existing manor house, whose Great Hall was incorporated into the new buildings. In the mid-18th century, Squire Buck, in order to keep up with the Jones', turned the college into a Georgian country house, with a superficial Palladian front. Behind this the mediæval floors were lowered, ceilings raised, and no less than three rooms were built into the Great Hall.

For 200 years this desecration went undetected, and it was not until 1971 that restoration work began. What you will see today is a fascinating portrayal of domestic architecture over five centuries. Outside, comparison between the east and west elevations make you realise that you are looking at a storybook of building, written in wood, stone and plaster. In the north and south chapels of the collegiate church are three fine monuments; just to the south is a lovely Georgian farmhouse, and an unspoilt pub.

The college is now the home of a flourishing annual season of arts and music. There are guided tours for parties and school children. The topiary and the old kitchen gardens just add to the scene of this splendid enterprise.

Wingfield College, The West Palladian Front

Diss, we think, is the most attractive country town in South Norfolk, probably because the Mere is in the middle of it. There is just something about Diss that makes you want to stay, and to seek out its secrets, and delight in the villages that are around the town. John Betjeman described it as his favourite Norfolk town, and Mary Wilson, wife of Sir Harold, lived here as a child.

Mere Street is so narrow that it is tortuous, but it does widen a little at the top, to form a small market place. It formerly had an important use, as a poultry market, but today it is dominated by St. Mary's church. The church is disappointing, because it has suffered from over-restoration inside, but it has an early 14th century tower, and 15th century west doors. The Corn Hall is a fine building, and along the street, on the other side of the Mere, are some very pleasant Georgian houses. Just north of the church is the Georgian manor house, with an elegant semi-circular porch on Corinthian columns.

We stayed just outside Diss, at **Scole**, at **The White Lodge Guest House**. The house is a lovely example of late Georgian architecture; big pillars on either side of the entrance porch, and shuttered windows, which show off the elegance of that era. The gardens reflect a desire for space, and make a welcome haven in summer, for guests to relax in, whilst fig trees and grape vines grow in warmth and seclusion.

Once the home of an Arch Deacon, it is now an ideal base for visiting the many historical towns that are within easy reach. Norwich is no distance, with its beautiful Cathedral, daily market and unique mustard shop. Thetford, the headquarters of the Danes in the 9th century, with its mediæval buildings, and the picturesque remains of the Abbey at Bury St. Edmunds, are all a must for visiting. If you would rather go to the beach, then Great Yarmouth and Lowestoft are only an hour's drive. As you know already from reading this book, there are very many places within easy reach, and Mrs. Cunliffe, the proprietor, will readily answer your questions, as she did ours.

The White Lodge Guest House

Flax Farm, which is also in **Scole**, takes its name from a blue flowered plant that was widely grown in the area. It is the only remaining building of a once flourishing industry that employed hundreds in Scole and nearby Eye. Flax was softened in the River Waveney; this allowed the inner fibres to be extracted and, after a long process, graded for future uses, such as rope, twine and sacking. A 100ft. chimney dominated the skyline; sadly, it collapsed in 1895.

Flax Farm

The building we see today was built in 1854, and has survived five severe fires (shows how well buildings were constructed in those days: no Wimpeys then!) It now houses craft shops, selling local merchandise, cards, gifts and souvenirs. Delicious home-made cakes and cream teas can be enjoyed in the tea rooms. Parking space is ample, allowing one to spend time exploring the nearby beauty spots and walks. A day at Flax Farm can be educational and relaxing, with much more to be learned than we can tell you here.

When a pub is as old as **The Kings Head** at **Pulham St. Mary**, Diss, it needs constant loving care to keep it up, and to retain as much as possible of the original pub. The Kings Head dates from the 12th century, so this one has needed particular tender loving care; Keith and Anne Standland do this. They have done a tremendous amount of restoring and refurbishing, which has given the pub even greater charm.

All the original beams are still there, and the original doors are still on view. The wood for the beams apparently came from a mediæval ship. One of the bars was brought from a hotel in Great Yarmouth in 1887, and has been in use ever since. There are inglenooks in the bar, one of which still houses a fireplace, and in another there is a huge open fireplace. It really is a pleasure to drink and eat here; the atmosphere is so steeped in history, and the welcome is warm and sincere.

The Kings Head

We were fascinated by a collection of extinct local beer labels, each one would have had a tale to tell, if the labels could speak! Research tells us that the pub was originally called the 'King Edmund', supposedly because he took refuge in one of the local churches, before the Danes tracked him down and killed him. You can imagine that folklore is rife in a pub of this age. Get the locals talking to you, and you will find out a great deal more.

Keith and Anne advertise that you can cook your own barbecues at the pub, from May to October; children love it. Apart from the history, which to us is always of supreme interest, the pub is one of the nicest and friendliest family-run pubs that we have come across.

The Pulhams are two very attractive villages in the Waveney valley. Pulham St. Mary the Virgin, where the Kings Head lies, is a small township, with the houses standing among a grove of trees. Its church is a magnificent

15th century building, which has been carefully restored by G. F. Bodley. This is very important, as many churches are spoilt by over-enthusiastic restorers, who end up destroying the original beauty of the church.

Pulham Market, or Pulham St. Mary Magdalen, is a village of plaster and colour washed houses, with high pitched roofs surrounding the village green. Here sadly we do have an example of a tastelessly restored church. Certainly, the Kings Head made it worthwhile visiting here, and we enjoyed ourselves looking at the buildings. On the way back to Diss, take a look at Harleston; it is a very pretty place. There is a long, straight street, with some fine Georgian houses, and elaborate wrought iron inn signs.

Brockdish comes next; it is a delightful village, with pretty houses on the banks of the stream. It has a super pub, **Ye Old Kings Head**, dating back to the 16th century. The bars are heavily timbered, with large open fires in the restaurant, just off the lounge bar. It has a feeling of history about it, particularly when you hear that the pub has a ghost, called Alice, who has been known to switch off the lights!

In recent years, seven en-suite chalets have been built onto the pub, which do not in any way destroy the old building, but rather, enable people to stay comfortably. There are four twin bedrooms, one double room, and one family chalet. The average price is £14.00 per night per person. The restaurant will provide you with good, inexpensive meals. For children, there is a menu that starts at £1.00, and at most is £1.75. For adults, you are looking at anything from £2.00 to £8.00, and we can promise you that, within that price range, you will be well fed.

Helen and Dave Dedman will make you very welcome, and will give you details of the live music that takes place there. You can entertain yourselves in the games bar, playing pool or darts.

Ye Old Kings Head

There is a lot to see in this rural area. The Otter Trust is a few miles away. Bressingham Gardens and Steam Museum is just ten miles away. If you want to go to the coast, then you will need to drive 20 miles; no great distance, is it? Diss is an interesting town to explore anyway, with a great deal of history attached to it. See if you can persuade Alice to stop turning off the lights, and let you into the secret of what went on in her time!

At **Bressingham**, you can enjoy the unique combination of Europe's most comprehensive steam museum, and an internationally famous garden, all in one day. It lies between Diss and Thetford, but is an easy run from Ye Old Kings Head at Brockdish. We heard someone talking about Bressingham while we were in the pub, and so we thought we would investigate.

There are all sorts of things to do there. You can ride on the footplate of a main line locomotive. There are three steam hauled narrow gauge railways going through five miles of track in the gardens, nurseries and woodland. You can take a ride on the nostalgic steam driven Victorian gallopers. There are road, traction and steam engines on view in the museum and, after all that, you can wander around Bressingham's renowned six acre Dell Garden, with thousands of varieties of hardy plants.

We saw several families enjoying a picnic in the picnic areas, and they all looked very contented after such an arduous time, covering all there was to see. You must be careful to check when they are open. The museum is only open Easter Sunday and Easter Monday, and Sundays in April. The museum and gardens are open Bank Holiday Mondays and every Sunday, from 1st May to 25th September, Thursdays from 1st May to the end of September, and Wednesdays in August. If you are slightly confused by these times, give them a ring on (0379 88) 382, and check it out.

Bressingham Live Steam Museum and Gardens

Hoxne is the legendary place of King Edmund's martyrdom in 870, by a flight of Danish arrows. He was betrayed by a newly married couple, who saw his spurs glinting under Goldbrook bridge, and that sighting sealed his fate. Some long time after, an old arrowhead was found buried in the tree where he was shot, and the site is marked now by a stone cross.

That little bit of history is only a tiny part of the richness of the past in this lovely area of Suffolk. When we came here, we saw another romantic sight of yesteryear. In a meadow behind **The Grapes**, in Cross Street, there were a number of those lovely old horse-drawn gypsy caravans, all so colourfully and beautifully decorated. We thought we had gone back in time, but in fact these are holiday caravans, and regularly use this meadow.

The Grapes, run by Val and Maurice Chaplin, is a friendly pub, built some time in the 15th century, and over the years has been lovingly cared for. It is a listed building of course. It has rustic timber porches, and a wonderful thatched roof. Inside, the original old beams are there, and lend character. We called in on a Sunday at lunch time, and found it was meeting day for some of the older members of the village, who use the 'Smoke Room' for a get-together every Sunday lunch time. They call themselves 'The Blue Tint Club'!

The pub serves real ale, and also real country wines and mead. Like all good village pubs, The Grapes has its sporting teams. In this instance, there are three, for darts, pool and dominoes respectively. Alternate weekends, there is live entertainment, and all the year round you will find very good and reasonably priced bar meals. The large garden area is lovely for summer days, and the big car park makes calling there simple. It allows too for motor caravans, and has facilities to deal with them.

The Grapes

We should have warned you that you must pronounce the name Hoxne as 'Hoxen', possibly because of the site of the village, which could have been compared to the shape of muscles in the heel of a horse.

From the middle of the 10th century until 1078, when the bishop moved to Thetford, Hoxne, like North Elmham, had a Cathedral. In the 13th century, a number of monks from Norwich established themselves beside the chapel, which was built to St. Edmund, and it could be that they started the legend of Edmund's death. Today there is not anything really that would make you realise the religious importance of Hoxne in those times, except possibly the fine 13th to 15th century church of St. Peter and St. Paul.

There are paintings of St. Christopher, and the seven deadly sins, on the north wall, where dragons are relishing the devouring of sinners; but for us it was the discovery of a marvellous bench end which made the church special. If you have read any of our other books, you will know that bench ends have become a hobby of ours. This one portrays the severed head of Edmund; a grizzly thought, but a fine piece of carving. Hoxne Abbey is still there, standing on the site of the former monastery.

Eye retains the peaceful atmosphere and character of a small 18th century market town, surrounded by superb Suffolk countryside. If you climb the mound that was once the old castle, dating back to 1156, you will have a very good panoramic view of Eye, and the surrounding countryside. East Anglia seems to be more than well blessed with beautiful churches, and the church of St. Peter and St. Paul is no exception. Founded in the 12th century, it has a magnificent tower, and the inside is superb; the rood screen is especially good.

The Village of Eye

To the south of Eye, just off the A140, you will come to Thorndon, and to The Black Horse Inn. The build-up of expectation you get, when you read that a pub is recognised by Les Routiers, featured in the Consumers' Association 'Good Pub Guide', also CAMRA's new 'Good Pub Food Guide', and in the 'Best Inns and Pubs in East Anglia Guide' is enormous. The let-down can be appalling; we have visited several well recommended pubs, and have been bitterly disappointed because, although everything was absolutely correct, there was one thing missing: a warm welcome.

The Black Horse Inn and Stables Restaurant at **Thorndon** has all the recommendations we mentioned above, but you could not wish for a warmer welcome anywhere. Paul and Kate Stephen work very hard to keep all of their customers happy. The Black Horse is a 16th century free house and restaurant, situated two miles off the main A140 Norwich to Ipswich road, in the centre of this pretty village, signposted from Stoke Ash, near Eye.

Once a trading post, in the days when the River Dove formed a turning circle for long boats in front of the premises. The Black Horse Inn is an olde worlde inn, with oak beams, low ceilings and huge inglenook fireplaces, as well as one of the village's two wells, now brought inside the property, with its extension and recent total restoration.

The stables restaurant was indeed originally a stables, and three of its tables are actually situated inside the horses' stalls, making a delightfully secluded dining area. It seats approximately 45 diners, and caters for parties, weddings and small business meetings.

They are open for lunch and dinner. Sunday roast is very popular each week, with a choice within three courses, including two different roast joints every week. There is a special seafood night every Friday; regular musical entertainments (jazz, folk, country), occasional Morris dancing and colourful Suffolk pony and trap meetings.

In the bar, a bar menu features no less than 40 different bar meals, plus daily chef's specials. On draught are Adnams, Greene King, Courage and John Smith's real ales, Fosters and Premium Kronenberg lagers as well. Their well reputed char-grilled steaks, at extremely competitive prices, are delicious. We found that because of the popularity of the Black Horse, it was wise to book in advance for dinner. There is ample car parking available.

The Black Horse Inn and Stables Restaurant

Next to the church in **Fressingfield**, quite close to Eye, is the **Fox and Goose**, a lovely old inn, dating from 1509. We just want to tell you a little about it, because the Clarke family, who have run it for over 20 years, have a unique way of making sure their customers can have meals to order, completely freshly prepared. They send out menus to people in advance; the customer telephones in with the order and the time and date, and 'hey presto' you have a very efficient system, which helps everyone. Do not worry, however, if you just call in. You will be very well cared for, as we were. They are open for lunch and dinner, but closed on Tuesdays. In the winter, they close on Sunday evenings as well.

One would not suppose that two counties so closely tied would be so different. In this chapter we have wandered from Norfolk to Suffolk and back again, but we have been aware that each county is very special, in its own individual way.

In the next chapter we will be completely in Suffolk, and we are looking forward to it; we hope you are.

Lowestoft to Southwold

Friary Gate, Dunwich

Area covered in Chapter 8

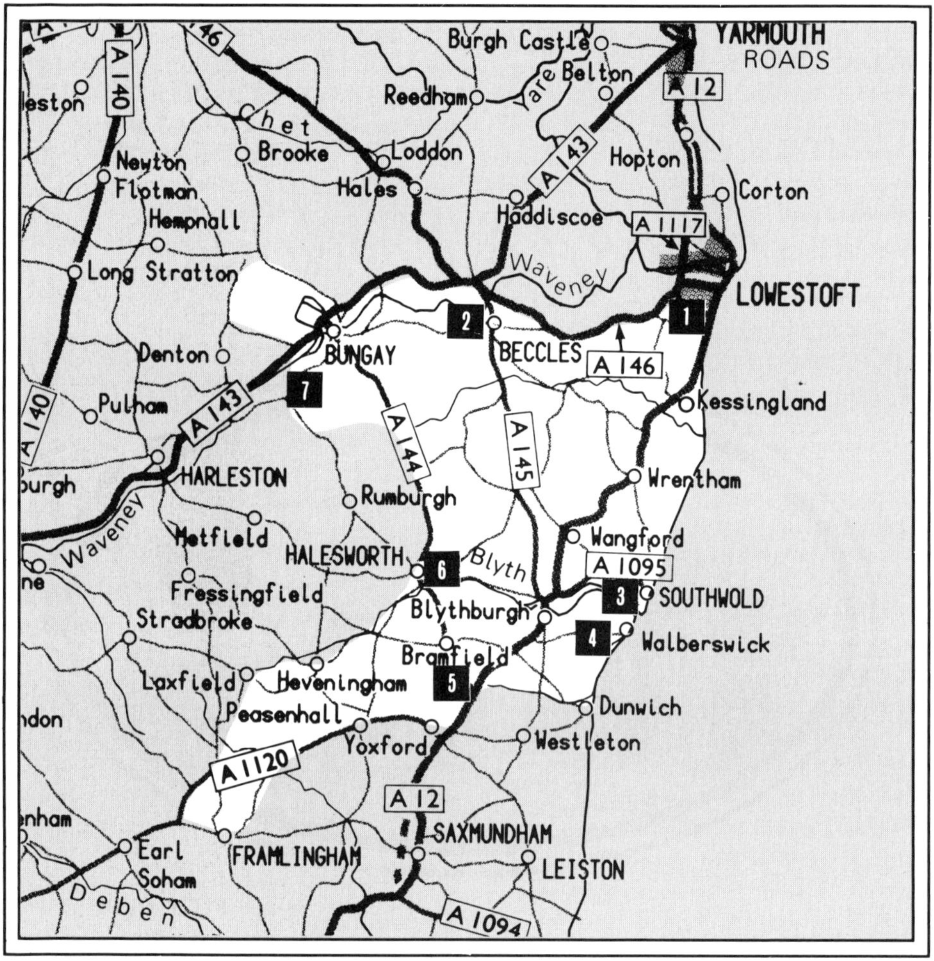

1 Pakefield Caravan Park *(Pakefield)*
2 Jenta Restaurant *(Beccles)*
3 The Sole Bay Inn *(Southwold)*
4 Marys of Walberswick *(Walberswick)*
5 Broad Oak Farm *(Bramfield)*
6 The Triple Plea *(Halesworth)*
7 The Cider Place *(Ilketshall St. Lawrence)*

CHAPTER 8

Lowestoft to Southwold

Lowestoft is an excellent starting point for a visit to this part of north east Suffolk. In fact if you are a collector of 'ultimates' you may like to know that Ness Point, in Lowestoft, marks England's most easterly point. Lowestoft combines successfully its role as a leading holiday resort with that of a busy, modern fishing and commercial port.

For those of you seeking good beaches, the firm golden sands here will delight you. The town has two beaches: South Beach is the pleasure beach with all sorts of events going on; Punch and Judy shows, two piers with amusements, and constant fun for the children. The North Beach is much quieter, but still has a fine sandy place with cliffs and sand dunes; you will find almost every possible holiday attraction, including an indoor sports and leisure complex at the Marina Centre.

Wandering around the town, you will come across parts of the ancient walls of this historic place. It is our premier fishing port, so there are many interesting displays and models of ships, fishing, lifeboats and shipbuilding in the Maritime Museum for East Anglia.

The town abounds with pubs and restaurants to suit all tastes and pockets. You can meet Woody Bear at Pleasurewood Hills, Lowestoft's American theme park. Children are always delighted with the Wild West village, the stereo cinema and the many rides and games.

Benjamin Britten, the composer, was born in Lowestoft, as was Thomas Nashe, the Elizabethan poet and playwright, hundreds of years earlier. When you wander down the lanes called the Scores, you can just imagine what Lowestoft was like then. The Scores eventually lose themselves amongst the few remaining curing houses, which once were a major part of Lowestoft.

In St. Margaret's Road, you will find St. Margaret's church, with its imposing 13th century tower and much flushwork decoration. Lions and angels wait at the entrance to the south porch, which is rib-vaulted inside. It is a spacious church with much to admire; graceful arcades line the continuous nave and chancel. There is a super east window, and the stained glass window close by, designed in 1819 by Robert Allen, is quite beautiful. There are mediæval brasses, skeletons in shrouds and many other interesting features to look at. The church is open daily from 8.30 am – 5 pm.

At the southern end of Lowestoft, with the sea and the beach on one side and beautiful open countryside on the other, **Pakefield Caravan Park** has every facility for family holidays. Upon arrival we were greeted by the park's managers, Terry and Judy. What a welcome, extended not only to us but everyone who comes to stay, perhaps one of the reasons why visitors return again and again.

Every holiday home has loos and showers, and both are available on the park, in clean modern blocks. A heated outdoor swimming pool and children's playground ensure the little ones are amused. The site's club-house offers good pub grub, and a takeaway service for Mums who do not feel like cooking.

Entertainment in the evenings is organised, with various artists appearing; it is great fun, so do join in. Within easy reach are the main Norfolk/Suffolk holiday centres, something for everyone, from theatres to fairgrounds. The choice is yours, whether to venture and explore or just spend your time in the relaxing atmosphere of the park.

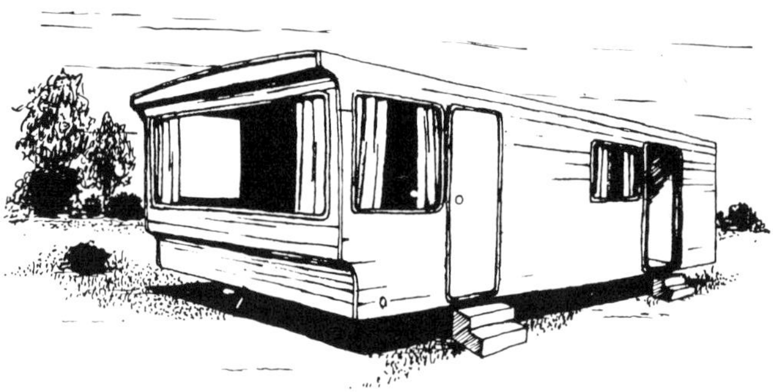

Pakefield Caravan Park

Just down the road from Pakefield is **Kessingland**, a small but increasingly popular resort with two and a half miles of sand and shingle beach. It is an excellent place for swimming and sailing, and we would describe it as bracing.

The Suffolk Wildlife and Rare Breeds Park is here. Naturally the main concern is the conservation of rare and endangered species of cattle, sheep, pigs and poultry, and there is a fine collection for you to see, but also the familiar attractions of the lion, lynx, leopard, tiger and Barbary ape are not forgotten. Children are encouraged to stroll among tame animals in the Pets' Corner and touch them; they live in really super natural surroundings.

We thought the miniature horses from Argentina were fascinating, and so graceful. Among the many animals we saw were miniature cows, less than 3ft. high, and tail-less Manx Rumpie chickens. There is a superb 70 acres of parkland, with a lake set in it, where there seems to be a never-ending display of water fowl, including geese and swans.

You can ride round almost one and a half miles in the grounds of the Suffolk Miniature Light Railway. It has four steam and two diesel engines, which operate regular trips in the summer, much to the delight of visitors, young and old. You will find the park is open daily from Easter to October although the Railway only runs from May to September daily, with the exception of Saturdays in May and June.

Another interesting place to visit is **The East Anglia Transport Museum** in Chapel Road, Carlton Colville, which is on the B1384, roughly between Pakefield and Kessingland. They have achieved a unique project here. It is a museum of street transport, showing the development of mechanised transport over the last three-quarters of a century. The essence of transport is movement, and they have made this a living museum, where vehicles of yesteryear can actually be seen in action. For those of us old enough it brings back half forgotten sounds of vehicles long vanished from our midst. You can even travel on a few of these vehicles along the museum's street. The curator told us that because so many old vehicles seem ill at ease in a rural environment, the aim is to develop a period street scene of houses and shops, complete with authentic street furniture of bygone days, which they have managed to rescue from many parts of the country.

You can feel the enthusiasm the staff have for this project. It is super, and although the whole project is still in its infancy, and put together by dedicated amateurs, you can imagine what it will be in a few years time. Already they have one of the widest ranges of preserved vehicles of any museum in the country. The money for this comes entirely from enthusiasts, and from money spent and donated by visitors. They have never received any development grants, and almost all the work is carried out by members. However they do admit to having occasionally to ask for specialised professional labour.

We are quite sure you will enjoy a visit here, and not be put off by the construction work, which is constantly taking place. We found it exciting to be there, whilst work was being carried out by such caring people. They feel very strongly that the encouragement, and the money from the visiting public, spurs them on. We hope you will tell others about your visit to the East Anglia Transport Museum, and go back again yourselves to see what has been achieved.

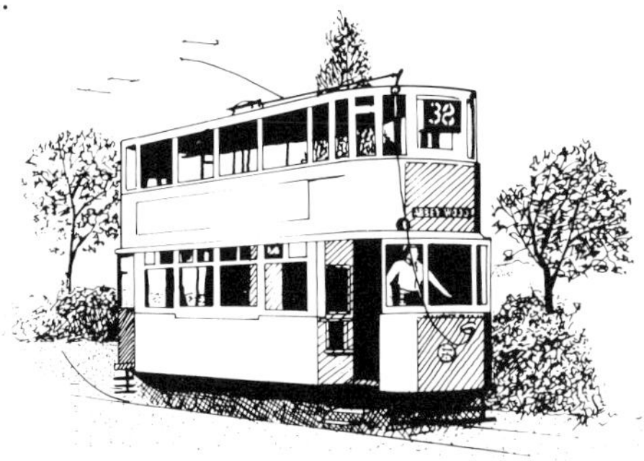

East Anglia Transport Museum

You can combine a holiday in Lowestoft with an exploration of **Oulton Broad**, which nestles to the west. It is one of the finest stretches of inland water in England, and the countryside around it is undulating and very beautiful. We have talked about Somerleyton Hall in a previous Chapter, but we should remind you that it is only six miles from Lowestoft, and in addition to the delightful Hall, Somerleyton village is charming. It is a Victorian estate village, with cottages and a school attractively grouped round a wide green. It was all the work of Sir Samuel Peto, a self made squire who was a railway magnate, and built Lowestoft Harbour. You can wander down past the Dukes Head to the banks of the Waveney.

There are several attractive villages and churches around Oulton Broad; tucked quietly away from the very busy Oulton itself is Oulton Church. It is a Norman building, looking westwards over the marshes to the River Waveney. There is nothing spectacular about it, but it is worth seeing. On the other hand, two miles outside the village of **Herringfleet** is the parish church, which is charming. It has a very early Norman round tower, a beautiful little Norman south doorway and a thatched roof. Inside it is 19th century, but very quaint, and has an intangible aura that makes you want to stay awhile.

Herringfleet Church

Fun has always been one of the priorities on Oulton Broad, and especially family fun. **Nicholas Everitt Park** is a great place for an outing. It is a setting where the natural beauty is paramount, and man-made fun has been blended into it in the most attractive manner. There is boating and fishing obviously, and a host of other things to do. The most recent development has been a remodelled children's play area. This has some of the most up to date equipment to delight children, and it has been designed with safety in mind. If you want a quiet picnic on the grass it is there for the taking, but if you want the noisier and very exciting power boat racing, you can watch one of their weekly races; quite spectacular.

You will find a cafe in the Boulevard Centre, providing food at reasonable prices. There is a swimming pool, and you can play crazy golf or jump on the trampolines. We found children enjoying the small Pets' Corner. We loved Oulton Broad, and would certainly recommend it to a family.

Beccles is an attractive ancient town alongside the River Waveney. Do not be satisfied by glancing at it as you go by on the new by-pass. There is so much to see here, and through the years it has become a holiday resort in its own right. It is a bustling market town apart from anything else, dominated by the fine church of St. Michael. There are several fine buildings worth looking at, such as the 16th century Roos Hall, the flint faced Waveney House Hotel, the 18th century Town Hall and the Swan House. You will find all of these as you wander round the town, but you will find much more to enjoy as well.

The Quay and Yacht Station is full of life, always with something to watch. For the avid shoppers among you, the shopping centre is excellent, and at the end of your day what better place to go to than **Jenta** (which if you have been to Beccles before you might have known as Chives); you will find it tucked away at 25a Smallgate.

Louise and her son Simon are the new proprietors of the Jenta restaurant. They are very fortunate in having a very good friend who is a master butcher in Smithfield Market, and it is from him they buy all their excellent meat. The excellence of the meat is of no virtue however, unless the cooking is superb. The Jenta have put both these factors together, and come up with a venue for an intimate candlelit dinner, which would be hard to beat. The atmosphere and quality have all the hallmarks of a five star restaurant, but do not worry, this is not reflected in the price! In fact we looked at our bill and expected to pay almost double for what we had. Had it been double we would have paid happily and still believed that we had been supremely well fed.

The Jenta Restaurant

Your dinner will be served at a table laid with crisp damask table cloths and fine cutlery. Your wine is equally cherished with good glasses; even a house wine tastes better when the glasses are right.

The menu caters for everyone, but whatever you choose the produce will be fresh. Vegetables come from Norwich, and the fish is locally caught. The sort of dish you can choose from is Crab Supreme, a combination of crab and egg garnished with peppered lemon mayonnaise, or perhaps Cantone Roti Sauce Plume, which is half a roasted duck, served with a plum and mushroom sauce. The sweets are changed daily, and when we were there we were served with delicious, individual Baked Alaskas.

You can relax and enjoy your whole evening here. No one will try to rush you.

After dinner we wandered to the bridge at the far end of the picturesque Northgate Street. Leaning over the bridge we took in the lovely riverside views, suddenly peaceful and tranquil after the busy day. You will not get better riverside views anywhere else in Beccles.

Just over the border into Norfolk, and only a few miles from Beccles, it is worth visiting **Burgh St. Peter**. The church tower looks as though it were built of toy bricks: it is believed to date from the 16th century, and looks out over the Waveney Valley towards Oulton Broad. The church has a very narrow thatched nave and chancel, which are of a much earlier date. The pulpit is particularly fine with copper plates commemorating the Boycott family who, one after the other, were rectors of this church for 135 years. At one time this must have been a very quiet backwater, but today the once peaceful staithe has become a fully developed marina, known as the Waveney River Centre, with a hotel and a shop, and the bonus of some very fine views across the Waveney, to the Oulton Marshes.

Beccles, Roos Hall 1583

There are several small villages around this area, but nothing really special. This does not mean to say that you will not enjoy the countryside; you will, it is beautiful.

In 1584 Beccles Marsh or 'fen' was given to the people of the town in a Charter granted by Queen Elizabeth I. The town sign commemorates this event. The Town Council are delighted to encourage people to walk round the system of tracks and paths, which form the Beccles Marsh Trail, following the yellow waymarks. They do ask you to keep to the marked paths, and keep dogs on leads at all times. If you enjoy walking and nature you will find this a rewarding experience. The marshes used to be liable to flooding, until a system of banks and dykes was made to allow the marshes to be farmed. Until 1965 it was only possible to graze cattle, but after the drainage was further improved crops were grown, and now there are cereals, vegetables, sugar-beet and horseradish grown. In the springtime you can watch the lapwings displaying themselves over the marshes.

Along the trail the Worlingham Wall is a bank built to carry water from higher ground to the River Waveney without flooding the land in between. The Wall separates the Beccles Level from that of Worlingham. You will see more dykes criss-crossing the grassland, forming smaller fields which are still grazed on the Worlingham side. Some of the dykes in Beccles Level are stained orange. This is an iron oxide formed when air comes into contact with the acid peat soil, and is a result of the deeper drainage system.

All along the dyke edges you can see wonderful wild flowers such as branched burreed and purple loosestrife. Wild ducks, moorhens and swans swim along the dykes, and dragonflies hunt for small insects.

Beccles Marsh Trail

The River Waveney is fringed with tall reeds, and willow trees. The banks are being eroded by the wash from passing boats, but you might see or hear reed or sedge warblers, and you might catch a glimpse of a kingfisher, but these are becoming rarer along this busy stretch of river. As you stand on the built up river wall, which stops the marshes from flooding, you can look back towards Beccles or over the Aldeby and Burgh St. Peter on the Norfolk side of the river.

Until 1960 when the line closed; the Beccles to Yarmouth railway line ran across the marshes. The pillars supporting the old swing bridge can still be seen spanning the river. Most of the line of the old railway is now the main route for farm vehicles, and is not included in the Trail. Near the swing bridge is a pump house, which helps to drain water from the marshes.

At one entrance to the Trail are some flooded pits, which were originally dug for mineral extraction for the building of the Beccles by-pass in 1980. Here you can see many types of wild waterfowl, and a great variety of waterside plants. The pits are privately leased for fishing, and public access is not available. It is a first class way to learn something about the marshes and how incredibly beautiful most of the area is; definitely different but rewarding.

We could not wait to get to **Southwold**, with its sense of timelessness. The ancient borough stands in splendid tranquillity beside the estuary of the River Blyth. If you have never been there, then you must be prepared to find it totally unlike the other seaside towns on the East Anglian coast. It is full of quiet pleasure.

Southwold is almost an island with the town boundaries formed by the River Blyth to the south, and Buss Creek to the north, which in many ways has been the reason why this charming town has retained its character, by limiting development.

To some people, the distinctive charm of Southwold stems from the haphazard grouping of houses of differing architectural design, some characteristic of Dutch and Flemish influence, resulting in a unique blend. To others the famous greens (each with its own particular attributes) embellish the town like scatter cushions, delighting the eye whichever way you turn. Most of the greens came about as a result of the Great Fire of 1659 which destroyed many buildings, never to be replaced.

The town has a remarkable Perpendicular church, of St. Edmund, where 'Southwold Jack', a 15th century oak figure of a man at arms, strikes the bell of the church clock. Jack also appears in the nearby Blythburgh church, and is used in promotions for Adnams Brewery, the town's major employer. Adnams brew succulent beers, which are supplied to all but one pub in Southwold. The brewery has expanded in recent years, and has also turned the Crown Hotel in the High Street into the showplace for its wine business.

We found the **Sole Bay Inn** nestling at the foot of the inshore, white-washed lighthouse. It is a small, old fashioned little house. The locals use it regularly, and they are welcoming to visitors like ourselves. We found the name interesting. The inn was named after the battle of Sole Bay in 1672, and a British victory over the Dutch.

The pub is Victorian, made up of two small houses, although the cellar is much older; a blocked up passage is believed to have been used by smugglers, who brought French brandy and other contraband up from the beach. Tiny though it is, the Sole Bay once had two bars, but they have long since been knocked into one, which currently has walls decked out with sailing prints and models of boats.

The pub is thought to have a ghost, and it is

Sole Bay Inn

said that a previous landlord had a strong rapport with it, especially when he'd had a few! Southwold has a string of excellent and unspoilt alehouses, but the Sole Bay Inn has pride of place; quiet, homely, expressing all that is best in the good natured Suffolk people.

Up on Gun Cliff, on one of Southwold's beautiful greens, stand six eighteen-pounder guns, with the emblems of the *Tudor Rose* and Crown on them. These are rare pieces, in that they were very large for their early period. They are said to have been captured by Prince Charles Edward from Edinburgh, recaptured by the Duke of Cumberland at Culloden, and later presented by him to Southwold. They had to be buried in the 1914–18 war, because the Germans bombarded Southwold from the sea on their account, claiming that it was a fortified place.

Adnams beer is brewed in Southwold, long recognised as the best real ale in England. Deliveries to the pubs and hotels within the town itself are made by horse-drawn drays, which is good trade for dealers in cameras and film: holiday makers are forever trying to find new angles on the horses and their cargoes, against the backdrop of this pub or that.

The inns themselves are a distinguished lot. The Red Lion on South Green is one of the few survivors of the terrible fire which swept through the town in 1659, after which the lovely greens were developed as firebreaks against any future catastrophe. The Lord Nelson, once called the Raven, until Nelson worship swept the country, has a small window on the seaward side of one of its dormer windows, from which, as from so many similar establishments along this coast, signals could be flashed to smugglers coming in below the cliff.

There are also tales of blocked up underground passages, which once led from the cliffs to the cellars. Certainly there are still some inexplicable passages, now choked with rubble, leading away from the cellars of the Sole Bay Inn, much photographed because of its picturesque proximity to the lighthouse.

Only one and a half miles south of Southwold, we came to another delightful place, **Walberswick**. It is quite lovely, and totally at peace with itself. We visited the little church of St. Andrew, which is right by the sea and heath where birds congregate. The little church is mediæval, and once was as grand as St. Edmunds at Southwold, and at nearby Blythburgh. In 1696 it was dismantled, leaving only the fine tower and south aisle, but you will find the church full of charm and character. It is open daily from 8 am until dusk.

Not only does Walberswick have this lovely church, but we discovered **Marys of Walberswick**, a charming and unusual restaurant with covers for 45 people. It was originally tearooms, and still has a flourishing trade for morning coffee and afternoon tea. We were told that people travel for miles to sit in the garden and enjoy a cream tea.

It was for dinner that we came to Marys of Walberswick. The interior is lovely and so informal. There are many nautical pictures on the walls, of local scenes and old fishing smacks. There are some splendid portraits of local fisherfolk, with their weatherbeaten faces. Here and there fishing nets are draped, and overall it gives a theme that is totally right for a restaurant in Walberswick, where fishing has been a major industry for generations.

The menu was a mixture of English and French, specialising in local produce, particularly fish and game. Fish is caught locally, and the game comes from the excellent shooting to be found in Norfolk and Suffolk.

The a la carte menu, which also has vegetarian dishes, is supplemented with the day's specials. There are always dishes like home-smoked cod roes or the very unusual Baked Banana with Stilton and Cream; mouth watering! The restaurant is licensed, and has a small but very well-chosen wine list; something appealing to everyone's palate, and pocket.

Marys of Walberswick

In winter and spring, Marys of Walberswick has theme evenings on the 3rd and 4th Friday in the month; they are very popular. Just before we were there, they had run a very successful Russian evening, and it was to be followed the next month by a Mediæval one. On New Year's morning they had a Victorian breakfast, which was a sell out! We want to go back there.

One of Southwold's most attractive features is the common, bequeathed to the Borough by the bailiff, William Godyll in 1509. It extends into the town marshes and down the River Blyth, beyond which lies Walberswick. The river was once a busy commercial waterway, but today plays host to a picturesque flotilla of yachts, pleasure craft and long shore fishing boats. On 12th April, 1590, 'Solemen and Walberswickers, foregathered to cut the harbour where it now runs in order to get a straight fall into the sea'.

The lighthouse, which was built in 1892, stands four square on the town and its beacon serves mariners in their quest for a landfall at Southwold Haven. It has become a landmark that signifies Southwold for many people.

You will find Southwold pleasing, whether you come there in the winter, spring or summer. Sometimes the winter shows Southwold at its best with marvellously invigorating walks along the windswept pebble beach, followed by a drink in front of a roaring open fire. The colours of the sea, even at their greyest, are ever changing and exciting.

To choose Southwold as a base for exploring will give you the best of several worlds. It is the centre of an area of great natural beauty; a paradise for the walker, the naturalist and the bird watcher or someone like ourselves who just like to commune with nature. It is so easy to explore the many facets of East Anglia from here. As you know, you are only a few miles away from Lowestoft and the Norfolk Broads. Going to the south you are in Constable country. Norwich is no distance, and there are innumerable lovely Suffolk villages for you to see.

We have paid a visit to Walberswick, but not yet **Blythburgh**, just four miles away on the A12. If you take your first look at Blythburgh at night, you will see immediately the impressive church of Holy Trinity, which rises above the marshes like a Cathedral, and is floodlit at night; a marvellous sight, making it visible for miles. In the 15th century Blythburgh was a very prosperous place with its own mint. The quays were always busy with shipping, and it was this wealth that was responsible for the size of the church. Sadly over the years, the silting of the river put an end to its prosperity. If you want to walk from Southwold to Blythburgh, then your route is over the Bailey Bridge, following the track of the old Southwold Railway, across Walberswick Common and on through the lovely countryside on the South Bank of the Estuary, into Blythburgh itself.

Dunwich Friary Gate

Dunwich is a magical place. It is full of mystery, and if you listen to some, they will tell you that this once capital of East Anglia was prosperous in mediæval times and finally engulfed by the stormy seas; it still sounds its muffled church bells beneath the waves. You should read a very good book by Rowland Parker called 'Men of Dunwich'. It was reviewed by the *Sunday Times*, when it was published, and they said "How history should be told; Parker's uncommonly personal approach to his subject is distinguished by intelligent imagination and supported by solid research". We were lucky enough to be lent a copy by Mr. and Mrs. Marshlain of the Ship Inn, Dunwich, Saxmundham, to whom we are indebted. Having read the book you will understand far more.

The few remaining cottages do not tell you much of its past. Gone are the six churches, three chapels, two monasteries and the Mint. There are a few ruins, and some narrow leafy lanes that once were streets, and now and then the bones of the long since dead are revealed in the crumbling cliffs. If you read Rowland Parker's book, and then visit the Dunwich Museum, you will be able to piece together the extraordinary and fascinating story of the town and its decline.

We spent some time at **Minsmere**, which justifies its claim to be one of the best bird reserves in Britain. It was awarded the Council of Europe Diploma in 1980 and attracts ornithologists from all over the world. In all, it covers 1,560 acres and there is general access to part of the reserve from Minsmere Cliff. There are several public 'hides' from which a wide variety of birds can be observed in their natural habitat; in particular the rare avocet.

Covehithe has been severely eroded by the sea, but it is the most striking place. Tall Scottish pine almost touch the sea, and there are vast salt-marshes stretching inland. The church is well worth a visit. Though enormous, it lies in ruins and has done so since the 15th century, when it became too large for the population, which had been reduced to three hundred. In 1672, using materials from the original church, a new smaller church was built inside the old one, a church within a church.

Looking for somewhere to stay whilst you wander around this area, you will not do better than to aim for **Bramfield**, just off the A144 on the south side of Halesworth. **Broad Oak Farm** at Bramfield is a spacious Suffolk farmhouse, with parts dating back to the 16th century. It was modernised in 1980 but has retained most of its historical features. It is a working farm, a

Broad Oak Farm

mile out of the village, and on the edge of the Heritage Coast. Pat and Peter Kemsley, who own this lovely house, welcome you to stay for bed and breakfast in their home. They have three comfortable double rooms, and we can promise you will have a terrific breakfast.

We came here because we wanted to take a look at Bramfield church, which is very unusual. It is thatched, and has a detached round roof; quite rare and lovely to see. Actually Bramfield is a good spot from which to take a look at the many attractive towns and villages around it, both on the coast and inland.

Quite near is the Royal Society for the Protection of Birds Reserve Sanctuary at Minsmore. Broad Oak is listed and has been inspected by the East Anglian Tourist Board.

A few miles away at **Haw Wood Farm, Darsham**, Pat and Peter Kemsley also run a Caravan and Camping Site. This is a secluded and well laid out site with modern facilities including excellent showers, washing area and toilets, and is looked after by the resident manager, Mr. Cecil Chapman, to the same high standards as Broad Oak Farm. The site is open from April – October.

Haw Wood Farm is situated half a mile east of the A12, and only four miles from the pleasant coastal village of Dunwich. It is also listed and inspected by the East Anglian Touring Board.

Whilst we were wandering the small roads around Bramfield, we came to **Laxfield**, a little to the west, and off the B1117. Coming from Halesworth, on the same road but south west, it is just six and a half miles. It was our intention to look at the church of All Saints, which is splendid. Flushwork distinguishes the Perpendicular tower, the roof and lovely nave. The font is very special, with the seven sacraments illustrated on it. There is a fine screen, box pews and delightfully ornate benches, with animals and a tower carved on the arms. The church is open daily from 8 am – 7 pm, except in winter when it closes at dusk.

Just opposite the church is the Laxfield and District Museum, housed in the Tudor Guildhall. There are displays of local archæology, natural history, farm, craft and domestic exhibits. It is only open Saturdays and Sundays, from the end of May until the beginning of October, but in July and August it is open on Wednesdays as well, from 2 pm – 5 pm.

By chance we found something in Laxfield that gave us great joy; **Jacobs Farm Museum of Childhood**. It offers you a unique insight into a child's life between the two world wars. There is a large collection of antique toys,

Jacobs Farm Museum of Childhood

trains and playthings. There is also a twelve acre working small holding, with lots of animals to feed. Inside the farmhouse there are room settings. Displays relating to education, shopping, the farmer's year, World War II and 'the home front' are all well laid out, and you will be shown a labourer's cottage. If the day is kind, then the Farm and Nature Trail is great, and the wildlife garden entrancing.

There is a picnic area, but you can also get tea and coffee in the Barn Gift Shop. It is open from Easter to October from 10 am – 5 pm, and Sundays all the year round from 12 noon until 5 pm. They do close all day Friday, Saturday and Monday however. You will definitely need your wellies though, if the day is wet.

Halesworth is a charming little market town, with some very pretty buildings. We spent a contented morning looking round the town and the church of St. Mary, with its 15th century tower battlements, well decorated with flushwork. The church is a mixture of 14th century arcades and many Victorian additions. When they were doing some restoration work on the church in 1889, they uncovered fragments of a 9th century Saxon frieze. The two mediæval doorways in the chancel are especially noteworthy; they have fleurons, shields, an angel and a monk over one, and the other has a lion at the apex, and the appeal in Latin, 'Pray for Thomas Clement and his wife Margaret who had this vestry built for you'.

There is an old wooden collecting shoe, and a font which is typical of East Anglia, with symbols of the evangelists and angels on the octagonal bowl. There are four lions and four wild men below, three of whom hold their clubs up to show they are reborn, whilst the fourth has his club down, implying that he has not yet been saved or seen the light, but is trying!

East Anglia has a number of unusual names for its pubs. Whenever we come across one that we have not seen before, we make sure we visit it. That is how we came to the **Triple Plea** in the Broadway at Halesworth. There is nothing outstanding architecturally about it; the building is only about 100 years old, but inside there was a cosy, beamed bar.

The Triple Plea

Apparently it became very popular with American servicemen, who were stationed at nearby Holton during World War II. The pub has a strong local trade, who enjoy Mrs. Foster's well kept beers, particularly Adnams Southwold Bitter. The bar menu has anything from steak, chips and peas to deep fried mushrooms, but we enjoyed the jacket potatoes, for which there are many fillings. The price starts at 95p and goes up to £1.95, and having eaten one you will feel more than satisfied.

The pub has just one letting room which is a double, at the cost of £15.00 per person, including an excellent breakfast. Halesworth is in lovely country, and there are many good walks round here, and our very favourite place Southwold, with its beach is only ten miles away.

In an old Elizabethan brick house, built from parts of former Almshouses, dating from or before 1478, we found the Halesworth Art Gallery in Steeple End; it was an enjoyable experience. The gallery houses various exhibitions of paintings and sculpture, and is open from mid-May to mid-September, Monday to Saturday 11 am – 5 pm and Sundays 3 pm – 6 pm.

Whilst there is nothing of special architectural interest at Halesworth, you must be sure to take a look at The Maltings, a very picturesque group of buildings round a courtyard. The little quay at the back exists under a wide archway.

Eight miles west of Halesworth on the B1116 is **Fressingfield**, a superb place: the lovely 14th and 15th century church of St. Peter and St. Paul, which stands on rising ground in the centre of the village, is beautiful. Stand back awhile and look up at the wonderful clerestory and the additional window at the east end of the nave. You will see, seated above it, and exquisite Sanctus bellcote, with miniature buttresses and a cross on the central pinnacle.

The 15th century porch was built by Catherine de la Pole, in memory of her husband who died of dysentry at the siege of Harfleur, and her son who was killed at Agincourt. It is gorgeously decorated with crowns and fleurons, flushwork and niches. When you have digested all this beauty, go inside and take a look at the very handsome roof. We were enchanted with the 15th century oak benches, wonderfully carved and traceried. The church is open for you to enjoy from 8.30 am to dusk, Monday to Saturday, and 10 am to 6 pm on Sundays.

The 16th century Guildhall is now the **Fox and Goose**, run by Adrian and Rachel Clarke who proudly continue the tradition of superb cooking, which has become famous over a quarter of a century. The food is excellent, and the whole atmosphere of the Fox and Goose is delightful. You will need to book your table well in advance (on Fressingfield 247) and if you can give them sufficient notice, they will send you a menu from which you can order your meal in advance.

Between Halesworth and Bungay and not too far from Beccles, there is a village called **Ilketshall St. Lawrence**, where you will find **Cherry Tree Farm**, the home of **The Cider Place**. It is a small family concern run by the

Coules. They produce a unique range of two year old ciders, apple juices, and country wines, which are all home products grown at Cherry Tree Farm. They use old crushing mills and a press, which are over 120 years old. These can be seen in working order, together with some 60 stillage and storage barrels.

The Press can be seen working on some days from Mid-September to December but do ring to make sure, the telephone number is Ilketshall 353. Mr. Coules showed us their range of 16 or so varieties of country wines, made from English hedgerow and soft fruits grown on the farm. There was some mead, and some grape wines as well. In fact when we looked around there were bottles of cider vinegar, jams, preserves, and some very exotic looking preserves and fruits in alcohol based syrup. There was some Norfolk and Suffolk honey as well.

We were told that the farm attracts a large number of people of all ages and all walks of life, who love to see that the produce is all natural and literally free from preservatives. If you are lucky you will be invited to taste some of the ciders and wines. Certainly you will get individual attention, and one of the Coules family will be delighted to explain the history and process of cider making. Cherry Tree Farm is open seven days a week all the year round from 9 am to 1 pm, and 2 pm to 6 pm, but they are closed Wednesday and Friday mornings.

Cherry Tree Farm — The Cider Place

Bungay was the last place we visited in this part of Suffolk. It is a fine and ancient market town, standing on Suffolk's border with Norfolk. The town stands almost as a sentinel to the meandering River Waveney, which skirts the town on three sides. Its history stretches back a long, long way. The Domesday Book noted five churches in Bungay and two of these remain. Holy Trinity is the oldest, dating from about the year 1000 AD. It has a fascinating 11th century round tower, which lends great distinction to the church, which also has a turret decorated with flushwork, and an angle of the 14th century south aisle.

The chancel was rebuilt in 1926, and the south chapel is very beautiful; we also like the pulpit of 1558, which is adorned with arabesques. The church is open from 9 am to 5 pm Monday to Saturday, and from 8 am to 7 pm on Sundays, although you will find it open later in summer. The other church is St. Mary's, with ruins of a nuns' choir at its east end. It has a truly magnificent Perpendicular tower. This flint-knapped building dates from 1160.

Bungay Castle, which was built, or we should say rebuilt, in 1300 by the last Bigod Earl, and passed to Edward I on his death in 1306, stands as a reminder of the town's turbulent past. Today the castle and the castle meadow provide a superb vantage point, to view the water meadows that stretch away to the west of the town towards the village of Earlsham.

Like so many town, it was largely destroyed by fire in 1688, and rebuilt with some fine Georgian buildings. The carved sills in the upper windows of one of the few properties to survive the fire can still be seen opposite the west end of St. Mary's church.

The market place stands in the centre of the town on gently rising ground, and contains the Butter Cross, a super octagonal building, with a dome shaped roof, on top of which, standing on a pedestal, is the figure of Justice, holding scales in the left hand and sword in the right hand. All the main streets and buildings of the town are easily accessible from here. The shops are good, and you will find many good antique and book shops in which to browse. The restaurants are varied, and offer something for everyone at different price levels. We found the pubs friendly and the locals helpful.

The River Waveney has long played an important part in the life of Bungay, and the town suffered badly in the early 17th century, when the river became clogged and ceased to be navigable above Beccles. This was remedied by an Act of Parliament in 1670, which rendered the river navigable once more by providing locks at Geldeston, Shipmeadow, Ellingham and Wainford. This helped the town to prosper as a large trade in coal, corn, malt and timber developed, as lighters and sailing wherries (many built in Bungay), plied between the town and the coast.

These days the Waveney has once more ceased to be navigable above Geldeston, but the river still plays its part as it meanders round the town. There is plenty of fishing and boating while the common has a gold course open to visiting golfers. There is an area where the public can stroll and enjoy the fine views of the lovely Bath Hills.

If you are really energetic you can walk the Bigod Way, that provides a whole range of varied country walks from two to ten miles in length. You will find a guide to the Way is available at the local Council office, or in shops and hotels. Bungay has a good sports centre, which welcomes visitors.

We have already visited one of the neighbouring villages, Ilketshall St. Lawrence, but there are a number of these small places popularly known as the Saints, from the churches whose names they bear. They fall into two groups, the Ilketshalls and South Elmhams. They are all worth a visit; do keep an eye on the signposts though, during your tour of these villages.

Even native East Anglians have found themselves travelling in circles in the village grouping known as 'The Saints'.

Another must on your visiting list is the famous Otter Trust near Bungay, which is renowned for its work in re-establishing this engaging, but rarely seen animal.

We were sad when we came to the end of our visits in this area, but no matter, we will find our next stop providing something new.

Bungay Butter Cross

Newmarket to Sudbury

Newmarket Race Course

Area covered in Chapter 9

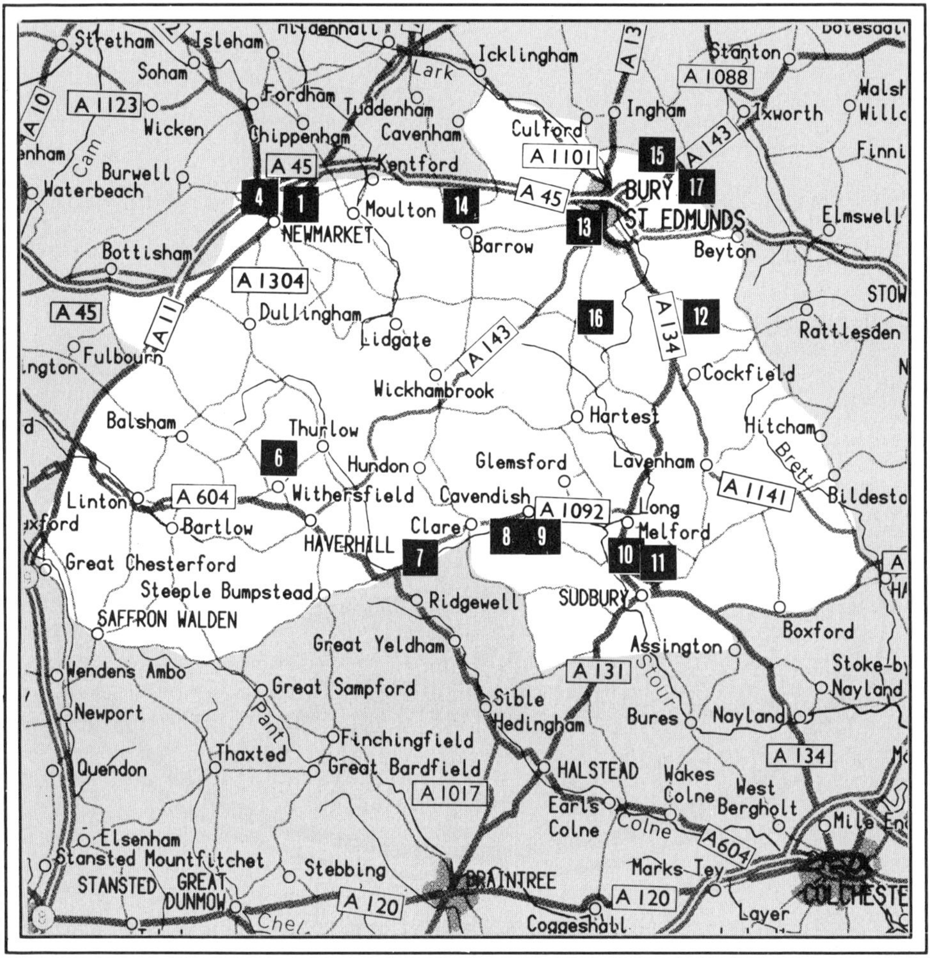

1 The Langtry Hotel *(Newmarket)*
1 Beechcroft Guest House *(Newmarket)*
1 The Old Plough Restaurant *(Newmarket)*
4 Rosery Country Hotel *(Exning)*
4 The Wheatsheaf Inn *(Exning)*
6 The White Horse Inn *(Withersfield)*
7 Boyton Vineyard *(Boyton End)*
8 The George Inn *(Cavendish)*
9 The Woolshed Craft Gallery *(Cavendish)*
10 The Cock & Bell *(Long Melford)*
11 The Black Lion Hotel *(Long Melford)*
12 Bradfield House Restaurant *(Bradfield Combust)*
13 Peggotty's Carvery *(Bury St. Edmunds)*
14 The Old Parsonage *(Higham)*
15 The Three Kings *(Fornham-All-Saints)*
16 The White Horse *(Whepstead)*
17 The Suffolk Barn Craft Centre *(Great Barton)*

Newmarket to Sudbury

We looked at the territory we were expected to cover for this Chapter, and tossed a coin as to whether we would start at Bury St. Edmunds, one of our favourite places historically, or Newmarket, which caters for our great love, horse racing. Newmarket won!

Newmarket is the 'Headquarters' of horse racing. The town has two race courses, The Rowley Mile and the July Course. Also in the town is Tattersalls (where bloodstock sales are held), the Jockey Club and the National Horse Racing Museum.

In Gazeley Road you will find **The Langtry Hotel**. The artist Millais said of Lillie Langtry, the darling of the Victorian stage,'Lillie Langtry happens to be, quite simply, the most beautiful woman on earth'. To say that the Langtry Hotel was the most beautiful place on earth would not be true, but Andy and Teresa Baron, who own and manage this building, which has considerable charm and character, have achieved a combination of modern convenience, together with the peaceful pace of life in the time when the building was owned by Lillie Langtry.

Langtry Hotel is home for Andy and Teresa, and this is what they wish their guests to feel: a home from home, where the service is friendly and personal as well as being highly professional. It is very well appointed, in keeping with the character of the building.

There are 14 bedrooms, each with shower or bath, radio and colour television, in-house video, direct-dial telephone and tea and coffee making facilities.

There is a special Lillie Langtry Suite, which was the Jersey Lillie's own bedroom. It is a very large, sunny room, decorated in blue, which was her favourite colour, and with a four poster bed. The views from the windows are of the gardens on two sides, quite lovely. They also have a King's Room, which was reputedly used by King Edward VII.

The Jersey Suite, formerly Lillie's elegant drawing room and billiard room, is the perfect venue for dinner dances, banquets, wedding receptions, conferences and parties. It is capable of taking up to 80 people for a buffet, or 60 seated. There is an excellent restaurant, offering a la carte meals prepared by a classically trained chef. It is not too large, seating 40, and so it retains a pleasing intimacy.

It is a thoroughly pleasurable experience staying there. Imagine living in the time of the famous Lillie Langtry, who started life as Emilie le Breton in 1853, daughter of the Dean of Jersey. She became the mistress of Edward VII and Oscar Wilde declared 'Lillie's beauty has no meaning; her charm, her wit, and her mouth — what a mouth — are far more formidable than weapons!

The Langtry Hotel

Newmarket is a very busy place but, just a short walk from the bustling High Street, the **Beechcroft Guest House**, at 13 Park Lane, offers you comfortable centrally heated accommodation, plus ample parking facilities. There are single, double, twin and family rooms available. Beechcroft boasts that it caters for all parties. Certainly the rooms are well furnished, and you are made to feel very welcome. The full English breakfast, served between 8.00 am and 9.15 am, will set you up for the day. If you need to get away early, then breakfast will be cooked for you at whatever time you wish, providing you have arranged it with Mr. and Mrs. Wren.

Everybody enjoys Newmarket, it is so alive and expectant. This probably has something to do with its racing connections. With the National Stud, the National Horse Racing Museum, Tattersalls, the Bloodstock Agencies and the headquarters of the Jockey Club, you are right in the heart of the sport of Kings.

Beechcroft Guest House

If you do not like horse racing, Newmarket has more to offer. There is a super sports centre and a fine swimming pool. However, we have to admit that perhaps to enjoy Newmarket it is preferable to have some taste for horse racing and breeding. There are some first class guided tours of the racecourses, the National Stud and the exercise areas etc. You can get all the information on these tours from the National Horse Racing Museum. This is situated in the High Street, and we found it a fascinating experience. The museum tells the story of Horse Racing over the last three hundred years.

In Newmarket you expect to hear people talking about horses, and if you visit **The Old Plough Restaurant** you are very likely to be seated at a table next to a trainer, or a well-known jockey. This building is over 400 years old, and has always been either a pub or a restaurant. It now belongs to Tony who is the chef, and Mick, who is a renowned race horse trainer.

What a delightful place it is, with original oak beams and huge open fireplaces. The menu is a mixture of traditional English and fine French cuisine. Turbot on the bone was on the menu the evening we ate there, something which we love but rarely see. However with Lowestoft not very far away one would expect to find good fish on the menu. A Yorkshire favourite, the Barnsley lamb chop, was another tasty dish available.

Sunday lunch time is always busy at the Old Plough, and with good reason, because they stick to the firm favourites. You can have prawn cocktail, French onion soup, chilled melon or fruit juice to start, and afterwards the choice is between roast Scotch beef, leg of pork, English lamb or Norfolk turkey, all served with the appropriate accompaniments and seasonable fresh vegetables, followed by sweets from the trolley or a selection of English and Continental cheeses from the cheeseboard, and finally coffee. All this, we may say, for an incredible £8.50 per head; no wonder they are busy!

The Old Plough Restaurant

The village of **Exning** is just two miles west of Newmarket on the B1033. If you leave the A45 Newmarket by-pass at the A142 exit, signposted Ely, and travel in that direction for about 200 yards you will see a turning to the left for Exning. Once you get to the village, turn left at the crossroads and the charming **Rosery Country House Hotel** is immediately on your right. It offers true country house hospitality. You will be personally welcomed and immediately made to feel one of the family. The lounge is spacious and comfortable, and has a well stocked bar which is at your disposal, enabling you to relax and unwind at the end of the day.

The Pidsleys openly admit to being more than a little proud of the good reputation they have for their restaurant. You will find that their pride is not misplaced, because you will be served with delicious meals from a select menu, which has been designed to cater for the most discerning palates. The wine list is equally well selected, and they will be delighted to recommend suitable wines to accompany your meal.

All eleven of the individually decorated rooms are equipped with colour television, telephone, radio alarm, tea and coffee making facilities and a degree of comfort guaranteed to bring you relaxed and refreshed to the breakfast table. The hotel, we should warn you, steadfastly upholds the traditional reputation of the English breakfast.

The Rosery Country House Hotel

There are small touches that make the hotel special and memorable. For example there is a laundry service available by prior arrangement, newspapers are delivered at 8 am; all you have to do is place your order the previous evening.

Shoe cleaning equipment is available from Reception; how often have you forgotten to pack this? You can also borrow a hairdryer if you wish. If you are off for a picnic, or you want a packed lunch for whatever reason, it will be prepared for you, and it will not be soggy sandwiches!

We got to know about the Rosery when we attended a conference there some time ago. It is an ideal spot for this, in surroundings conducive to getting the best out of anyone. It will be of no use to you if you want a big occasion, but the Conference Room will hold up to fourteen seated boardroom style, or twenty theatre-style.

All the equipment you need is there: telephone, flipcharts, video equipment, a projector screen and photocopying service. Coffee and tea can be provided throughout the day. Meals are served in the restaurant, but if you want a working lunch then that can be arranged in the Conference

Room. It was after one of these conferences that we first stayed here; something any delegate can do by arrangement.

There are two roads that go straight through the little village of Exning, which is signposted on the A45 between Cambridge and Bury St. Edmunds. One is the main road, and the other one leads to the duck pond. **The Wheatsheaf Inn** is on the latter, a typical Suffolk flint building which has been added to, a bit like the house that Jack built.

Mr. Johnson, the landlord, told us that the building is at least 200 years old, and he is still researching its history. It is a good traditional two bar pub, with a public bar which has bar billiards, shove ha'penny, darts, dominoes and the fine old game of cribbage.

The dining room is open every night except Wednesday, but at lunch time the only cook to cater for bookings by telephone, because the Wheatsheaf is such a hidden place. If you arrive unannounced you will not starve, there is usually good cold food to be had. The ploughmans lunch with stilton or pâté, and home-made chutney, is very good value, and very substantial. It is well worth seeking the Wheatsheaf out; the food is first class. The specialities include home-made soup, pâtés, local game and traditional puddings. The food is imaginative, with herbs and vegetables from the garden in use whenever available.

The garden is a pleasure to be in. It used to be a famous bowling green, but now you can play Petanque in summer, a game that was new to us. The pub also has bowls you can borrow. You are not far from Ely and the fens from here, nor Devil's Dyke and Newmarket Race Course.

The Wheatsheaf Inn

Anyone who appreciates a traditional pub atmosphere, good beer and food, will enjoy a visit here, and want to come back.

From Newmarket we made our way south towards **Haverhill**, through countryside that sometimes took us over the Cambridgeshire border, and then eased us gently back into the soft Suffolk sunshine. Haverhill is a pleasant little place, but if you are an architectural buff you will not be excited by what you see. The church of St. Mary was destroyed by a fire in

1665, and has since been restored, much of it in the 19th century, and like so many other churches restored at this time it has been overdone.

Nearby we found a little village with some lovely thatched roofs. We have always loved thatched roofs and **The White Horse** at Hollow Hill, **Withersfield**, was the epitome of what one would expect from a true country inn.

Since the 17th century, this former coaching inn has served travellers on the Cambridge to Colchester road, which has now been by-passed by the A604.

Jill and Douglas Morrison took over this free house about five years ago. They are a very welcoming, friendly couple, who told us that, before they moved in, the inn was more like an ale house than anything else. Lovingly they have restored it to a traditional country pub, which is both picturesque and charming, with old beams and original features.

Jill Morrison does most of the cooking herself, and it is no wonder that the pub has gained such a reputation for first class food. Jill makes a delicious spicy tomato soup, which is a marvellous starter, although you may choose from several others, including a good coarse country pâté.

The White Horse Inn

The main courses are all simple, but very well cooked and presented. If you have room for dessert then you will find a choice of Jill's spicy bread pudding or apple pie and cream; weight watchers beware! The wine list was not vast, but had very helpful descriptions which allowed us to get to know the wines before we made our choice. There was something for every taste and every pocket!

We were very interested to hear Douglas Morrison's background. He was a contract furnisher before buying the pub, and his knowledge came in very useful when he and Jill started refurbishing the White Horse. They have done it well; the two bars are both full of character, and serve real ales.

There is a very comfortable, friendly atmosphere in the Stable Bar, and next door the comfortably furnished Suffolk Lounge opens out into the restaurant area, where there is seating for 24.

The White Horse is set in an acre of land, and on a fine evening you can sit at the tables outside looking over open fields and gently rolling hills. What better place to go to one evening, or lunch time? Bear in mind it is only 10–15 miles from Cambridge, Newmarket, Bury St. Edmunds and Saffron Walden.

Taking the A1092 you will come to a part of Suffolk that we think is wonderful. First to the hamlet of **Boyton End**, some three and a quarter miles from the village of Stoke-by-Clare, just off the A604 between Cambridge and Colchester. Here **Boyton Vineyard** is run by Roy and Christine Williams, where it forms part of Hill Farm, and was planted in 1977.

Their Boyton Muller Thurgau 1986 is a delicious medium dry white wine, with a good depth of flavour and a very pleasant clean finish. But do go and visit the vineyard and find out for yourselves. It is a fascinating and informative outing, and is open most days between May and October.

One of the outstanding features of the vineyard is the Tudor farmhouse, dating back to the 16th century. The house boasts many interesting period features and, like most local houses, was built of a sturdy timber framework, filled with wattle and daub and covered with hair plaster. The steep pitched roof originally supported a thatch, and the tall chimney stack was added later, during the Stuart period. Inside the farmhouse there is a wealth of exposed beams and several inglenook fireplaces. The house is protected by a conservation order, and is listed grade II.

Just before you enter the vineyard glance to your right, and where the lawn ends and the rose bed begins you will be able to see the remains of an ancient bridle path. It is understood that this path was in existence before the farmhouse was built. The path runs the whole length of the vineyard on the north side.

The vines directly in front of you are the variety known as Huxelrube. The grapes from these German vines produce a medium dry white wine, with a full flowery bouquet, and we thoroughly recommend it to complement white meat and fish dishes.

As you stroll by the vines you will see they are grown and trained to posts and wire supports. Looking down the rows to your left you are facing due south; the vineyard was purposely designed and planted in this manner to capture the sunlight on one side of the vine leaves in the morning, and on the opposite side of the leaves in the afternoon. In this way they are able to ensure that the maximum sunlight is directed onto the vines.

Planting the correct distance between the vines is very important, and here at Boyton the vines are planted four and a half feet apart, and eight and a half feet divides each row. The distance is essential, to allow the vines to develop their large root system unhindered: vines have been known to root to depths of 20 feet or more.

Depending on the severity of the winter, pruning begins in January or February. From the centre of the vine two or four canes are chosen as being suitable for carrying fruit later in the year, and all remaining canes are cut away. When the sap begins to rise, in late March or early April, the wood becomes supple, thus allowing the vine to be trained onto the wire to form a wide 'Y' shape. It is from these canes that the crop is harvested.

You have now reached the top of the vineyard, which is approximately 27 feet higher than the eastern end and over 250 feet above sea level. The vines growing here are the Muller Thurgau variety, which produce a medium dry white wine similar to a Mosel: the wine is full bodied and fruity, complements the finest food, and is thoroughly recommended for all occasions. We have chosen the Muller Thurgau and the Huxelrebe wines specifically because they were developed by German specialists in viticulture for producing high yield, quality wine in similar growing conditions that are experienced here at Boyton.

Whilst you wander through the vineyard you may be interested to know that:

1) Each year over 1000 hours are spent tending the vines.
2) Thirty miles of wire is needed to train the vines.
3) The rows of vines stretch over three miles.
4) The posts supporting the vines would stretch for two miles if placed end to end.
5) Staples and nails weighing a half hundredweight are used to secure the vines to the posts.

As you can see this represents a great deal of hard work, which hopefully will be rewarded by an excellent wine.

The vines flower early to mid July, and it is important that during this time the weather remains warm and dry, in order that a good flower setting is achieved. In an average summer a further 100 days is then required before the grapes can be harvested, and this normally happens in the third or fourth week of October.

Silver poplars have been planted at the eastern end of the vineyards, to provide additional protection against the elements.

Boyton Vineyard

At the end of the trail you will be very welcome to visit the Wine Lodge and taste the wine. The Lodge is fully licensed for the sale of wine, should you wish to buy a bottle or a case.

Stoke-by-Clare has a number of charming timber-framed and plastered cottages, which stand by the green; truly a lovely place to be on a fine summer's day. The Perpendicular church has a 14th century tower, and adds grace to the village. Castellated capitals crown the nave pillars, and we found a profusion of poppyheads carved on the benches. The pulpit is a gem, and there is some superb 15th century stained glass. Seek it out for yourselves: the church is open from 9.00 am to dusk daily.

Whenever you feast your eyes on beauty such as we have found in so many of the Norfolk and Suffolk churches you can only marvel at the craftmanship and think what was achieved with so little in the way of tools to do the work.

Whoever wrote that excellent hymn 'How Lovely Are Thy Dwellings O Lord God Of Hosts' must have visited some of these churches.

From Boyton to **Clare** is no distance at all. Although it is little more than a large village today, its past is very evident, with a number of preserved buildings and monuments. There are several examples of the pargeter's art. A superb example of this decorative plasterwork, which was so popular in the eastern counties during the 17th and 18th century, can be seen on the gable of the former priest's house, which stands beside the churchyard and displays a strong floral design. The house is now a museum and bears the date 1473, although pargeting did not start until at least two centuries later. Three 'musts' for you to see are the Globe Inn, with its Georgian facade, the Swan Inn, with its heraldic sign, and the Post Office in Callis Street, with its wonderful carved brackets. Nethergate House was remodelled in 1644, and there are more fine houses on Nethergate Street. There is a shop above a vaulted cellar on Market Hill, which dates back to the 14th century. You will be able to feast your eyes wherever you look here.

There are the fragmentary remains of a castle built by Gilbert de Clare, whose family wielded great power in the realm. He married the daughter of Edward I, but had no male heirs after his son fell at Bannockburn, and the castle passed to a daughter, Elizabeth. Edward III stayed several times in the castle when he visited his cousin.

In Victorian times, when the railway yard was being constructed, workmen unearthed a priceless pearl-encrusted cross, which is believed to have belonged to Edward III. The castle motte still remains impressive, but the Victorians obliterated the inner bailey when they constructed their station. No longer required, it serves as an information centre for the very attractive country park.

The church of St. Peter and St. Paul in the High Street is elegant, loft and Perpendicular. The tower is 13th century, and the whole church is very beautiful. Inside you will find it light and airy. The chancel was practically rebuilt in 1617, but is in total harmony with the remainder. The east window has some fine heraldic glass. The screen at the east end of the south aisle is very special, and we loved the Jacobean gallery pew. The church is open daily from 9.00 am to 6.30 pm or dusk, and to 4.30 pm in winter.

An Augustinian priory was built by Gilbert de Clare in 1248, beside the River Stour. The object was to provide the Order with their first English house. The Benedictines used to have a house in Clare, but around 1100 they removed themselves to Stoke-by-Clare. The infirmary is still there, along with the remains of the walls of the church. The priory was dissolved in 1538, but the Augustinians returned to Clare in 1953 to establish a house for the training of their novices.

Clare Castle

Without doubt one of the most picturesque villages in East Anglia is **Cavendish**, with its pretty timber-framed and colour washed cottages, grouped around a large village green. Behind these cottages the tower of the mediæval church of St. Mary completes this beautiful, serene English picture. It is a village to be savoured.

The church, which is open every day from 9.00 am to 6.00 pm will delight you. To get the best out of this lovely part of the country we stayed in **The George Inn**, overlooking the green. This 15th century pub is a warm and friendly place with a great atmosphere. Mike and Jill Vincent, who run it, could not be better hosts.

The George Inn

We has a very comfortable room complete with a shower, although we understand the other two rooms have just hot and cold facilities. The rooms have televisions, full central heating and, after a good night's sleep in this peaceful village, we were served with a super breakfast. The price was only £13.00 plus VAT. During the day there is a range of excellent home cooked fare, either in the bar or the dining room. At lunchtime meals and bar snacks are served between 12.00 and 2.00 pm, and in the evenings from 6.30 to 9.30 pm.

The village and the George have much more history than we are able to tell you, but you will find Mike and Jill only too ready to tell you more.

In Cavendish we met two exciting people who in 1987 were an Editor with the *New York Times* and the Picture Editor of *The Daily Telegraph*; their names are Erica Brown and John Hodder. When we came across them late in 1988 they had become **Hodder Brown Ltd.**, owners of one of the best kitchenware shops we have ever seen. Sleepy Suffolk might not seem to be the expected venue for such a business, however East Anglia has become a hunting ground for different committees, and the people of Suffolk are alert and alive to all that today's market offers.

Erica and John realised in 1984, when they bought a cottage near Bury St. Edmunds, that the county was waking up, but it was not until they both parted company with their respective employers, within three months of each other in 1987, that they seriously considered the kitchen shop. Erica had been thinking ahead for six years.

Why a kitchen shop, we asked. 'Because I love pots and pans' Erica replied, 'and because for years we have both been devoted to searching out good food and wine'. We discovered subsequently that Erica is a member of the Guild of Food Writers and a founder member and Fellow of the British Gastronomic Academy; John is a talented cook.

At first they considered renting a shop in Bury St. Edmunds, but an estate agency offered them a property for sale in Cavendish, on the tourist route from Clare to Lavenham and only three miles from Long Melford. This former village store, with 1,000 square feet of selling space and a three storey former woolshed next door with planning permission for a flat, were all for £73,500. They bought it, of course, and say now how wise they were.

The rise in property prices, and a sympathetic bank manager, has enabled them to turn the village store into the reality of what Erica had been planning for years. The shop has brick piers, simple white shelving, and non-slip navy blue tiles. We saw how wonderfully inexpensive Texas Homecare doors could look, polished with two coats of marine varnish (a useful tip for anyone). The shop design is very clean, and there is no concession to country kitchens in the choice of goods.

Hodder & Brown is a must for anyone interested in kitchenware. Erica's choice of stock highlights her love of pots and pans. Only the best, but not necessarily the most expensive, ranges are kept. There is Danish Eva Trio, Calphalon from America, Cuisinox from France, Kuhn Rikon from

Switzerland, Castle brand Copper from Ulster, Apilco crockery and Bill Goldsmith's American designs in Lomoges porcelain by Site Corot, and so on. If your kitchen and cooking is your delight, then you will find yourself in a seventh heaven. They also sell Cartwright & Butler, Sam Taylor, Lake condiments, and, since they inherited the village off-licence, wines.

The ground floor of the barn-like woolshed has been converted to offices. The first floor is the **Woolshed Craft Gallery**, a permanent exhibition space to members of the Suffolk Craft Society, whose shows at the Aldeburgh Festival have already proved Suffolk is the most beautiful crafts county in Britain.

They intend to follow a French plan of opening until seven at night, and on Sundays in the gallery, but they are closed on Mondays and Tuesdays through January and February. They are also launching a promotional series of wine tastings in the gallery, and cookery demonstrations in the shop. They are also already talking of a second branch, in Norwich if possible, but otherwise perhaps King's Lynn and Diss, "and the important thing" they say, "is that we are absolutely loving it".

Hodder & Brown — Woolshed Craft Gallery

From Cavendish to **Long Melford**, the Roman Road runs in an almost straight line to the towers, turrets and trees to the town itself. Perhaps calling it a town is not quite correct, because it is really a very large village with a great air of spaciousness. It is this sense of space that makes it able to cope with the vast number of visitors who come every year. It became prosperous, as so many East Anglian town and villages did, with the growth of the mediæval cloth industry. It still has some industry, but relies quite largely on the tourist industry.

There are several splendid buildings, but pride of place must go to the church of the Holy Trinity. It sparkles in the sunlight like a palace, because its 97 windows pick up the light. The church was erected between 1460 and 1496 in the Perpendicular style. There has been a lot of discussion about its tower over the years, and we have read different opinions: one said it was a fine tower built by Bodley, and another says that in 1903 the discordant brick tower, built in 1725, was encased in stone to resemble the churches of Oxford rather than Suffolk. We thought it looked lovely, and was in total harmony with the rest of the church.

As you might imagine, the memorials throughout the church, and there are many, are all in memory of the 15th century clothiers, whose wealth built the church. Those of the Clopton family, the leading benefactors, are predominant. The church is a place of grace: the soaring clerestory is complemented by the superb flushwork. There is a marvellous 15th century stained glass, and the figures kneeling are of donors.

You will see the rather stout Elizabeth Talbot, Duches of Norfolk, who was John Tenniel's model for Alice In Wonderland. The Clopton Chapel is superb: John Clopton, who died in 1497, is buried here. The Lady Chapel has a very distinctive ambulatory. From our enthusiasm you will realise that you are in for a treat. The church is open from 8.00 am to dusk, and 9.00 am to dusk or Evensong on Sundays.

Melford Hall is the church's neighbour on the green. It is a mellow red-brick house, dating mostly from the mid-16th century. You approach the Hall via a pepperpot turreted gatehouse. The house was built by Sir William Cordell, a shrewd lawyer who became Master of the Rolls. He entertained Queen Elizabeth I here in 1578, and it is said that '200 young gentlemen in white velvet, 300 in black and 1,500 serving men were in attendance'! They must have needed a further army to contend with the washing up!

The exterior of Melford Hall has changed little over the years and, with its dramatic skyline of tall chimney stacks and fanciful octagonal turrets, it is one of the loveliest and finest houses in East Anglia.

Inside there are fine pictures, furniture and porcelain, displayed in rooms of varying styles. The original banqueting hall is still there, and an 18th century drawing room. The Regency Library is quite beautiful, and you can see a Victorian bedroom.

The gardens are traditional, with fine trees and clipped box hedges. The octagonal brick pavilion, which overlooks the village green, is a beautiful example of Tudor architecture. Part of the moat survives, while the drained north section serves as a sunken garden.

The Hyde Parker family have owned Melford Hall since 1786, and the family is still in residence today. The house contains many reminders of the sucessive generations of Hyde Parkers, including many family portraits, naval pictures and a superb collection of Chinese porcelain, much of which was taken from a Spanish Galleon captured by Captain Sir Hyde Parker the 5th Baronet in 1762.

Beatrix Potter was related to the family, and often visited Melford. Her signatures and sketches in visitors books, pictures of the house and grounds, and her model of Jemima Puddleduck are on display in two rooms specially furnished in her memory.

Sir Richard Hyde Parker, the 12th and present Baronet, and his family live in Melford Hall today. Recent works carried out by Sir Richard include the restoration of the fish ponds and the cultivation of oak saplings from the acorns of existing mature oak trees in the Park.

You will find a definitive guide to the house is available, which is very useful, and there is a special publication for young visitors; a practice that we wish more places of interest would adopt.

Melford Hall

When it was suggested that we met some friends for coffee in the 'Pit' we wondered what on earth it was. It is part of the charming old **Cock and Bell Inn** in Hall Street, Long Melford, and was originally used for cock fighting. The building is Georgian, and is a typical traditional pub, with lots of attractive furniture, and fresh pots of flowers everywhere. The locals tell us that it has always been the number one pub in the village, dating back to the 17th century.

The food is very good, and whilst the menu covers a range of Mediterranean food and pastas, we thought the traditional English roasts were particularly nice. In the bar we noticed a variety of ploughman's lunches being served, with crisp fresh bread and trimmings.

Local beers, together with Charrington beers, seem to dominate the ales, and the barman was no mean hand at shaking a cocktail. The wine list was not vast, but contained good French and Spanish wines. They are open all day from 10.30 am to 11.00 pm.

Cock and Bell

If you would like to stay there, you will find the accommodation comfortable but unpretentious. It will cost you about £15.00 per night. Personally we would rather enjoy the atmosphere of warmth and friendliness that you get from a well-run pub like this than one of the more expensive 'bed factories' that so many hotels are today.

The Black Lion Hotel is a converted coaching inn, also situated in the delightful picturesque Suffolk village of Long Melford. The hotel, which is thoughtfully run by the owners, overlooks the traditional village green.

The hotel is open all year round to offer its many facilities to residents and non-residents. The charming public rooms are tastefully furnished with many antiques. The drawing room overlooks the village green, and is available for morning coffee and afternoon tea, or pre-dinner drinks.

The ten spacious bedrooms are individually decorated, and all have superb views over the green or village. Each room has its own private bathroom, television and full coffee and tea making facilities.

Dinner and lunch are served in the restaurant, overlooking the walled garden, which has an informal atmosphere and superb modern English cuisine. A comprehensive and well-chosen wine list is offered to complement

The Black Lion Hotel

the varied menu, including many regional French and Australian wines, all of which are reasonably priced. For celebrating a special occasion, or simply enjoying your evening without the worry of having to drive home, they invite you to take the opportunity to relax over your meal and wine, and then stay the night.

Businesses are also welcomed, and facilities are offered to hold product launches, meetings or seminars, with a choice of two rooms to accommodate twenty and thirty people respectively. A complete package for business clients is offered, with lunch or dinner menus, accommodation and use of the rooms.

The village of Long Melford has a tree lined main street leading up to the village green, which is dominated by a magnificent church. There is a wealth of 18th and 19th century houses and shops: of particular interest are Long Melford's 26 antique shops. The village also boasts two halls, Melford Hall, and Kentwell Hall, both of which are open to the general public.

Luke and Amelia Brady, owners of the Black Lion Hotel aim to create, and welcome you into, the relaxed and amicable atmosphere of their country house hotel. They offer you excellent quality and value for your money, probably unrivalled in East Anglia. As well as rooms and cuisine, they pride themselves on their breakfasts, serving a traditional English breakfast, with freshly squeezed orange juice and, at weekends, home-baked croissants or brioches. Your stay there will be a happy one.

Kentwell Hall is hard to describe, so we will tell you how it was explained to us. Firstly, since 1971 Kentwell has been the subject of a unique attempt at restoration and refurbishment. This fine Tudor house is still a family home, as it has been for 400 years, with an old style Home Farm based upon rare breed farm animals; new gardens are being created out of the long established layout. Gradually the house and the outbuildings are being improved, and much has been achieved, but there is still a great deal to be done.

Now for the question we asked: 'What is different about this restoration project?' The answer was 'This is an Historical Recreation, an attempt to recreate, as authentically as possible, everyday life at this Tudor manor at the date chosen. This is achieved by some 200 participants who seek to live, dress, behave and talk as their Tudor forebearers did. They use Tudor style tools and artefacts, and have authentic accessories of all kinds. The unique feature is that those participating never leave their Tudor roles, so that visitors to the Recreation feel they are meeting figures out of history'.

When you read material about Kentwell you will see it always asks the question 'Have you seen the Progress'? We went to see the Progress and found it exciting. We hope to go back again before too long and see the next Progress. The opening times are varied, so we suggest you ring the Hall before you go. The number is (0787) 310207.

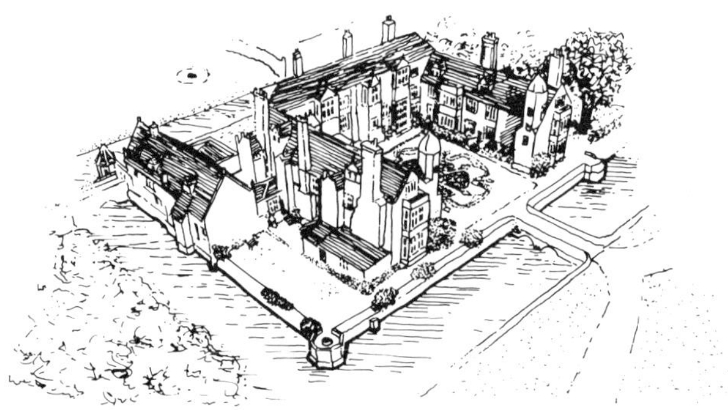

Kentwell Hall

We found that Kentwell has an air of timeless tranquillity. It is beautiful, and the gardens are a delight: intimate yet spacious. We hope you will feel the same way.

Lavenham's failure in the 17th century to develop adequate replacements for the dying cloth industry has served Suffolk well. Today it is much as it was in the 17th century, and its residents fight hard to keep this lovely village as perfect as possible. The mediæval buildings are timber-framed, and have seldom given way to the intrusion of the Georgian brick houses and facades, as has happened with a lot of Suffolk villages, and even more in Essex, such as Thaxted and Dedham.

The church of St. Peter and St. Paul is set at the end of this matchless old wool town. The church in all its glory was built by rich clothiers to celebrate the end of the Wars of the Roses in 1485. The screens of the early 16th century chantries are fabulously carved, and you will find beautiful wood carving on the 14th century rood screen, with flowering tracery, and again in the figures on the misericords.

There is only one thing to mar the beauty of this church. Lavenham, like Clare and Walberswick, did not escape the attention of the Puritan William Dowsing, who smashed all the stained glass. The glass is now coloured Victorian.

Visitors who have a head for heights can climb the tower of flint and Barnack stone; it is a landmark for miles around. You will need to be fit, as it is about 141 ft. high! We were told that there is a legend that says it would have been even higher if the master mason had not fallen off the top whilst building it. Certainly when you reach the top, and have had time to get your breath back, the reward is enormous. Below you is the marvellous site of this near perfect village.

Thomas Spryng and the Earl of Oxford both have their coats of arms carved around the tower. The former was so proud of his newly awarded coat of arms that he paid for it to be carved no less than 36 times!

Even the Post Office had empathy with the beauty of Lavenham, and removed the posts and wires in 1967, leaving the village unspoilt apart from the traffic. The streets are quaint, and will lead you everywhere into delightful mediæval prospects. The Corpus Christi Guildhall, in the market place, was built in the 16th century, when Lavenham received its Charter from John de Vere. Since that time it has served the town as guildhall, prison, workhouse, almshouse and woolstore. It is now in the ownership of the National Trust.

The Swan Hotel is a fine example of timber-framing. It was built originally in the reign of Queen Elizabeth I, and then in 1965, in the reign of our present Queen Elizabeth, an extension was added in which the old building technique was retained. One of Lavenham's three guildhalls is now an extension at the back of the Swan, where there are frequently some very fine music recitals. The cross in the market place has stood there since 1502 and, in Prentice Street, the 15th century Woolstaplers was the home of the last surviving wool merchant. De Vere House on Water Street was built at the same time.

Having taken in all this beauty, we looked at some of the more modern businesses which fit beautifully into the whole. The One Bell we found fascinating. It is absolutely bursting at the seams with small collectable items of antiques and militaria. The Old Tea Shop and Suffolk Restaurant is a pretty thatched cottage serving coffee, lunches and teas, and has a pretty garden. Baker Antiques in the High Street has a fine selection of 17 – 19th century antiques as well as paintings, porcelain and collectors' items.

The priory is a beautiful, timber-framed house listed Grade I, which houses the Bossanyi Art Collection and, in total contrast, has a fine Herb Garden.

We would defy anyone not to like Lavenham, and indeed this small area with Clare and Long Melford is, for us, very special.

Lavenham Guildhall

We back-tracked from Lavenham south to **Sudbury**. Set in the heart of Stour valley, Sudbury is a good centre for both business and pleasure. It is an ancient market town with roots dating back to Saxon times. The Domesday Survey of 1086 mentioned the market, which was held every Saturday at the junction of School Street and Stour Street. When the town expanded in the 14th century, the market moved to the old market place at the east of St. Peter's Church, and it was moved again in 1840 to its present location on the Market Hill, where you can have a good time browsing round the stalls on Thursday and Saturday each week.

Sudbury received its Charter of incorporation from Queen Mary in 1554, and was granted its borough arms by Clarencieux King of Arms in 1576, during the reign of Elizabeth I.

For centuries the weaving and silk industry prospered in Sudbury, and with the wealth came great houses and churches. The whole area has a wonderful historical legacy, and will provide anyone who is interested in history and art with a great deal of joy. It is no wonder that Gainsborough and Constable were so inspired, and painted many wonderful pictures from scenes that are so superb, and yet we found that the people of Sudbury tend to take their good fortune for granted.

Gainsborough was born here in 1727, and Gainsborough House, in the centre of the town, is the only birthplace of a great painter open to the public in England. It contains a valuable collection of the artist's work, and some of his family possessions, as well as work by many other painters, including Frost, Heins and Dupont — not a patch on Gainsborough in our opinion, but everyone's ideas of beauty vary, do they not?

The Quay theatre provided us with a very good evening's entertainment. It was built in a restored maltings on a cut on the Stour. You can get a good, inexpensive meal in their bistro, and a drink at the bar.

Sudbury is set in a river hollow, and the River Stour wanders attractively around the town on three sides. The mixture of rolling hills and water meadows provides a constantly changing scene.

Sudbury — a view across the Water Meadows

Who could resist visiting a village with a name like **Bradfield Combust!** The village gets its name from a riot in the 14th century, when the locals burnt down the Hall; it is hardly a village at all now, just a few houses on the road to Bury St. Edmunds.

On driving along the A134 Sudbury Road, between Long Melford and Bury, you cannot miss this wonderful timber framed property, **Bradfield House Restaurant**, overlooking the village green.

Roy and Sally Ghyben run their 17th century home as a restaurant, with rooms serving English and French country cuisine. They have retained the feel of a country home, with log burning fires in many of the rooms, and an old French enamelled wood burner in the entrance hall. The bedrooms have been tastefully refurbished with solid English pine furniture and new en-suite bathrooms.

The dining room overlooks a beautiful Victorian garden, with spacious lawns bordered by scented flower beds, yew hedges and a large kitchen garden where unusual salad items and herbs are grown. The menu changes monthly, with a choice from an a la carte menu, with only fresh produce used. Starters may include various souffles such as prawn or mushroom, and stuffed fresh mussels with garlic butter. Main courses could include fresh salmon, poached and served with a green herb sauce, or fillet of beef panfried with garlic and mushrooms. Desserts include butterscotch meringue, creme brulee and home-made sorbets. The average cost for a really lovely meal for two with wine is about £35.00. Sunday lunch is an excellent value table d'hote menu, after which you may well feel the need to walk in the nearby Bradfield Woods.

Bradfield Woods are the most ancient worked woodland in England, where much wildlife can be seen, including deer and unusual plant life, such as wild mushrooms and rare wild flowers.

Bradfield House is four miles south of Bury St. Edmunds, and is well situated for Lavenham and Long Melford, and an easy run on the A136 from Norwich.

Bradfield House Restaurant

Bury St. Edmunds is one of our favourite Suffolk towns. For its size it has an astonishing number of archæological treasures and places of interest. It takes its name from the Saxon king, Edmund, killed at Hoxne and later canonised. His body was eventually enshrined in the monastery here, and the town became a place of pilgrimage. Miracles were attributed to Edmund.

King Canute gave the monastery the status of an abbey in 1032, and its precinct is unchanged, even though many of the buildings are now in ruins. In 1327 there was bitter fighting between the townspeople and the monks, and the abbey was virtually destroyed. The town was hit again, by fire this time, in the 15th century, and almost totally rebuilt by the 16th century.

At Angel Corner there is a superb collection of clocks and other timepieces, and you will find a very good museum at Moyses Hall, a Norman building believed to be the oldest private house in the region.

We already knew what an interesting place Bury St. Edmunds was, but until this visit we had not found **Pegotty's Carvery** in Guildhall Street. It is an attractive place with latticed windows, built some time in the 18th century.

As you would expect in a carvery, the speciality is roast meats, and succulent they are. There are, of course, other options on the menu, and every day there is a home-made lunch time special. An excellent self service salad bar is also available, with a whole range of cold meats and imaginative, freshly prepared salads. For just £5.00 you can get a very substantial lunch, which will give you the energy to continue sightseeing, and perhaps take in the Abbey Gardens nearby, or the Cathedral.

Pegotty's Carvery

If you are a vegetarian do not worry, you have not been forgotten. There is a full vegetarian menu. Peggotty's is open six days a week from 12.00 to 2.00 pm, and from 6.30 to 10.00 pm, and it is fully licensed, with a good, well selected wine list. Warning: do not go there on a Monday, that is the one day they are not open.

After an excellent lunch at Peggotty's we went to the abbey, and it was here that a group of nobles decided to force King John to sign the Magna Carta. This is incorporated in the town's motto: 'Sacrarium Regis, Cunabula Legis' (Shrine of a King, Cradle of the Law).

If you enjoy military things, then you will certainly find pleasure from a visit to the Suffolk Regiment Museum. We spent some time there learning much of the regiment's proud history, and quite a lot about the men of Suffolk who took arms.

Looking for somewhere just outside Bury to stay, we found the village of **Higham**, just off the A45, mid-way between Newmarket and Bury St. Edmunds. It is a quiet, restful place where instinct tells you that you could stay awhile and recharge your batteries.

To do this you would need somewhere to stay, and we found just the place, **The Old Parsonage**, run by Susan Ram, a very amiable lady, on whom you could depend to ensure your comfort. Mrs. Ram runs the house for people who want a restful holiday; she offers a very good breakfast, and dinner can be arranged if you require it. There is a large drawing room comfortably furnished, where you can relax, or read a book perhaps, from the many on the bookshelves, watch television or just sit and enjoy the views.

On a fine day the large garden, of almost two acres, is a delight. You can use the grass tennis court if you wish, although you may well find you have Sue's rare breed sheep looking on. At the end of the day, when you are ready for bed, you will find the bedrooms spacious and very comfortable. Both her rooms have private bathrooms, and one en-suite. The house is open all the year round, and is kept beautifully warm in winter; not easy in a house of this size.

Apart from anything else, the house is charming to look at. It was designed using flint stone by Gilbert Scott. If you want the theatre or some night life then, apart from Newmarket and Bury St. Edmunds, Cambridge and Ely are only half an hour's drive. We felt that people working or visiting the area for business would find the Old Parsonage a great place to stay. For whatever reason you go there you will not regret it.

The Old Parsonage

There are delightful places whichever way you go outside Bury St. Edmunds, and we found one of them at **Great Barton**, just north east of Bury on the A143.

Nearly ten years ago Margaret and Geoffrey Ellis opened a combined craft centre and tea shop in their restored old traditional **Suffolk Barn** at Great Barton. Around it they sell a selected range of herbs, wild flowers and other plants, and have also established a herb and wild flower demonstration garden.

They claim to be one of the few East Anglian centres selling crafts made entirely in the east of England. These include ceramics from a range of potters, fine and domestic woodwork, basketry, glass flowers and animals, toys, jewellery, home-made jam and honey and a wide range of dried flower bunches and arrangements: popular, they say all year round. The barn also houses an increasing range of secondhand country books, including some on gardening dating from early in this century.

The tea shop caters for teas and light lunches, and the wide selection of cakes are entirely home-made on the premises, using recipes collected from a number of sources. Especially popular are passion cake, honey fruit loaf, walnut tea bread, Dorset yum-yum, Canadian fruit cake and traditional Chelsea buns.

The herb and wild flower garden was developed following increased sales of herbs and a growing interest in wild flowers and the environment. In a formal, octagonal-shaped setting, it shows how both can be used within the average garden. Also open to the public are the ornamental gardens, containing a number of unusual plants. Admission to the garden is free.

Craft at the Suffolk Barn

After a visit to Craft at the Suffolk Barn we went to the little village of **Fornham-All-Saints**. It is really a part of Bury St. Edmunds today, but the locals like to hang on to their village identity. Suffolk has some lovely names, and one such name is Fornham-All-Saints. Not only does it have a nice name but it has a very good pub, **The Three Kings**, built somewhere about 1843. The pub is two things really: a good traditional English pub, serving fine ale and good bar food in a large, attractive beamed bar. The

Kings Carvery — The Three Kings

second is the **Kings Carvery** which seats 34, and serves a first class choice from the carvery every day. The roasts are succulent, and always accompanied by crisp fresh vegetables. Cold meats are always available too, from chicken to beef, and you can make a pig of yourself, if you wish, from the wide selection of salads. There is always a blackboard special every day as well. If you wish, you can choose from the a la carte menu, which gives you a wide choice.

The Patio Bar and the beer garden all lend to the very pleasant atmosphere of this pub. It is well run and, although it gives you a welcoming feeling in its old world atmosphere, the landlord ensures that the strictest hygiene standards are kept: important today when we are all aware of the health hazards that any relaxing of standards can bring.

Each time we went back into **Bury St. Edmunds** there was always something more to see or to re-discover. There are three particularly interesting buildings: the 15th century Guildhall, the Cupola House, built in the 17th century; and Hengrave Hall, which is now a convent, it was built in the 16th century, and was once moated. You will also come across the Angel Inn, which appears so vividly in Dicken's Pickwick Papers.

Going towards Haverhill, about four and a half miles from Bury, you will come to **Whepstead**, which has a lovely 17th century pub. **The White Horse** is charming. It has a comfortable lounge bar, with a farmhouse type bar, exposed beams and real log fires in the inglenook fireplaces. The tap room, which dates from the early to mid-19th century has regulars, one of whom has been coming there for sixty years, and there are some newcomers who have only been using the taproom for thirty to forty years! The pub is supposed to be haunted, but David and Rosemary Woolf, mine hosts, say they have never had any experience of the ghost.

There is no restaurant, but anyone wanting food is in for an unexpected treat. Rosemary Woolf, who has French/Chinese background, produces some delicious curries and spicy chicken dishes, which are served in the bar. For £3.75 you can have a veritable feast.

You will find a lot of business people use the pub at lunch time, knowing that there will be something to tempt their palates. Rosemary does not only produce her native dishes; you will find a mix of English, vegetarian, Indian and Chinese! Something to suit everyone. Do go and look for this pub, you will enjoy it!

The White Horse

Lavenham Tower

A trip to **West Stow Anglo-Saxon Village**, which is off the A1101, five miles north west of Bury St. Edmunds, will round off your visit in this area perfectly. It is a strange place: during excavations of a low hill beside the River Lark at West Stow, the diggers unearthed the footings of some 80 Anglo-Saxon houses, together with many personal and domestic items, such as bone combs, bronze brooches and dress-fasteners. There were weaving pins, pottery fragments and animal bones. From the evidence available, it has been possible to reconstruct a group of thatched wooden houses and a communal hall, using only the tools and techniques which the Anglo-Saxons would have known. The village is right at the centre of West Stow country Park, which is a lovely spot. Footpaths wind round a lake, which is frequented by many migrant birds. The paths will take you through woodland and over the sandy Breckland heath, in a world full of wildlife. There is a nature trail which draws your attention to the plants, animals and birds that can be seen. The village is only open between April and October, but you can wander through the park any day throughout the year.

We are off to Ipswich next, a place we know well for we used to live at Woolverstone, a delightful spot.

Ipswich to Stowmarket

Otley Hall

Area covered in Chapter 10

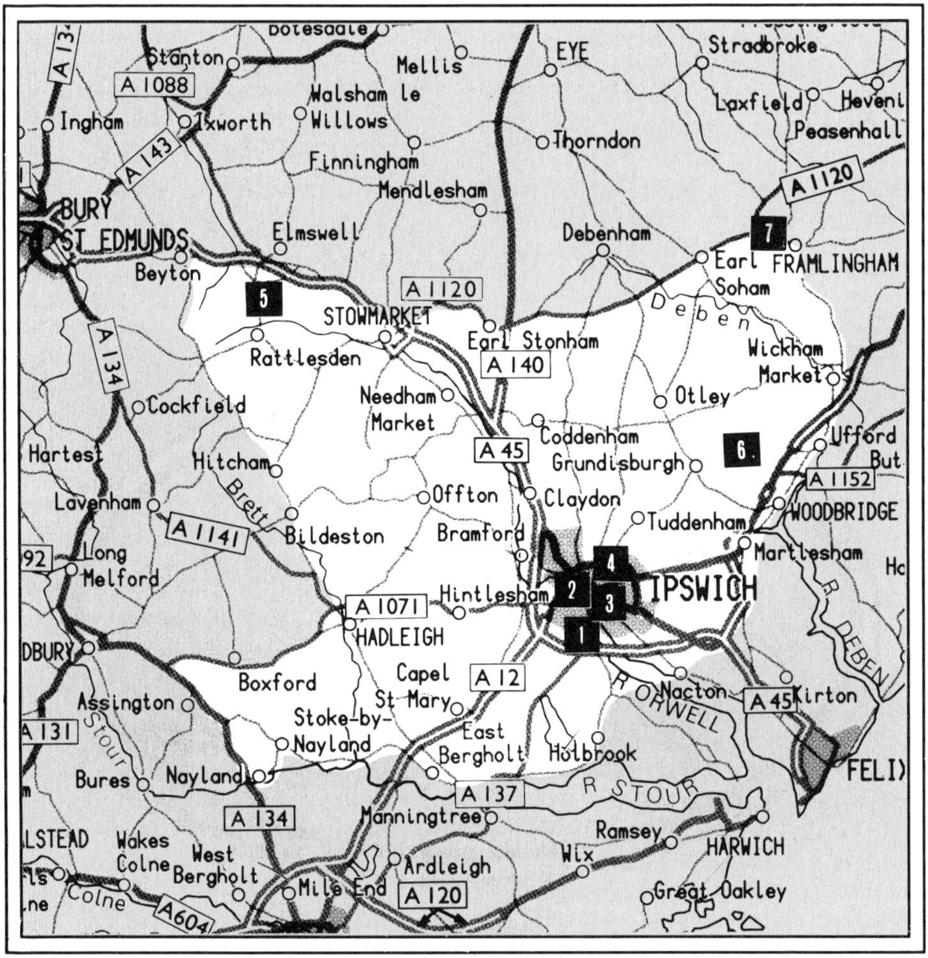

1 Burlington Lodge *(Ipswich)*
2 Koh-I-Noor *(Ipswich)*
3 The Golden Key *(Ipswich)*
4 The Lions Head Hotel *(Ipswich)*
5 Grange Farm *(Woolpit)*
6 The Crown Inn *(Bredfield)*
7 Shawsgate Vineyard *(Framlingham)*
8 Museum of East Anglian Life *(Stowmarket)*

CHAPTER 10

Ipswich to Stowmarket

Ipswich is the oldest English town. It was already a borough when the Normans arrived, but there has been a settlement here since the Stone Age. The Anglo-Saxons developed it into a port in the 7th century. King John granted it a charter in 1200, by which time it was thriving with its merchant community, which has expanded until today when it is enjoying the fastest growing economy in the country, as is most of East Anglia.

Ipswich has had its ups and downs. The decline of the famous Suffolk cloth in the mid-17th century did not help the economy, and it was not until the 18th century that it regained a little of its wealth because it was so favourably situated for the distribution of food to the Continent during the Napoleonic Wars. Since the 19th century it has grown steadily.

There are a lot of interesting people who have helped to make Ipswich great. Cardinal Wolsey was perhaps its most favourite son and certainly one of the most powerful during Tudor times. That wonderful painter, Thomas Gainsborough, lived and worked here creating beautiful portraits. Dickens stayed at the Great White Horse Hotel as a young reporter, and left a good description of it in the Pickwick Papers. Visit the Great White Horse while you are in Ipswich; it is one of the country's great coaching inns. We wonder if we may include Sir Alf Ramsay as one of Ipswich's famous. He was the manager of Ipswich Football Club before he became the England manager, and with the team won the World Cup in 1966. Such is greatness in our eyes!

Like the county itself, Ipswich does tend to sprawl, but it contains so many gems that it is worth making the effort to unearth them. Take a look at the Ancient House in the Buttermarket, reputed to have been used as a hiding place by Charles II. It contains the finest pargetting in the county. It is now a very charming bookshop, which hopefully will stock this series of Hidden Places.

Ipswich is the region's second largest port, with exports going out to the world. You should look at the Old Custom House on Wet Dock, which houses the Ipswich Port Authority.

In Christchurch Park there is a stately Tudor mansion that now is a splendid museum with paintings ranging from Constable and Gainsborough to Steer and Munnings. You can arrange a personalised day or evening tour of this fine country house, led by a knowledgeable guide who will help you to enjoy the excellent collection of furniture, glass, china, paintings and clocks etc. This service is provided by the Friends of Ipswich Museums, and they would appreciate it if you wrote a month in advance of the proposed tour. Your letter should be addressed to the Curator, Ipswich Museums and Galleries, High Street, Ipswich.

Whilst we are talking about the Ipswich Museums, we must tell you that the activities there are imaginative and great. Apart from the regularly changing exhibitions, they run such things as 'Hands On', where you can find out what fish's skin is used as sandpaper, what is the largest egg in the world, or how a dolphin eats.

Bob Markham, who is an assistant curator of the museum, gives some marvellous lectures. We heard one entitled 'Enthusiasts and Eccentrics'. He described it as a story of Victorian earnestness and intrigue, of dinners, debts and shootings. Tactile 88 is a guided tour service for the visually handicapped. The Friends of the Ipswich Museums quite obviously give enormous support to the Curator and his staff, and this becomes very apparent when you visit the museum which is open daily, except Sundays and Bank Holidays, from 10.00 am to 5.00 pm.

Ipswich is a city we know well, having lived at nearby Woolverstone, on the banks of the River Orwell, some years ago. If you want to explore this town then book yourselves into **Burlington Lodge**, a late 19th century house at No. 30 Burlington Road. It is in a quiet residential area, yet it has almost immediate access to the A12 and the A45 on the southern ring road via Handford Road. It is a family run guest house, with a friendly, homely

Burlington Lodge

atmosphere. There are five rooms, not en-suite, but all the rooms contain washing facilities, colour television and tea/coffee making facilities. There are no evening meals here, but with sixty restaurants and a vast number of pubs in Ipswich, we do not think you will starve.

The owners Jean and David Wickens amused us when they told us that cats and dogs were welcome provided they brought their own beds! Cots and high chairs are available for children too. Mid-week bookings are accepted, and they open all the year round. It is always good to know where you can stay comfortably without breaking the bank.

Talking about the evening meals, fourteen years ago the unlikely combination of a Bangladeshi and an Italian wife opened the **Koh-I-Noor** in Upper Orwell Street. But what a success they have made of this Indian restaurant, which is run now by their son and his wife. Koh-I-Noor means 'Mountains of Light' and this is the feeling the restaurant generates. It is light, friendly and cheerful. The food is traditional, and prepared to a high standard. Whether you like your curry hot, medium or mild, it will be given to you as you request. We had an excellent, leisurely meal there. There was a well stocked bar, and the average price per head works out to approximately £10.00, which is more than acceptable.

All the way round the walls of the restaurant there are paintings which tell an Indian story 'The Wishing Tree'. We asked about the paintings, and enjoyed the story the very pleasant staff told us while we waited for our meal.

If you are football minded then we can tell you that the restaurant was opened by Bobby Robson while he was manager of the Ipswich football team.

Mr. and Mrs. Rahman, who started the Koh-I-Noor, have lived in Ipswich for twenty-nine years now, and have devoted much time to community work, for which they are highly respected.

Koh-I-Noor

Ipswich has no less than 12 mediæval churches. St. Margaret's, which is the finest in Ipswich, is built of flint and stone, dating mainly from the 15th century, with a double hammerbeam roof. There is a fine hexagonal clock on the tower which dates from 1737. St. Mary-Le-Tower church is the civic church which, although of mediæval origins, was mostly rebuilt between 1850 and 1870. It still retains some of its earlier features, including a fine 15th century font.

St. Mary at the Elms church is mainly 15th century, behind which stand the town's oldest cottages, which date from 1467. The Unitarian Meeting

House, erected in 1699, is one of the earliest non-conformist chapels in the country. The interior features a fine carved pulpit and a 17th century Dutch brass chandelier.

Time to take you to another pub we think. When we called at **The Golden Key** on Woodbridge Road, we were met by a very friendly Great Dane, who introduced us to his owners, Mac and Chrys McPherson, who run this local family pub, which was built around 1860.

The saloon bar has a collection of World War I artefacts and other militaria; Mac runs occasional tours of the battlefields of France and Belgium for his customers, and anyone else who is interested.

The Lounge Bar has a more horsey theme, and features a 'Rogues Gallery' of photos of customers, taken during various events, some of which are most amusing.

There have been only ten landlords in the pub's history, and it has always been known as a friendly local, with some local characters who have been enjoying their pints in the bar for forty years or more.

One advantage is that there is no juke box. There is background music only, with a folk night on Thursdays, featuring many local performers. There is a dart board in the saloon bar, and dominoes are also available. There are three traditional bitters provided, Adnams, Burton and Tetleys.

The Golden Key

Bar snacks are available Monday to Friday lunchtimes, some of which are home-made, at prices which range from 65p to £2.00.

At the rear of the pub there is a pleasant patio area, and a children's play area and playroom with many toys provided. There is also a large car park.

The pub is twinned with the Copper Kettle in Nijmegen, Holland. Darts matches and exchange visits between the two pubs are another feature of this traditional local.

Mac and Chrys have run 'The Key' for thirteen years, and are proud of the fact that it is still a pub where ladies visiting alone can feel comfortable.

For swimmers and those who like fun in the water, and out of it, you should discover the magic of the Crown Pools. It is one of Europe's finest and most imaginative swimming complexes, incorporating the very best in leisure and competition facilities. There are large shallow beach areas, a wave machine, waterfalls and fountains. There is also a tropical fun pool, with lush tropical and sub-tropical planting areas, including bananas, coconuts, pineapple etc. There is a teaching pool for very young beginners.

It is open Monday to Friday from 7.45 am to 9.10 pm, and on Saturdays and Sundays from 7.45 am to 4.55 pm. The last tickets are sold 25 minutes before closing time, so do not leave it too late to get the maximum fun out of it.

For the princely sum of 55p you can find fun for adults at the Council's Whitton Sports and Community Centre, or Gainsborough Sports and Community Centre. The former is open on Mondays from 1.00 pm to 4.00 pm and the latter on Wednesday mornings from 9.00 am until noon. Everyone is welcome, and there is no need to book. You can enjoy badminton, indoor bowls, keep fit, snooker and racquet ball. In the phase 2 fitness studio supervisors will assist you in finding the best fitness programme to suit your needs.

If you like to dance, the centres have tea dances too, on Monday from 2.00 pm to 4.00 pm at the Gainsborough Centre and Friday from 2.00 pm to 4.00 pm at Whitton. We are informed that these sessions are very popular, but new members are always welcome. Just turn up, there is no need to book.

If you want to have a night out and see something of Ipswich you can do this without taking your car. Ipswich Buses run trips of special interest to all those who enjoy a good drink: Real Ale Runabouts! These trips are operated in conjunction with the Ipswich and Suffolk branch of the Campaign for Real Ale, and run throughout the year on Wednesday evenings.

For full details of the service call into the Tower Ramparts Enquiry Office, or ring Ipswich 55586. We tried it out and had a great evening with lively companions, and we also got to see a lot more places than we would have done on our own.

One of the pubs we visited had decorative plates everywhere around the walls, some 200 of them. They were the first things that caught our eye as we went into **The Lions Head Hotel** in Cauldwell Hall Road. It is a busy pub, built in 1890, with one large horseshoe-shaped public bar, where darts seem

The Lions Head Hotel

to be the 'in' game. The lounge bar was comfortable, and the whole atmosphere of the pub was friendly. They have a good local trade, catering mainly for the over 25s. The landlord is proud of his selection of beers, which are all well kept. There is no restaurant, but bar food is available.

The hotel has accommodation, three twin rooms and one single room, at the good price of £12.00 per person for bed and breakfast.

At **Wherry Quay** there is an excellent water sports centre. It offers an exciting variety of water-based holidays for all ages. You can choose from a fleet of ocean going yachts, sailing dinghies, sailboards and canoes. There is a choice of single or multi activity holidays with full R.Y.A. training if required. Do not be afraid of being a complete novice, you will be equally as well cared for as the experts. It is a marvellous place to go, whether you are by yourself or with a family.

We went on a nostalgic pilgrimage, taking the B1456 out of Ipswich towards **Shotley**. The road runs along the River Orwell through the small hamlet of Woolverstone, where we once lived in a converted farmhouse. At that time filming was taking place below us on the river. It was used to reconstruct location shots for 'The Yangtze Incident' a famous naval occasion which happened in 1948 in the Yangtze when H.M.S. *Amethyst* was trapped up river and had to fight her way out with great bravery and some loss of life. We were in Malta at the time, and met some of the officers on their way home. Therefore it was especially interesting to us to see the filming.

Wildfowl on the River Orwell

In 1955 when we were at Woolverstone the Royal Navy had a strong presence in the area. The Minesweeping Squadron was based at Harwich, with the parent ship H.M.S. *Mull of Galloway* watching over all her chicks as they came and went, ever busy in recovering World War II mines or keeping an eye on the fishing fleets. Most of the families lived on the Shotley side of the river. Shotley was still home to H.M.S. *Ganges*, the Naval Training Base for young seamen.

We were amazed to see that Shotley had become a flourishing marina, with no trace of the navy to be seen, and we met an entirely different breed of seafarers. One thing mercifully had not changed, that was **Pin Mill** on the Orwell estuary, which has a wonderful pub 'The Butt and Oyster'. This was a favourite meeting place for the navy, and held very happy memories for us. One regular visitor at that time, who has since achieved fame as Master of the Queen's Household, was Sir Paul Greening, then a young lieutenant.

Sunday lunchtime was the most popular meeting time. We all went to the little church in the park and afterwards walked across to the pub. Unusual bar games were played there which we have seen nowhere else: Shut the Box and Pass le Temps.

Thames barges are often moored on the hard at Pin Mill, near the Butt and Oyster, which has a history of associations with smugglers and the books of Arthur Ransome.

The whole of the Shotley Peninsula, which lies sandwiched between the wide estuaries of the Stour and the Orwell, is a nature lover's paradise. The Orwell, in spite of its commercial channel carrying heavy traffic, is home to no less than eleven species of wildfowl and waders. The Stour estuary is of particular interest, because of the very large number of over-wintering birds who feed on the extensive mudflats.

As we wandered back from Shotley Gate we drove to **Holford** where we had friends, and the magnificent Royal Hospital School takes pride of place. Since we were there thirty odd years ago Alton Water Reservoir has been developed to provide opportunities for many water sports and recreations.

From Holford to **East Bergholt** is no distance. Randolph Churchill, son of the great man himself, Sir Winston, and father of the M.P. Winston Churchill, lived here at Stour House. He was always a sad man, never quite achieving the greatness of which he was capable. He entertained quite considerably and, if you were lucky enough to dine there when he was at his best, you were privileged to see and hear a brilliant man, very much his father's son.

Constable first met his future wife, Maria Bicknell at the Rectory, now known as the Old Rectory. Constable had a studio there in a small cottage, now called Moss Cottage, which stands next to the garage. If you take a look around the churchyard of St. Mary's you will see Constable family tombstones.

East Bergholt is large and scattered, and just on the edge you will come to **Flatford Watermill**. It was built in about 1773 and of course became famous through Constable's painting. John Constable loved his birthplace, East Bergholt, and this was the landscape that was to influence him always. He went away to London but he returned regularly, sometimes for whole summers. He walked or rode through this lovely fertile valley, with his small sketchbook his constant companion.

Flatford Mill and Willy Lott's Cottage look today much as they did when John Constable painted them, and when his father was the mill owner. His father had hoped than John would take over the business, and John did try to learn the corn business but his heart was never in it. We thank God today that it was not.

The Mill, Willy Lott's Cottage and Valley Farm are owned by the National Trust, and are not open to the casual visitor, but you can enjoy looking at them as they cluster picturesquely along the Stour. Nestling under Flatford Bridge, a replacement for the one Constable loved to paint, is Bridge Cottage, which has a tea garden and a National Trust shop which we found a

Willy Lott's Cottage

super place to bide a while. You will find a display here of many aspects of John Constable's paintings. If you would like to take to the water, then there are boats to be hired. What has become known as Constable country is truly beautiful. It is not difficult to understand from whence Constable got his inspiration.

One way of seeing much of this lovely countryside is to take a guided tour with **Eandee Tours**, 75 Lacey Street. Ring them for details on (0473) 55530. They define their role as being 'able to take visitors to reach parts that other tours do not reach!' We went with them on one tour and found it to be a very enjoyable experience. They visit such places as Debenham, Hoxne and Framlington on one tour; Flatford, Lavenham and Woolpit on another, and yet another takes you to Debenham, Laxfield and Snape. The standard tour starts at 10.00 am and returns about 5.30 pm. The tours include morning coffee, afternoon tea and a traditional ploughman's lunch in a Suffolk pub.

Eandee are based in the centre of Ipswich, but they will collect and return you to your place of residence or hotel anywhere in the vicinity of Ipswich.

If you are interested in the gossipy type of history you may like to know that the courtroom at Suffolk County Hall is where Mrs. Wallis Simpson obtained her divorce in 1936, so that she could marry the King, which she did after his abdication. In retrospect she did the country a favour. George VI gave so much more to the monarchy than his brother would ever have done.

A visit to **Stoke-by-Nayland** is definitely a must. If you are a golfer then it has fine golf courses, but if you are just a lover of charming places then you are in luck. You can have bed and breakfast if you wish at the Tudor and Queen Anne Vicarage, which will give you more time to see the timber and plastered buildings which are quite lovely, with overhanging second storeys dating from the 16th century. The National Trust have preserved the Guildhall and Maltings built in 1620, which are gems, and one and a half miles east of Stoke is Thornington Hall, a fine oak-framed Tudor mansion which can be visited by appointment.

The church of St. Mary the Virgin is a grand Perpendicular church, parts of which, including the carved oak south doors, date from the 13th and 14th centuries, although the main part of the church was built in the 15th century. The ornamented tower, which local merchants left money to build, appears in scores of paintings by Constable. Behind a Perpendicular screen in the south chapel you will find mediæval brasses. There is one of a knight in shining armour with a curly beard, Sir William Tendring.

Stoke-by-Nayland

On your way back to Ipswich you should also take in **Dedham**, which has many fine buildings as well, some dating from its heyday when it was a centre for the wool trade. It did not decline after the decay of the East Anglian cloth industry, so it has far fewer mediæval timber framed frontages than some of its neighbours. It derives its character and charm from the large number of Georgian houses which gracefully line its streets, some painted white and some displaying the natural brick.

The church of St. Mary was built on the wealth of the prosperous 15th – 16th century clothier families. It has a magnificent flint and stone tower, which was financed by the Webbe, Hawke and Dunton families, and was the last part of the church to be built. Unusually the tower was breached with a passageway that allowed religious processions to circle the church without leaving hallowed ground. Dedham welcomed John Constable and understood his dreams. The English School was housed in Sherman's Hall, built originally as the home of a clothier, who was, incidentally, an ancestor of the American Civil War General.

Southfields was another merchant's house, and Castle House was the home of Sir Alfred Munnings, famous for his horse paintings. The house contains much of his work, and is open to the public from May to October each year.

Wherever you roam in this part of Suffolk you will not be disappointed, and we have only touched on it. Ipswich makes probably the easiest base to use for touring, and will certainly give you a lot to see in its own right.

From Ipswich we took the A1071 to **Hadleigh**, a small town steeped in history. Its main street has an excellent architectural facade, and the town, whilst welcoming visitors, makes you realise that it is a working community. Hadleigh is fortunate in having a town centre that is worthy of much praise. The High Street is a gem of vernacular architecture, representing every period of 600 years of history.

King Guthrum the Dane reigned here in 870 AD, and after his defeat by King Alfred the Great he built the church that now lies hidden beneath the churchyard turf. The church of St. Mary is vast, as are so many of the churches built from the wealth of the spinners, weavers and cloth processors.

The tower belongs to the 13th century, built to replace the Saxon one, and the rest of the church would seem to have been built and added on to between 1350 and 1450. The vaulted ceiling of the porch has never been finished, probably because the Black Death killed off both the masons and those paying for it. It is fine and for us was extra special because we found a bench end to add to our collection: King Edmund's head in the mouth of a wolf.

Hadleigh Guildhall

Across the churchyard stands the Guildhall, for many centuries the centre of the town's commercial and social life. The central three-storey portion is the original Market Hall, given to the town by William de Clopton in 1438. The other timber framed portions were added in 1451. We were fascinated by the brickwork of the Corn Exchange built in 1813, which has been scored by generations of children sharpening their slate pencils as they went into school. The Corn Exchange is on the east side of the town, but on the west are the remains of the Mediæval Kitchen, in which guild banquets were prepared. Just over the wall is Topplesfield Hall, once the home of William de Clopton, but now the headquarters of the East Anglia Tourist Board.

The town has good shopping facilities and a good selection of pubs and restaurants. Parking is free, which is a bonus. We enjoyed wandering, and before we went further we took a gentle walk which wandered from Duke Street as far as the mediæval Topplesfield Bridge, over the Brett, and along the river path to Bridge Street. It was about one and a half miles until we got back to the High Street. It took us past many different buildings, and underlined the fact there are many examples of different styles of brickwork and they are worth looking for.

Just a little north of Hadleigh on the B1113 you will come to **Little Blakenham**, with its Woodland Garden. There is a five acre bluebell wood with a large collection of varied trees and shrubs, many of them rare and vigorous specimens. In the spring you can wander through paths of bluebells, camellias and rhododendrons, and in the summer there are an abundance of shrubs and climbing roses. The autumn brings hydrangeas and coloured maples. It is a joyous place of sheer beauty and tranquillity.

Kersey, a few miles to the west of Hadleigh, is almost too beautiful to be true, and this is no doubt the reason why it ends up on so many scenic calendars. It is set in a delightful valley and has an old world charm. There are a fascinating range of historic buildings lining the main street: weavers' cottages, merchant houses, which are somewhat grander, and some splendid mediæval pubs, all jostling for pride of place.

If you are driving through the main street, the middle is crossed by a stream, and you must take care to avoid the ducks when negotiating the ford. The ducks have the right of way! At the head of the village stands the church of St. Mary, mentioned in the Domesday Book. It is a fine church, with a 15th century tower and a delightful flushwork parapet.

The south porch is very special, with a glorious display of flushwork and crocketed pinnacles outside, and graceful traceried panels forming the roof inside. The 14th century nave arches are charmingly decorated. The church opens in summer from 8.00 am to 7.00 pm, and in the winter from 10.00 am to 4.00 pm. Kersey is an enchanting place, and lives up to its idyllic image.

Nearby **Lindsey** has houses scattered along narrow lanes, which remind one of how the cottage industry developed during the 14th and 15th centuries, to produce Lindsey-Woolsey, a coarse woollen cloth. Take a look at St. James Chapel, which was built in the 13th century and somehow became a barn; it was restored in 1930.

A little further north, **Chelsworth** will reward you if you venture off the main tourist tracks. The village is so picturesque that once a year almost every property opens its gardens to the public.

From Lindsey we went wandering through the small roads, enjoying all the delights of this lovely county on our way, until we came to **Stowmarket**, where we intended to base ourselves for a few days, staying with friends.

We had stayed here before but, in order to refresh our memories of the elegance of the Georgian houses in the town, and to revisit the church of St. Peter and St. Mary, we spent our first day doing just that. Stowmarket is a gentle town, and the church which overlooks the market place has a wonderful Perpendicular tower, married to a 14th century church with beautiful, flowering window tracery.

There is a very touching inscription on a 17th century brass of Ann Tyrell inside, wearing a small shroud, which says 'By Reason and Religion She, at Seven, Prepared Herself and Found her Way to Heaven'. Also in the church is a remarkable iron wig stand of 1654. The church is open daily from 9.00 am to 5.00 pm, and until 7.30 pm on Sundays.

The **Museum of East Anglian Life** is a remarkable place. It is only three minutes walk from Stowmarket market place, and occupies a large meadowland site, extending for nearly half a mile to the River Rattlesden. It has constantly changing exhibitions, and there are frequent lectures on a whole range of subjects, but just to wander around is pleasure enough.

You can see Alton Windmill, which was carefully constructed on the museum's site in 1970. Its original site near Ipswich is now flooded by a large reservoir. The watermill dates from at least the 18th century and possibly earlier. The machinery is usually turned by water power every afternoon from 2.45 pm to 4.45 pm, and since last year grain is ground on special demonstration days.

Museum of East Anglian Life

The Boby Building is the largest structure to be erected on the museum site for a decade. It was originally part of the engineering workshops of Robert Boby of Bury St. Edmunds, and dates from the 1870s. The large spaces inside the building have been used for new exhibitions. The building was formally opened by the Duke of Gloucester in June 1986.

Inside the space is well used. There are six reconstructed craft workshops on the ground floor: rake-maker, wheelwright, basket-maker, cooper, printer and harness-maker. All will be in use from time to time by demonstrators during the museum's open season. Visitors will see a short video in the cooper's and basket-maker's shop, showing the craftsmen at work. Michael Marsh, the museum's wood-turner craftsman, can usually be seen at work in the wheelwright's shop, except on Tuesdays and Saturdays.

There is also a Steam Gallery. East Anglia was the home of important engineering companies, who built steam engines for agricultural and industrial use. One of the museum's three Burrell steam traction engines will usually be displayed on the ground floor, as well as a rare surviving horizontal steam engine by the Suffolk engineering company, Whitmore and Binyon of Wickham Market.

On the first floor gallery is an exhibition about steam and its use in East Anglia, which includes working models and tape-recorded reminiscences of a former steam engineer.

Much in the style of the 1851 Great Exhibition in the Crystal Palace, the museum tells some of the story of industrial development in East Anglia. There are so many varied industries. Artificial fertilisers, brick-making, tanning, glove-making, rope-spinning and, of course, agricultural engineering, all find a place.

In a corner of the Industrial Heritage Exhibition we were able to seize the chance to rest our weary legs, whilst we sat and watched a short selection of historical films about industries in the region, specially made for the museum by the East Anglian Film Archive.

The museum is lucky enough to be the proud owner of 'Remus', a super Suffolk Punch who is very much part of it all. He can regularly be seen at work on the site. When we were there they were excited at the prospect of having a special vehicle adapted by museum craftsman Michael Marsh, which will enable Remus to give horse-drawn rides round the site.

There is a constant programme of happenings from April to October, many of them organised with the help of the Friends of the Museum, who were formed to raise funds and to help with the development of the site and to stimulate public interest in the work of the museum. This they do splendidly. Every season the Friends organise a varied programme of lectures, followed by a buffet supper and a glass of wine in the Museum Education Centre. Do write to them for a programme; the occasions are very enjoyable. For those of you who might think that it would be heavy going, come and see; you will be very agreeably surprised.

Just five miles north of Stowmarket there is a Mechanical Music Museum, which has a mighty Wurlitzer theatre pipe organ in a reconstructed cinema. There are a whole range of organs, street pianos and many other unusual items. We passed a happy couple of hours there.

Between Stowmarket and Bury St. Edmunds is **Woolpit**, and there you will see how the Tudor character of the village asserts itself, with prominent chimney stacks and timber-framed houses with diamond panes. The 19th century is there too, with the charming canopied village pump.

There are times when even the finest five star hotel loses its charm and you long for the simplicity of a comfortable, friendly home to stay in, and **Grange Farm** at Woolpit answers this need. The Grange is a farmhouse on a working farm, where the accent is definitely on a family home rather than a hotel or guest house. It is set beyond a paddock, and surrounded by ponds with plenty of wildlife in residence. There are four letting rooms, one double, two twin-bedded and one single, so it is ideal for families. Cots are provided for little ones, and there is a baby alarm system. Well behaved dogs are welcome also. Mrs. Parker only provides breakfast; we say only, but you should see the size of the excellent breakfast!

Hidden away from the farmhouse are facilities for caravans and campers. This lovely secluded spot is a marvellous starting point for visiting places in the area. There is a farm shop on the premises, with produce and preserves, dried flowers and local crafts. You can also buy soft fruit in season.

The Grange is about two hundred years old, and has always been in the family. You will find many portraits of Parker ancestors hanging in the dining room and the hall. It is a happy house and we are sure you will enjoy staying there.

Woolpit has a lovely 15th century church, of St. Mary the Virgin. Queen Elizabeth I is said to have presented the church with its fine lectern, but that is overshadowed by the feathery angels who rest against the marvellous double hammerbeam roof, with wings that spread as if they want to enfold you.

Grange Farm

Angels abide in the aisle roofs too, and you must see the beautiful canopy at the east end. We found our favourites there too: bench ends with saints and animals on the traceried ends. Before you leave, take a look at the 15th century porch. It has an eye-catching stone face, and is superbly decorated with an agee gable stretching up to statue niches and a lacy openwork crest.

The name Woolpit was originally Wolf Pit, and appears in the Domesday Survey of 1086 as the place where wolves were taken to be destroyed and buried. There is a derelict brickyard that once made bricks for export. Some were actually used in the building of the White House, in the States.

Lady's Well, in the village, was supposed to provide water that was able to cure bad eyesight. We hope you do not suffer this way, because we are not at all sure the cure will work and we do want you to enjoy the beauty of this charming place.

Leaving Stowmarket and travelling directly east, you will come to **Helmingham Hall**, with its beautiful gardens and park which are open to the public. Helmingham Hall is a Grade I listed building of extreme beauty. Helmingham and the Tollemache family have been together for many hundreds of years. Let us tell you something about the home first. When Lionel Tollemache started work on Helmingham in 1510, it was built in the traditional half timbered style, with an overhang to the upper floor both

Helmingham Hall

outside and inside the courtyard. There have been a number of changes in external appearance, but the basic form of a courtyard manor house has never altered, and many of the brick chimneys are original, although some have had to be repaired over the last two centuries.

Helmingham has been lucky over the centuries, in that whenever the Hall has been in danger of falling into disrepair a later generation has come along who, by their energy and love for the place, have rebuilt and restored their family home. Two in particular were both called John Tollemache.

In 1840 the first Lord Tollemache, on his succession, found the house in a deplorable condition and a great deal of restoration, particularly on the garden front, had to be done. Just over a hundred years later John, the fourth Lord Tollemache came to Helmingham, in 1953, and again found the Hall sadly neglected. There was no running water, no electric light, no bathrooms and many holes in the roof. The wall tiles and bricks were lying everywhere. It must have been so disheartening.

However with vigour and enthusiasm the late Lord Tollemache and his wife tackled the problems and saved this lovely house from the sad ranks of so many other family homes which have been pulled down and disappeared forever.

The two drawbridges are pulled up every night, as they have been since 1510, and the Hall thus becomes an island, protected by its wide moat which is stocked with several kinds of fish.

Queen Elizabeth I is said to have come here twice, first in 1561 and later to attend the christening of one of the ten consecutive generations of Lionel Tollemaches as her godchild. She left as a gift on one of these visits the Helmingham lute or orpharion, built by John Rose in 1580. It is the only one of its kind, and is exhibited all over the world. History was repeated four hundred years later in 1976, when the Prince of Wales became godfather to Edward, the eldest son of the present Lord and Lady Tollemache, and in 1983 when Her Majesty the Queen and H.R.H. Prince Philip stayed for two nights at Helmingham.

The Gardens and the Park are splendid. When visitors enter the main garden on the western side of the Hall they will see a large sundial. From this point you can either go straight on to the Shrubbery Walk and up to the tennis court, passing a collection of shade-loving plants, or take several different routes through and around the walled garden. On the left of the wall is the Spring Border, with a profusion of tulips, irises, peonies, tree peonies and a collection of hostas.

Straight ahead through a parterre of box hedges and viola cornuta lies the main garden, divided as in Elizabethan times into four large beds with cruciform shaped herbaceous borders around each. On the fencing are many different varieties of old-fashioned roses, most of which have been identified and labelled, some going back to the 19th century. The kitchen garden grows prize-winning vegetables every year, and the produce goes both to the Hall and for sale to the public.

At the far end of the garden a bridge leads to the tennis court, and to the Meadow Garden, which in early summer is a carpet of primroses, cowslips, orchids and ox-eye daisies.

Before crossing the bridge, on either side stands the West Border, which is designed on a theme of silver, pink and white, and contains perennial shrubs and plants, and nicotiana to fill the air with scent on a summer evening. From this point it is possible to return along the Apple Walk or back through the Shrubbery Walk.

In 1982 the present Lady Tollemache, herself a skilled and knowledgeable gardener, began the new Herb and Knot Garden on the eastern side of the Hall. It is possible that a 17th century garden such as this previously existed at Helmingham. Certainly there is one at Ham House, which is another Tollemache seat. In the library there is a recipe book written by Catherine Tollemache in about 1600, explaining ways of cooking vegetables, and the making of jams and herbal cures. Although not open to the public, it is possible to glimpse the new garden, in which only plants and flowers which existed in English gardens before 1750 have been allowed.

An afternoon at Helmingham will always be a happy one, but there are different ways of finding that happiness. For some it may be the extensive gardens, where they can wander at will down the long herbaceous borders and compare notes on the flowers and vegetables with the head gardener. Others may wish to buy a ticket and go on a safari ride around the Park. For this you may climb onto a large wagon drawn by a Landrover, and for some thirty minutes gaze at the deer and watch the young fawns with their mothers.

There are few places in Europe where some 600 deer may be seen all at once, especially in such beautiful surroundings. A herd of Highland cattle and a flock of wild Soay sheep are also in the park. The park itself, which encloses 400 acres, has large herds of both red and fallow deer. Every year the stags grow antlers which they shed in the spring, and as they mature they grow to huge proportions. The deer have been in the Park for many centuries; the earliest mention of them being killed for the pot is about 1600.

John Constable, whose brother was steward of the Tollemache woodlands, lived for some time at Helmingham Rectory and painted a number of versions of a Dell in Helmingham Park. The oak tree in that picture, with its singular curved trunk, is still standing. Some of the famous Helmingham oaks in the Park are estimated to be up to 900 years old, and many have immense girths, but the splendid oak avenue leading up the front drive was planted about 1700.

The church of St. Mary, standing at the edge of the park, is known to have existed in 1258, and is well worth a visit. Although the tower was completed in 1543, it was in 1488 that John Tollemache subscribed £30.00 to commence the building of it.

The church is filled with magnificent and beautiful memorials to a number of generations of Tollemaches. These were cleaned and renovated

Highland Cattle at Helmingham

in 1976 in memory of the fourth Lord Tollemache, who had brought Helmingham back to life in the 1950s, and who died in 1975. Contributions are gratefully received to ensure the upkeep of this famous Suffolk church.

From Helmingham the B1077 will take you to the often forgotten **Thornham Parva**. There is a little thatched church here, huddling in the middle of a field, and it houses a remarkable mediæval altar painting, one of the finest to be produced in England. The artist is unknown, but it was painted around 1300. It consists of three panels, and the centre panel depicts the crucifixion, with four saints on each of the side panels.

The painting was discovered in 1927 amongst a lot of junk bought at a farm auction in a nearby village, Stradbroke, and it still carries the auctioneer's tag to this day. Because of the enormous value of the painting the church has to be kept locked, which is sadly a sign of the times. If you want to take a look at it then go to the house nearest to the church, where the key may be obtained. It is worth the effort.

Debenham comes next, a village that is often missed. The ancient craft of rush weaving still flourishes here. The weavers have a workshop near the river at the southern end of the village. You can watch them at work, and their products, including baskets, table mats and carpets are on sale.

At the other end of the village is the church of St. Mary, which has a very old core, and the lower parts of the tower seem to date from the Norman Conquest or a little before. Inside there is a fine roof of alternating hammerbeams and crested tie beams on arched bases. The church is famous among bell ringers for its peal of eight bells cast in 1761.

Although a fire in 1744 is believed to have destroyed no less than thrity eight houses, many attractive buildings remain. At the top of the hill is the Guildhall, which dates from the 15th century. It is a lovely timber-framed building, with a bricknogging infilling on the upper floor. We particularly liked the porch.

Hitchams School is another splendid building dating from 1666. It has an overhanging upper storey and decorated beam. Look at the 16th century Red Lion Hotel, which is not only very hospitable but when you look around you will see it has its original decorated plaster ceiling.

One and a half miles from Debenham to the south east is Crow's Hall, which is a splendid example of an early 17th century moated mansion. It abounds in oak panelling, and as you approach the mansion you will pass 'The Barracks', a fine range of farm buildings. We thought it was a strange name, but we discovered it goes back to the Civil War, when Crow's Hall was a Cavalier base.

On our way to Framlingham we found **Bredfield**, and there you will find a brass plaque on a building that is **The Crown**. It says 'On this spot 1742 absolutely nothing happened'. Of course we immediately went in! Bredfield is a lovely sleepy place where genuinely not a lot happens. The Crown is a real pub, and its history is fascinating. It is more than 450 years old, a Grade II listed building which first became an inn for cattle and sheep drovers bringing their flocks along the old trails from the North to London.

The Crown, Bredfield

The atmosphere is marvellous, and the name 'Old English Pub' is not a misnomer. So often today a pub is not really that; it has far more emphasis on its restaurant or live music nights than on the intrinsic ingredients that make up a true hostelry. The pub is thatched which, apart from making it so attractive, keeps it beautifully warm in winter and cool in summer.

There is a super beer garden, where children can play in total safety. It is well away from the main road and the half acre of land has climbing frames, ropes and swings made from old trees and all manner of things to enchant children. The little pond at the side is home to ducks and moorhens, with geese and chicken clucking alongside. At the rear there is a caravan park, which is registered and has all the amenities one would expect.

Last but not least the pub serves very good food. Mr. and Mrs. Grice have only been at the Crown for three years but they have acquired a reputation for their high standard.

Bredfield is half way between Framlingham, with its castle and quaint street, which is our next stop, and Debenham which, in addition to all the other things you have to see there, has some wonderful antique shops for which it is famous.

The hilltop castle at **Framlingham** glowers down on the town as if it is remembering its lengthy past. It was built by Roger Bigod, second Earl of Suffolk, at the end of the 12th century. The thirteen towers and linking walls are still in almost perfect condition.

The castle was only under siege once by King John in 1215, so it did not suffer the ravages of war as so many of our castles have done. In the 17th century the castle was turned into a home for local paupers, and the present poor house was built during the 18th century against the inside of the west wall. This is now the home of the custodian of the castle.

There are many fine buildings in Framlingham of various periods. The streets are quaint and very narrow, which adds to the delight if not helping the congestion.

Framlingham Castle

The church of St. Michael is formidable and majestic. It is Perpendicular, and the tower is embellished with flushwork. Sitting lions form alternative pinnacles at the corner of the battlements. The hammerbeam roof of the nave is nothing short of magnificent with its ornate fan tracery. That cruel man, Thomas Howard, third Duke of Norfolk who was such a power in Tudor times, started the rebuilding of the chancel and chapels to form a family mausoleum. Its completion was ordered by Edward VI. Without doubt the most splendid of these outstanding Renaissance monuments is for the third Duke who died in 1554.

It was erected at a surprising time in history, when religious images everywhere were being taken down. There are many such monuments to see, but for us the most beautiful thing was the 17th century organ case and the reredos with its sacred painting.

While you are in the Framlingham area do take a look at **Shawsgate Vineyard**, managed by Rob and Penny Hemphill, who have a deep love of, and understanding for, the vines and their fruit.

The 13 acre vineyard is only a mile from Framlingham. It was established in 1973, but it was not until Ian Hutcheson bought it in 1985 that major restoration was undertaken. New post and wirework has been constructed, windbreaks have been planted and gaps in the existing vineyard filled. A further four and a half acres of vines have been planted, making Shawsgate one of the largest vineyards in East Anglia.

Shawsgate Vineyard

The majority of the grapes are Miller Thurgau and Seyval Blanc, but they have introduced Bacchus and Reichensteiner. All these varieties of grape produce white wine.

In 1987 the winery was built. It has been fully equipped with stainless steel winemaking equipment, including a press, grape trailer, bottling line and vats used for the fermentation and storage of the wine. The grapes are picked in October and the wine is then bottled in April. Great care is taken during winemaking to ensure that the highest standards are maintained, so the best quality wine is produced.

A walk round the vineyard is available to those who choose a guided tour: a very worthwhile choice. The tour comprises a half hour tour of the winery, a walk round the vineyard and a wine tasting.

The shop sells not only the vineyard wines but many wine-related items. There were some beautiful dried flowers grown on the property, and vines. From time to time they cater for Wine Societies, other associations and clubs (frequently there are evening visits, by prior appointment of course, although normally their opening hours are 10.00 am to 5.00 pm) who come to learn more and enjoy the experience. It is an excellent outing for someone who is disabled, because the area is completely level. There is a children's play area, and a picnic site which you are welcome to use. We spent a very contented and informative three hours there.

Our visit to Framlingham was sheer pleasure at the end of quite an extensive tour of the area.

Saxmundham to Felixstowe

Choir Arcade, Orford Church

Area covered in Chapter 11

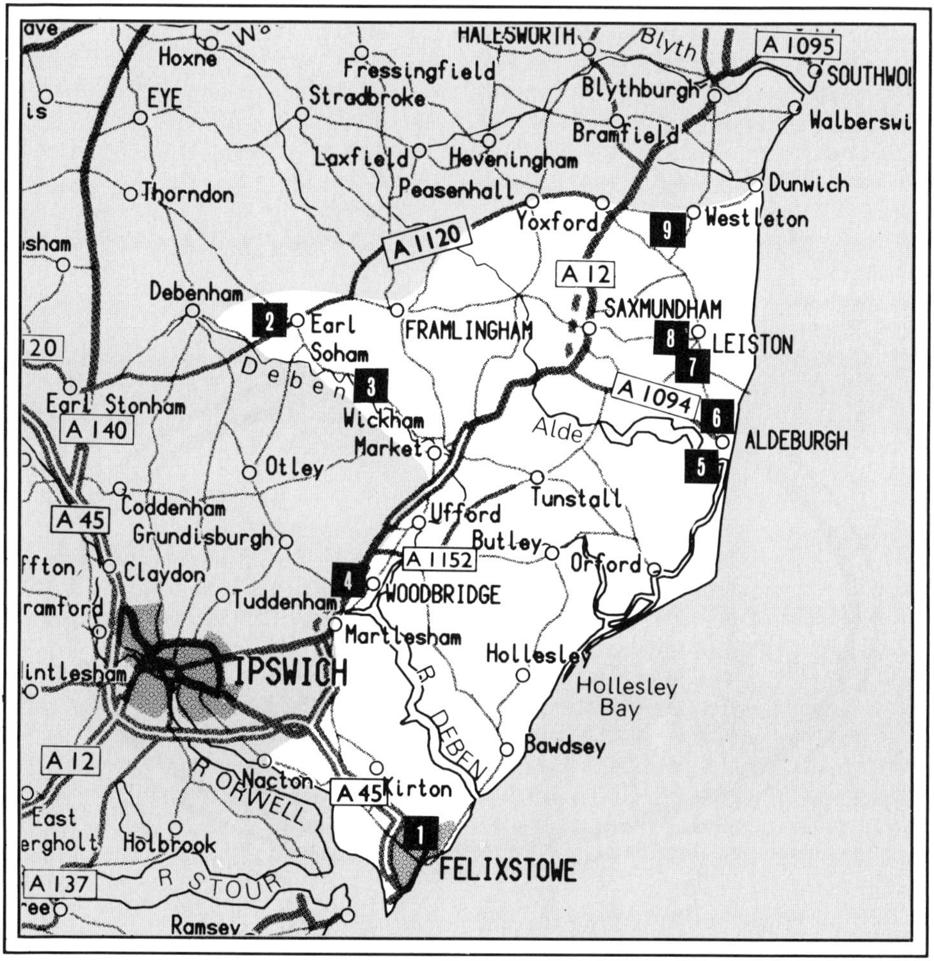

1 Felixstowe Beach Holiday Park *(Felixstowe)*

2 The Cider House *(Brandeston)*

3 Easton Farm Park *(Easton)*

4 The Georgian House Restaurant *(Woodbridge)*

5 The Mill Inn *(Aldeburgh)*

6 Austins Hotel *(Aldeburgh)*

7 The Parrot and Punchbowl *(Aldringham)*

8 The Volunteer Inn *(Leiston)*

9 The Central House *(Westleton)*

CHAPTER 11

Saxmundham to Felixstowe

The Felixstowe Peninsula is one of the prettiest parts of Suffolk. It lies between the Rivers Deben and Orwell, and abounds with attractive winding lanes through small villages that offer you a wealth of beauty in their churches, and excellent refreshment in the welcoming inns.

Both rivers are tidal, and have extensive boating activity; it is an area of magic for yachtsmen, experienced or beginners. The beautiful stretch of the Deben between Felixstowe Ferry and Woodbridge includes the Yachting Centre of Waldringfield and at Felixstowe Ferry a passenger ferry connects the peninsula with the village of Bawdsey on the north bank.

Whichever anchorage you use, or gaze at, you will find constant movement and become absorbed in the activity. We loved watching the fresh fish being sold on the water's edge by Felixstowe Ferry, and apparently this is a daily occurence.

We have already looked at the River Orwell from the Shotley side, but at **Levington** there is a concentration of boating activity, with an extensive marina. The river is the avenue to the sea from the port of Ipswich, and this traffic is coupled with vessels using the ports of Felixstowe and Harwich. You can imagine just how much traffic there is, can you not? It is certainly never dull!

Funnily enough you will find a complete contrast if you walk along the low wooded cliff on the northern bank from Levington to **Nacton**. It is totally peaceful and one of the most delightful walks we have been on in the county.

If you want to explore the peninsula on water, then there are special river cruises available at Waldringfield and Felixstowe. We went on one or two cruises on craft that were fully equipped with on-board facilities.

Felixstowe itself is a super place for a good holiday. It is very sheltered, and not only has a high sunshine record, but it does not rain all that often! The beaches are safe even for the youngest child at all states of the tide. The beach is a mixture of sand and shingle, but it makes a great playground for a family to have fun.

We were given definite instructions as to how we found **Felixstowe Beach Holiday Park**. Take the A45 Ipswich to Felixstowe road, turn right at the first roundabout, straight across at the second roundabout and, 200 yards on the left, there it is. It is a fun-filled place, and even if we had not been given such precise instructions we would have found it by following the sound of happy people.

The caravans are superbly equipped, including bed linen, which is quite unusual. Free gas and electricity is provided, giving you constant hot water in both the kitchen and the shower room. There is colour TV, and in the Super Luxury models you will find even more creature comforts. Every caravan is thoroughly cleaned after departures, and you can be sure that you will walk into your holiday home and find it spotless.

There is so much to do that if you did not wish to leave the Park for the whole of the time you are there you would not be bored. At Felixstowe Beach you can truly say that you are never far from water. There are beaches at Felixstowe, and in the Park there is a superb heated outdoor pool to splash around in. When you are tired of dipping there is plenty more fun to be had with a playground and paddling pool for the children, not forgetting the fun-filled games room. In the evening you have a choice of dancing, cabaret or exciting competitions in the Felix Family Club.

The Constable lounge bar is a very pleasant place to sit and enjoy a drink. The children have their own club to which they have automatic membership: The Children's Tiger Club.

For more mundane needs there is a fish and chip shop, a supermarket and a launderette. Having experienced a taste of the luxury of a Haven Caravan you might want to buy one; just ask.

Felixstowe Beach Holiday Park

One of the pleasures we found in Felixstowe were the lovely sea-front gardens. Brilliant splashes of colour in the well-kept flower beds, surrounded by the lushness of trim lawns, made a walk along the front a delight. It always amazes us that, even in a place as sheltered as Felixstowe, plants can stand up to the buffeting that sea breezes produce.

The sea-front has a lot to offer in addition to these super gardens. Most of it is designed to entertain children, and if we had to define our feelings about a holiday in Felixstowe we would say it was essentially for families. The town is served with many good shops and restaurants to suit all budgets, there are twinned cinemas, putting greens, crazy golf, sea floats, roller skating, coach tours, river cruises and boats that will take you longer distances if you wish — and do not suffer from sea sickness!

We watched the happiness showing through on people's faces, of all ages, as they had fun on the pier, and the vast Charles Manning Amusement Park must be every child's idea of heaven.

The Spa Pavilion has entertainment ranging from symphony concerts to star cabaret, brass bands and amateur dramatics.

Four years ago the leisure complex was opened, with three swimming pools, impulse pool, entertainment hall, sauna and sunbeds, as well as indoor bowls, a restaurant and bars. What more can you want?

It is quite surprising that Felixstowe has been developed over the last fifty years. It has an air of greater maturity.

On South Hill one older part of the town manifests itself at Q Tower, with its exhibition room on Martello Towers. It has a nice tea room and garden, which is situated in the dry moat of one of the Martello Towers. The cakes were delicious, and we could smell the enticing aroma of freshly ground coffee. They are open daily from May 1st to September 30th.

Are you a snooker fan? If you are, and you want to play at a club which has first class facilities, try The Felixstowe Snooker Social Club, which is quite a luxurious place and you will find them friendly and welcoming. From what we could see their members are quite dedicated to snooker, and to the apres snooker scene as well! It certainly turned into a very entertaining evening for us.

Woodbridge lies at the head of the picturesque Deben, and where once it was a busy centre of ocean trade, it is now a popular sailing centre, but if water sports are not for you just take a look at this charming town, with its wealth of historic buildings. The buildings and the life of the town were heavily influenced by one Thomas Seckford, who became Lord of the Manor in 1580. In addition to building the distinctive Seckford Almshouses in Seckford Street, he constructed the Shire Hall which dominates Market Hill. His family home has become a successful, well-appointed hotel. We had two nights of great comfort there, and found the food good and the staff efficient and friendly. There is quite a lot of accommodation at all levels in Woodbridge, and a phone call or letter to the Tourist Information Centre will provide you with a lot of information about the facilities on offer.

Edward Fitzgerald, the Victorian poet and translator, lived in a house near Market Hill, and his many friends included Lord Tennyson, who stayed at the Bull Inn when he visited Woodbridge. In the stable of the Bull you will see a strange memorial to an ostler, George Carlow, who was buried there in 1738 because he wanted to remain near his beloved horses.

That extraordinary man John Fox was born in the Crown Hotel in 1528. Can you remember reading about him? The Turks captured him and held him in slavery for 14 years. That very nasty time in his life gave him celebrity status in Woodbridge after his escape.

Woodbridge has a wonderful church, which is totally in keeping with the dignity of the town. It has a 15th century tower and north porch, both of which are magnificently decorated with flushwork, including friezes of initials and tracery. The most delicately ornate pinnacles crown the porch, and the front is yet another of the type that is only found in Norfolk and Suffolk, depicting the Seven Sacraments. There are some painted panels which have managed to survive from a 15th century rood screen, which was given to the church by John Albrede, a twill weaver, and his wife Agnes. Surrounded by so much that is old, it is quite amazing to turn to the east window and find some beautiful stained glass of the 20th century by Martin Travers. Thomas Seckford, who built the Seckford Chapel, was buried there on his death in 1587. One amusing story about him is that he rose to great power and wealth in the reign of Elizabeth I, in spite of the fact that she objected strongly to the stench which arose from his boots!

Woodbridge Steel Yard

The narrow streets will please everyone, except the motorist; they provide the town with much of its charming atmosphere. Dominating the river scene there is an equally charming sight; the restored Tide Mill. In 1956 this 18th century mill was the last of its kind in the country, and stands on a site used for this purpose since 1170.

The town offers many modern amenities, including a fine golf course, a covered swimming pool, a sports centre and a superbly modernised Riverside Theatre, which doubles as a cinema from time to time.

If you are a lover of antiques, then Woodbridge will give you great joy. There are several very good antique shops, where you can indulge browsing to your heart's content. The proprietors are very tolerant about this, although they will not say no when you are irresistibly tempted into making a purchase.

The history of cider has always interested us. We found out quite a lot when we were in Somerset, which you may have read already. Since then, we have seen an article in the *Sunday Times* writing about a panel of experts, who were asked to compare 45 major brands of apple juice from all over Europe. After tasting them blind, the panel chose James White's Cox's apple juice in second place and the James White Russett in sixth. Two out of the top six in Europe made us put a visit to **The Cider House** at Bridge Farm, **Brandeston**, Woodbridge a priority. To get there you take the A12 between Woodbridge and Saxmundham, and you will find Brandeston just four miles off the A12.

Cider has had its ups and downs in history. It has been savoured by

Englishmen for thousands of years, and by the 17th century it had become a valuable commodity, often being used to pay tithes. Until then, cider has been simply the juice of the crushed fruit, fermented for months in oak barrels. Gradually it became considered too good to give to the peasantry, so it became the practice to add water to the left-over mash, and then press it again. This inferior watered-down drink was often given to labourers as wages.

When later it became fashionable among the wealthy to drink imported French wine, the original real cider was doomed. Since then we have been subjected to the inferior kind until in recent years standards have slowly risen, and discerning cider drinkers have become very particular in what they choose.

James White's cider, which we had come to see in the making at the Cider House, is made from the juice of crushed apples and nothing else, maturing in oak casks. It is the true taste of real cider. We were allowed to taste the two ciders on offer today. James White's Suffolk Cider brings the original taste of ancient English cider, but be careful with this one, it is very strong.

James White's October Gold is a vintage cider, treated with as much care as one would expect of the finest wines. It is pure English apple juice, fermented and allowed to mellow in oak casks for a whole year. This gives October Gold its distinctive and delicious character. James White's Cider Royale Mix is just the sort of drink for a cold winter's evening in front of a crackling fire. It is mulled with carefully selected spices.

We had read about the non-alcoholic juices in the *Sunday Times*. The Cox's apple juice, which is pure and simple with nothing added, is a perfect drink for a summer picnic. Original Apple Juice is something different. It is blended from the finest local English apples, and has a slightly smokey taste and aroma; it would be excellent in place of a dry white wine with lunch. To drink chilled on a summer's afternoon, the Russet would take a lot of beating; it is sweet and delicate. James White also has pure cider vinegar available.

The Cider House

Mr. Hall, of the Suffolk Cider Company, will be able to tell you much more than we have written here. What we can tell you is that it was a very enjoyable experience, and we have learned much more about cider.

Easton Farm Park is a delight to visit, and will give you and your family a wonderful day out. It was opened to the public in April 1974, and has given enjoyment to thousands of people ever since.

Set in one of the most picturesque parts of the Deben valley, the farm buildings were built by the Duke of Hamilton as a model farm in 1870. Buildings on the site were either cleared or refaced to fit in with the new design. No farmhouse existed on the site. The Duke lived at Easton Park, which was demolished in 1929, but surrounded by the serpentine wall still visible in the village today. However there are two cottages, one for the farm foreman and the other for the laundry and dairymaids. At that time there were also two small cowsheds for the milking of the Red Poll dairy herd, stables for the Suffolk Punches which worked on the farm, poultry units, a laundry, an unusual octagonal dairy, as well as the usual barns and cart sheds.

The estate was split up and sold in 1919, following the death of the Duke, who had no male successor. Since then the estate has been sold on more than one occasion, and improved farming methods and changes of lifestyle have rendered most of the buildings unsuitable for modern agriculture. However as listed buildings they lend themselves very well to be used as the centre for the Farm Park.

On the low-lying water meadows you can see the farm animals. Some are commercial, and some have become quite rare due to their unsuitability for modern requirements. The same meadows, along with the wooded areas, some natural and some cultivated, make up the Nature Trail which, along with the rest of the Farm Park, won the Farming and Wildlife Advisory Group — Bayer Farm Trails Award.

It is interesting to note some of the facts about Easton Park because, as well as providing a pleasant day out for all the family, it is capable of producing 1.5 million litres of milk, 1,500 tonnes of wheat, 750 tonnes of barley, 300 tonnes of sugar, 150 tonnes of oilseed rape, 300 tonnes of freezing peas and 300 tonnes of freezing beans. Impressive isn't it?

The Dairy Centre was built specifically for the use of the public, with walkways over the top of the cow cubicles and a viewing gallery over the milking parlour. It gives the public a better insight into where their daily pint of milk really comes from: not a bottle as some people think!

Easton Farm Park really is a mine of information. We all take so many of these things for granted, do we not? We suppose one should know that it is necessary for a dairy cow to have a calf once every year to enable it to produce milk; common sense if you think about it. The herd here has been produced from the nucleus brought down from Ayrshire in Scotland. Since then the herd has gradually grown until the present day.

Although it was originally founded on the Ayrshire breed (red and white) it has for some years gradually been changed to British Friesian, by breeding with British Friesian bulls, presumably to produce the higher milk yield that you get from Friesians. They are black and white, and we have always thought them less belligerent than Ayrshires. This sounds very knowledgeable, but it so happens that some years ago we were lucky enough to attend Friesian bull sales in Holland, and learned something about them.

The nutrition of the dairy cow is a complex problem, and the herdsman and herd manager make it one of their primary functions to observe and detect any changes in the individual cow's appetite and requirements. Without this care milk production would inevitably fall.

The national average production for the dairy cow for one lactation (ie as a result of one calving, with production spread over about 300–320 days) is about 10,200 pints (6,000 litres).

All milk is refrigerated on the farm, and you will see the stainless steel milk tank in which the milk is kept. If you are there at the right time you will also see it collected by the road tankers of the Milk Marketing Board. This happens every single day of the year, Christmas Day included. After it leaves the farm it goes for processing and distribution.

The cattle are housed in the main part of the building, which is subdivided into rows of cubicles. They really are very well cared for. They can go into these cubicles when they wish to lie down, or they can take themselves outside for water and exercise.

We were able to look down into the milking parlour and see the herdsman fitting the milking machines onto each cow's udder as she comes into the parlour. The herdsman knows all the cows individually, and this is very important, because he needs to give each cow the correct amount of concentrated feed from the automatic feed dispenser.

It is important to be quiet when you are watching in the Dairy Centre, because the herd does not like being disturbed particularly during milking time.

In total contrast to the very modern Dairy Centre is the **Victorian Dairy**, an ornate building with marble shelves and painted doors, with a fountain

The Victorian Dairy at Easton Farm Park

in the middle which was used to keep the air moist for the butter and cheese etc. It is a unique building, we do not remember having seen one anything like it. It is especially interesting because of its octagonal shape.

Do not miss seeing the 'Suffolk Trinity', the three breeds of Suffolk in their home county: Red Poll cattle, Suffolk Punch horses and Suffolk sheep; it is a rare combination. Today Red Poll cattle are a rare breed, and in today's world the Suffolk Punch horse is becoming almost as rare. It is the Suffolk sheep that are still used commercially in modern agriculture.

What wonderful animals the Suffolk Punch horses are. Powerful and lovely, they give you constant joy to watch. They are not as tall as shire horses, as they have shorter legs, but this gives them a lower centre of gravity and makes them very effective as pulling horses. They also differ from the shire in that they do not have 'feathers' on their feet. Have you

Cattle at Easton Farm Park

noticed the long hairs just above the hooves of the shire horses? It helped in Suffolk when the Suffolk Punches were used as working horses, because they were much cleaner animals to work the Suffolk clay-soils. The lack of these long hairs prevented so much mud getting stuck to their feet.

We were lucky enough to see the forge on the one day in a six week cycle that horses were in for shoeing. It was a process we had not seen in action before, and we found it fascinating. One thinks of a forge being a building solely for the shoeing of horses, which primarily it is, but with the mechanism of farming it became the forerunner of the modern workshop, and the blacksmith was a mechanic, mending and making machinery. The difference between the farrier and the blacksmith is distinguished here, with the latter not being qualified to shoe horses.

The open part of this building is the **Travus**. This is where the horses are tied up, under cover, for the farrier to work on. The first operation is to remove the old worn shoes. This is done by lifting the clenches with a buffer and hammer, and then drawing the nail out through the bottom of the hoof with a pair of pincers.

Since a horse's foot grows rather like one's own finger nails, the extra length is then rasped to take the new shoe comfortably. Horses, like us, have different size feet, so it is important to have not only a shoe of the right size, but of the right shape too.

Shaping the shoe is a craft on its own. Modern farriers have to undergo a four year apprenticeship. If they are accepted into the 'Worshipful Company of Farriers' at the end, we are to be comforted in the knowledge that they are employed as a craftsman.

Shoes start life as a straight piece of metal bar heated in the forge. This is then shaped on the anvil with a hammer in the traditional way. Once the shoe reaches the basic shape, the nail holes have to be hammered through. The tool for this job is a hardened steel pritchel. This leaves a V-shaped hole to take the special nails.

The hole must be the right size and at the right angle for the nail, which in turn must be the correct size for the hoof. The hoof having been rasped to make sure it is square across the foot, is then ready to take the shoe. To make sure the fit is as perfect as possible the shoe is left hot and burnt on the hoof. This may appear to be dramatic, but the horse feels no pain or discomfort. This done, the shoe is put on the 'bosh' on the front of the forge to cool down before it is nailed on.

Easton Farm Park

You will notice a shoe has seven holes, four on the outside and three on the inside. The nails go into the hard wall of the foot, which is about half an inch thick. The well trained farrier gets the nail to come out in a nice line around the hoof. The points of the nails are hammered home, then the jagged end rasped into the hoof so the clench will lay flat when knocked down. All that is left to do after this is to rasp the foot back to the shoe.

To some of our readers this description may have seemed heavy going, but we certainly had no idea how intricate a process shoeing was, and we often wondered if the horse felt any pain. We all know that is not the case.

Old steam engines are always good to see. At Easton there is a splendid steam engine called 'Little Ben', which was built in 1878 by Ransome Sims and Jefferies. He can often be seen at work about the Farm Park.

In between seeing all these things, we found time to enjoy the tearoom which had a wide range of refreshments, including dairy cream teas and home made cakes. We also paid a visit to the gift shop, which is full of nice things, most of them at affordable prices.

There is something very special about Easton Farm Park; the ambience is right. You do not feel overpowered by commercialism, as so often happens. Visitors are free to wander about at their leisure and take in the beautiful countryside with walks down the farm trails and along the banks of the Deben.

We watched children enjoying themselves, because they can really get close to the animals. Even toddlers can get friendly with the smaller animals, such as rabbits and chickens etc. Grandparents will enjoy the sense of the past; the beautiful Victorian buildings and the vintage machinery will remind them of the 'Good Old Days'.

You will have guessed by the amount we have written about Easton Farm Park that we had a wonderful day, and we wholeheartedly recommend it for all the family, no matter what the age.

After a day out at Easton Farm Park, on returning to Woodbridge it was lovely, and a rarity, to find a really good tearoom where you can indulge in delicious home-made cakes. This delight we found at **The Georgian House Restaurant** in the Thoroughfare, Woodbridge. It is also a licensed restaurant, where you can have hot meals all day long. All the food is prepared on the premises, and it is beautifully presented. Special care is taken with vegetarian meals and there are childrens portions. Another nice touch in this friendly place is the special portions for Senior Citizens.

The restaurant is licensed; they serve red or white house wine, sherry and lager. The Georgian House is open from Monday to Saturday from 9.30 pm to 5.00 pm and on Sundays 11.00 am to 5.00 pm. The hours are slightly extended in the summer.

Georgian House Restaurant

On the B1084 between Woodbridge and Orford we discovered the Tangham Campsite at **Butley**, and it is a superb site. There are 5,000 acres of Forestry Commission forest in which the site is set. You can imagine how much there is to see in the way of wildlife and flora and fauna. We got a constant glimpse of deer and birds all in their natural environment. The site was well laid out, with flush toilets, hot water and showers, a site shop, gas supplies and electric hookups. It would be a great place to stay if you are touring the Suffolk Heritage Coast. We did not get a chance to take a photograph for you, but if you want more details ring (0934) 450707.

Having a drink in the Bull Hotel, a fine 16th century coaching inn on Market Hill, we got talking to a member of The Sutton Hoo Society, which was founded in 1984 as a local support group to the professional archaeologists excavating the site. If you do not know anything about **Sutton Hoo** let us explain that it lies just a few miles east of Woodbridge. In 1939 archaeologists working there revealed the outline of a Saxon rowing boat nearly 90 feet long. Amidships lay a spectacular treasure, comprising personal jewellery, weapons and domestic articles, perhaps for use in an afterlife. The grave was thought to be possibly that of Raedwald, the greatest of the Kings of the Angles.

Nearly 50 years have elapsed since that discovery, but interest in the site has never waned. During World War II excavations were obviously curtailed, but work started again in the 1960s, and yet another team is excavating the barrows and the ground between them, led by Martin Carver and a team from Birmingham University Field Archaeology Unit.

Returning to the Sutton Hoo Society, they organise visits and circulate information, raise money to fund the work and produce a magazine called 'Saxon' which provides articles of interest and reports on excavation news and views. Not everybody's cup of tea perhaps, but for anyone who finds archaeology even vaguely interesting you would benefit from joining the society. If you are interested just write to The Sutton Hoo Society, c/o Nat West, Cumberland Street, Woodbridge.

Orford, on the coast just about five miles south west of Aldeburgh, is a very strange place. The brick and timber quayside village is charming and gives you a sense of seafaring, but the vast gravel bank of Orford Ness has gobbled up what was once a seaport, which makes it slightly eerie, but it has a unique wild beauty.

If you are feeling very fit we suggest you scramble up the hummocky ramparts to the top of the Orford Castle keep, which is 12th century and gazes sternly over a vast area, affording those who have enough puff to make the climb a wonderful view over coast and countryside.

The church of St. Bartholomew at Orford is in keeping with the little village. It has a ruined Norman chancel, which extends from the Decorated church, whose tower top crumbled and finally toppled in 1830. For 140 years it remained this way, until in 1971 it was replaced. There is a truly wonderful font of the 14th century, which has four proud lions and four wild-looking men round the stem, and boldly sculptured signs of angels and evangelists, with the Trinity and a Pieta above. You will enjoy the beauty of this church. It is open daily from 8.00 am until dusk.

Looking around the quayside and at the fine old Kings Head you can imagine that it was once a very popular haunt for smugglers.

St. Bartholomew's Church, Orford

What a lovely place **Aldeburgh** is. Even today, having achieved fame as the home of the late Benjamin Britten and Peter Pears, it has a slightly 'behind the times' feel about it.

Moot Hall must surely be one of the best-loved and most photographed buildings on any seafront. Its herringbone brickwork and its 1650 sundial stand bravely up to the winds which never quite die.

The Moot Hall is a 15th century building, and is still the Town Hall, and used for council meetings. There is a museum in the building as well.

The charming 400 year old **Mill Inn** stands in Market Cross Place, just opposite the Moot Hall. In fact through its leaded windows you look straight at the Hall. The Mill is very pretty, with its grey slates matching the colour of the waves pounding the beach just yards away.

The Mill Inn

The inn hosts three small bars, where visitors and locals come together. You will find fishermen talking quite happily with city lawyers and businessmen. There is no place for children at the Mill Inn, except on the beach stretching as far as the eye can see. The restaurant specialises in local fish dishes in season, and there are good lunch time specials, like steak and kidney pie, or seafood pie. In addition to the wonderful fish, there is a selection of grills at night.

There are three letting rooms, and at what better place could you have to stay in such an entrancing area? The inn was quite heavily involved in smuggling in days of yore when the local population, rich and poor alike, took part. At that time the inn was much farther from the shore. A 1559 plan of the town shows that the church, which stands just behind The Mill, was at least half a mile from the sea and separated from it by denes and downs similar to those at Yarmouth. This area has now been swallowed by the sea.

Each time we return to Aldeburgh we get a sense of well-being. It remains unspoilt in spite of its international reputation, and this is probably why it feels such a good place to be. There is always something to do or see, although it has none of the more obvious holiday attractions. Take a look at the Royal National Lifeboat Station, which houses the famous Aldeburgh lifeboat. You will be made welcome there, and they will talk proudly about the R.N.L.I. whilst you take a close look at this remarkable vessel.

For a quiet hour or two the Adair Lodge Gardens will give you complete relaxation whilst you sit and take in the beauty of the lawns and flower beds around you. What is it about the quietness of a lovely garden that is so special? Two things in our busy lives that we certainly find therapeutic are gardens and the sea.

We dined one night at **Austin's Hotel** which is very conveniently situated at the end of the High Street, close to the beach, the yacht basin and the marshes with their abundant wild life. Austin's Hotel has become very well known in Aldeburgh and the surrounding area for good food and wine in attractive, welcoming surroundings.

Guests staying at Austin's should not expect identical rooms, as a great deal of thought has gone into creating six bedrooms with very different styles, all of them with bathrooms or shower rooms en-suite. Each room has a theme, realised by using different furnishing fabrics and antique furniture, so visitors may find themselves in a Chinese room, an oak room or among the peonies of Greece.

The restaurant is furnished and decorated with the same attention to detail and seats about thirty. Close by is a comfortable drawing room and the 'Theatre Bar', filled with theatrical posters, signed photographs and momentoes. The food served in the restaurant is a blend of French and English styles, with an emphasis on local fresh fish.

Austin's House has the atmosphere of a private house, and offers quiet, relaxed surroundings in the lovely little town that has escaped the ravages of the 20th century.

The owners told us an interesting story about Austin's. Originally it was two shops: a greengrocer's and an ironmonger's. When the hotel was being refurbished they found and old door to an outbuilding, with the signatures of all the staff who had worked in the shops from 1910 to the 1950s; a link with the past and with the present, as many of the people who signed, or their children, still live in Aldeburgh.

Austin's Hotel

The area around Aldeburgh reflects the nature of this superb part of Suffolk. Only two miles north is the unusual coastal village of Thorpeness, where visitors can see the amazing 'House in the Clouds'. Thorpeness has a first class golf course, and if you fancy boating on the mere it is simple to hire a boat.

The village of **Snape** is the home of the Aldeburgh Festival, and it is a remarkable place. It is set right on the banks of the River Alde, and has a remarkable collection of 19th century buildings, which includes the world-famous concert hall, restaurants, galleries, shops and a centre for activity holidays. It is a wonderful place.

The Aldeburgh Foundation is a registered charity which promotes concerts, principally in the Snape Maltings Concert Hall, from Easter to the New Year. Included in this is of course the world famous Aldeburgh Festival of Music and the Arts, in June. Apart from listening to concerts, there are also guided tours. It is a very special place, and reflects all the love for beautiful music that has been poured into it by its founders.

The Snape Maltings Riverside Centre is a lovely place to visit any day of the year. The granaries and malthouses are built of that lovely mellow red brick, and there are shops and galleries for you here. There is also a super tea shop, which is a part of an old quayside granary; they serve very scrumptious home baked cakes and savouries. There is a pub too, the Plough and Sail which is very much a traditional country pub.

If you want to take a river trip and have a peaceful look at the Alde Estuary, with its abundant birdlife, then you can do so aboard the *Lady Moyra* between April and October.

If you can spare a weekend and would like to paint or print, or learn about countryside subjects, then you can arrange it at Snape Maltings Riverside Centre. (072888) 303/5.

You will realise by now that we quite like this part of Suffolk.

Just north west of Snape is **Aldringham. The Parrot and Punchbowl Inn** is right on the crossroads of the B1122 and the B1353, opposite the well-known Aldringham Craft Market, whose galleries offer a wide range of sensibly-priced products of a very high quality. Founded in 1958 the Craft Market is open daily throughout the year. Having spent some time there, we were more than ready for a drink in the Parrot and Punchbowl.

Although the old 16th century sign depicting a parrot sitting on a punchbowl has been replaced by a more modern sign, and the thatched roof of this old inn has gone, much remains of the Aldringham "Parrot" to remind visitors of its antiquity.

It was built about 1596 when it was called "The Case is Altered Inn" and was changed to its present title when it became the property of the Kemp family in 1604, who occupied the premises without a break until 1834.

Its chief interest however lies in its association with the smuggling days of the 17th century, when Aldringham was the centre of these activities. Many stories are told in the district of the adventures and daring of the smugglers of spirits, tobacco and lace in these romantic times, and of their many rough collisions with the Excise Officers and soldiers, who were stationed on the coast. The last capture at the Aldringham "Parrot" by the Excise Officers was of 300 tubs of smuggled gin!

The Parrot and Punchbowl

The layout of the bar and restaurant areas are on three split levels, which adds to the attraction of the inn. With a building of this age, you would expect the old beams which add a great feeling to the place. We asked Mr. Skinner which type of customer he looked for. His answer was clear, "we like people who appreciate good beers, wines and food, and enjoy a friendly old world atmosphere". You would have lost all sense of taste if, after a meal in the Parrot and Punchbowl, you did not savour the quality of the food.

Whether it is simple bar meals or supper in the restaurant, everything is well prepared, and well cooked. Start your meal with fresh local smoked salmon cornets, filled with melon balls and garnished with a seasonal salad, and follow that with Beef Wellington, with the succulent filled steak covered with a mushroom and onion puree, wrapped in bacon and cooked in puff pastry, served with Madeira sauce, chef's potatoes and fresh seasonal vegetables. The wine list is well selected, and the prices are very reasonable.

At lunchtime you can eat well on home-made dishes for a very modest price.

The home-made soup served with fresh local baked granary bread is almost a meal in itself. On Sundays there is always a traditional roast sirloin of Scottish beef. Good Beer, Good Food in a friendly pub, what more do you want?

We went to see **The Long Shop Museum** at **Leiston**, on the B1119. It is an industrial museum based on the work of the Garrett family who started the business in the late 18th century. It developed from simple beginnings in a local forge to the manufacture of ploughs, threshers and cast iron work, and then exploited the new market for steam powered units in factories, farms and mills. Richard Garrett the Third went to the United States to take a look at their mass production methods, and came back full of ideas for his own assembly hall. Locally it acquired the nickname of 'The Cathedral' but officially it was known as The Long Shop, this helped to expand construction of road rollers, steam engines and steam tractors.

During the World War II the firm made shell lathes, gun mountings and sections of the Mulberry Harbour used in the Normandy Landings. The works closed in 1980, but the memories linger on of this remarkable place as a result of the restoration work that has been done. Among historic Garrett manufactures preserved on the site are road haulage tractors and rollers, an 1846 fire engine, a trolley bus, a thresher and seed drills. It is open daily from April to September and is a super place to visit.

It is thirsty work visiting museums! John McGuire of **The Volunteer Inn** at Haylings Road, Leiston says that he keeps good ale and delivers quickly.

The Volunteer Inn

We were in dire need, and he was as good as his word. Busy people will appreciate this. There is nothing worse than having to wait ages for a round of drinks.

This is a friendly, real pub. There is nothing pretentious, but it is the sort of place where you are happy to have a drink, and for the incredibly low sum of 55p you can have a roll or a sandwich made to order. For £1.95 you can have home made shepherd's pie and vegetables.

There is one large main bar, with seating for 35 people and a pool room, or you can play darts and waste your money on the machines!

The pub has three letting rooms, and for £10.00 per person you can have bed and breakfast. There is parking, and although the pub is only two miles from the beach, you feel you are in a pleasant rural setting.

Saxmundham is a typical small East Anglian market town, historically important because of its strategic position on the London to Great Yarmouth road. The parish church is yet another of these beautiful Suffolk ones, with a superb 14th century tower and a quite exceptional hammer-beam roof. Every alternate Wednesday there is a busy market, and it is fun to wander around looking at all the wares and listening to the market chatter. Afterwards it is no bad thing to wander over to the Bell Hotel which is comfortable and will feed you well. The building is 19th century, but it stands on the site of a much older inn.

We came to Saxmundham this time because we were going just a little further north to see Richard and Liz Morris at Westleton. This was to be our last stopping point this time in Suffolk, and we knew we were in for a very special treat.

Situated almost opposite the village Post Office in the pretty village of **Westleton**, is **The Central House**, a cosy licensed restaurant, with twenty covers, and tea rooms with an interesting history. Dating back to the 18th century, the restaurant has been a drapers shop, wheelwrights, general stores, Post Office and cafe.

Richard and Liz Morris, who became the owners in November 1988, returned from ten years in the Dordogne, France, where they own a 350 acre farm, and Liz had an outside catering business, cooking for anything from small dinner parties to large buffets held at a local chateau owned by Nick Ryman (of stationery family fame).

Before going to France, Elizabeth trained at the Chelmer Institute of Higher Education and went on the cook lunches for the directors of Security Express in London.

They are now putting their joint experience of French food and wine into practice, and do French style table d'hote evening meals with dishes such as Boeuf Bourgignon, Confit de Canard and Salade Perigourdine regularly available. The menu also includes vegetarian dishes. Special events are also planned, such as Bastille Day celebrations on July 14th.

Richard brings back wines from France, and therefore has a very comprehensive wine list. He also hopes to start a wine club in the near future, and provide reasonably priced meals with free wine tasting. The wines will then be available for sale by the case.

Sunday lunch remains a traditional English meal, with a choice of starters, roasts, desserts and coffee at a very reasonable price.

Teas have a slightly international flavour, with the ever-popular English cream tea rubbing shoulders with American chocolate chip cookies and French croissants.

The restaurant garden runs down to the village duck pond, which is inhabited by 70 ever hungry ducks, and during the warmer months, meals and teas are served in the garden under colourful umbrellas. Evening barbecues are also planned, weather permitting!

The Central House

We were quite right to come to Westleton and now, having had such an enjoyable experience, we are heading for home. Our journey has been a wonderful re-acquaintance with much that we knew about, but as always there is an abundance of new experiences, sights, sounds and smells to discover.

Reference Guide

to

Inns, Public Houses, Hotels, Guest Houses,

Self-catering Accommodation, Farm Accommodation,

Camping and Caravan Parks, Restaurants

and Cafes, Riding Schools,

Tourist Attractions and Places of Interest

Details in this section are for guidance only.
For more information please contact the individual establishments
who will be only too pleased to help.

Inns & Public Houses

Name Address	Tel. No.	Open	Credit Cards	Restaurant	Bar Snacks	Children's Room/ Garden	Car Park	Accom-modation	Disabled Facilities	Page
Black Horse Inn, The Street, Thorndon.	0379 71523	All Year	●	●	●	●	●		●	133
The Black Lion, Long Melford, Suffolk.	0787 312356	Flexi	●	●	●	●		●		171
The Bull Inn, 39 High Street, Lakenheath.	0842 861443	All Year			●	●	●			117
Buxton Mill Tavern, Buxton Mill, Buxton.	060546 8194	All Year	●	●	●	●	●		●	77
The Chequers, Church Road, Wimbotsham, Norfolk.	0366 387704	All Year			●	●	●			55
The Coachmakers Arms, Market Place, Great Yarmouth, Norfolk.	0493 844324	All Year			●				●	98
Cock and Bell, Hall Street, Long Melford.	0787 79807	All Year		●	●	●	●	●	●	170
The Crown, Church Lane, Bedfield, Nr. Framlingham.	072876 431	All Year		●	●	●	●	(Siting for Cara-vans)		202

Name Address	Tel. No.	Open	Credit Cards	Restaurant	Bar Snacks	Children's Room/ Garden	Car Park	Accom-modation	Disabled Facilities	Page
The Crown Hotel Downham Market, Norfolk.	0366 382322	All Year	●	●	●		●	●		56
Dolphin Free House, New Street, Jetty-Cliff, Cromer, Norfolk.	0263 512204	11–11 Not Sunday		●	●	●			Access-ible	37
Fisherman's Return, Winterton-on-Sea, Norfolk.	049 376 305	Trad. Pub Hours			●	●	●	●		94
The George Inn, The Green, Cavendish.	0787 280248	11–3 6–11			●	●	●	●		166
The Golden Key, 438 Woodbridge Road, Ipswich.	0473 723916	All Year			●	●	●		●	188
The Grapes, Cross Street, Hoxne.	0379 75473	All Year			●	●	●	Field, Touring Caravans or Tents	●	131
The Hall Inn, Woodham Road, Sea Palling, Norfolk.	069261 323	Flexi		●	●	●	●	●		38
Henry IV, Greenway Lane, Fakenham, Norfolk.	0328 2804	10.30am to 11 pm	●	●	●	●	●	●		18
The Kings Arms, Dereham Road, Garveston, Norfolk.	0362 858190	Flexi			●		●		●	80

Name Address	Tel. No.	Open	Credit Cards	Restaurant	Bar Snacks	Children's Room/ Garden	Car Park	Accom-modation	Disabled Facilities	Page
The Kings Head, 2 Dereham Road, Shipdham, Norfolk.	0362 820861	All Year			•	•	•			85
The Kings Head, Station Road, Pulham St. Mary.	0379 76318	Flexi	•		•	•	•			129
Kings Arms, Middle Street, Watton, Thetford.	0953 881863	Flexi		•	•					108
The Lions Head, 213–215 Cauldwell Hall Road, Ipswich.	0473 727418	Flexi		• Phone before	•	•	•	•	•	189
The Mill Inn, Market Cross Place, Aldeburgh.	072885 2563	Flexi		•	•			•		220
The Norfolk Hero, Swaffham, Norfolk.	0760 23923	Flexi			•		•			62
Parrot & Punchbowl Inn, Aldringham, Suffolk.	0728 830221	Flexi	•	•	•	•	•		•	223
Rose and Crown, Bridge Street, Hilgay, Downham Market.	0366 385414	All Year		•	•	•	•	•		58
Sole Bay Inn, 7 East Green, Southwold.	0502 723736	All Year			•	•	•			144

Name Address	Tel. No.	Open	Credit Cards	Restaurant	Bar Snacks	Children's Room/ Garden	Car Park	Accom-modation	Disabled Facilities	Page
The Three Kings, Fornham All Saints, Bury St. Edmunds.	0284 766979	11–2.30, 7–11, Sun. 12–2.00	•	•	•	•	•		•	179
The Plough Inn, Icklingham, Suffolk.	0638 713370	Flexi			•	•	•		•	113
The Ship, 29 Lynn Road, Gaywood, King's Lynn.	0553 775418	All Year		•	•	•	•		•	47
The Swan Inn, East Harling, Norfolk.	0953 717951	All Year	•	•	•	•	•	•		122
Swannington Hall, Church Lane, Swannington.	0603 868412	All Year		•	•	•	•	•	•	77
The Triple Plea, The Broadway, Halesworth.	098 673753	Flexi			•	•	•	•	•	150
The Volunteer Inn, Haylings Road, Leiston.	0728 830641	All Year			•		•	•		224
The Vine, Hopton, Diss.	095 381466	Flexi		•	•	•	•		•	121
The Weavers Arms, Aylsham Road, Swanton Abbott, Norfolk.	069269 655	Flexi		•	•	•	•		•	41

Name Address	Tel. No.	Open	Credit Cards	Restaurant	Bar Snacks	Children's Room/ Garden	Car Park	Accom-modation	Disabled Facilities	Page
The Wheatsheaf Inn, 45 Chapel Street, Exning.	063 877237	Flexi		•	•	•	•			161
The White Horse, White Horse Green, Rede Road, Whepstead.	0284 88542	All Year			•	•	•			180
The White Horse Inn, Hollow Hill, Withersfield.	0440 706081	Open Trad. Hours		•	•	•	•			162
Ye Olde Kings Head, The Street, Brockdish.	0379 758125	Flexi		•	•	•	•	•	•	130

Hotels & Guest Houses

Name Address	Tel. No.	Open	Credit Cards	No. of Rooms	No. of En-suite	Tea/ TV	Licensed	Children	Disabled	Car Park	Smoking or Non Smoking	AA/RAC Listed	Page
Anser Guest House, 18 New Street, Sheringham, Norfolk.	0263 823861	All Year		5		Tea/ Coffee in Rooms	•	•	(Limited)	•	Smoking		28
Barton Angler Lodge Hotel, Neatishead, Irstead Road, Wroxham.	0692 630740	All Year	•	7	5	•	•	•		•	•		89
Beechcroft Guest House, 13 Park Lane, Newmarket.	0638 669213	All Year		10		• TV		•	(Limited) Room on ground floor	•	•		158

Name Address	Tel. No.	Open	Credit Cards	No. of Rooms	No. of En-suite	Tea/ TV	Licensed	Children	Disabled	Car Park	Smoking or Non Smoking	AA/RAC Listed	Page
Brandon Lodge Motel, Market Hill, Brandon, Suffolk.	0842 814410	All Year		7	All	●	● (Partly)	●		●	●		111
Bunwell Manor Hotel, Bunwell Street, Bunwell.	0953 898304	All Year	●	10	10	●	●	●	(Limited)	●	●	●	123
Burlington Lodge, 30 Burlington Road, Ipswich.	0473 251868	All Year		5 Twin		●		●		●	●		229
Chiltern House, 2 Trafford Road, Norwich.	0603 663033	All Year		7	1	●		●	●	●	●		75
Church Farm Guest House, 20 Church St., Southrepps, Nr. Cromer, Norfolk.	026379 248	All Year		3		●		●		●	●		39
Church Farm Motel, Elsing, Nr. Dereham, Norfolk.	0362 83/ 8236 (8436)	All Year	●	7	7	●	●	● Plus dogs	●	●	● Discretion		79
Crossford Hotel, 15 Nelson Road North, Great Yarmouth.	0493 857252	All Year	●	16	5	TV L'nge	●	●			●		99
The Dial House, Railway Road, Downham Market.	0366 388358	All Year		4	2	●		●		●	Lounge only		58
El Santo Guest House, 81 North Denes, Great Yarmouth.	0493 843864	All Year		15		●	●	●		●	Not in Dining Room		101

Name Address	Tel. No.	Open	Credit Cards	No. of Rooms	No. of En-suite	Tea/ TV	Licensed	Children	Disabled	Car Park	Smoking or Non Smoking	AA/RAC Listed	Page
Griston Hall, Hall Farm, Griston, Thetford.	0953 881626	All Year	●	3	3	●		●		●	Smoking		107
Langtry Hotel Ltd., Gazeley Road, Kentford, Newmarket.	0638 750007	All Year	●	12	12	●	●	●		●	●		157
Old Parsonage House, Higham, Bury St. Edmunds.	0284 810308	All Year		2	1	●		● Over 12		●	●		178
Rosery Hotel & Restaurant, Church Street, Exning, Nr. Newmarket.	0638 77312	All Year	●	11	8	●	●	●		●	●	●	159
Skeet Hotels, 5-7 Riverside Road, Norwich, Norfolk.	0603 622556	All Year Except Xmas	●	21	13	●	●	●	●	●	Smoking		67
Stubbs House Hotel, Stubbs Green, Loddon, Nr. Norwich.	0508 20231	Flexi		9	4	●	●			●	●	Listed	101
Titchwell Manor Hotel, Titchwell, Branchester.	0485 210221	All Year Except Xmas	●	10	10	●	●	●	●	●	● Discretion	2 Star	12
The White Cottage, 19 Wodehouse Road, Old Hunstanton, Norfolk.	04853 2380	All Year		5		●		Not Under Three		●	●		3
The White House, 27 The Street, Holywell Row, Nr. Mildenhall.	0638 713015	All Year		5		●		●		●	●		115

Name Address	Tel. No.	Open	Credit Cards	No. of Rooms	No. of En-suite	Tea/ TV	Licensed	Children	Disabled	Car Park	Smoking or Non Smoking	AA/RAC Listed	Page
The White House, 44 Hunstanton Road, Dersingham, Kings Lynn.	0485 41895	All Year		4	1	•		•	•	•	•		7
White Lodge, Diss Road, Scole, Diss.	0379 740226	All Year		7	2	•		•	•	•	•		128
Worlington Hall Country House Hotel, Worlington.	0638 712237	All Year	•	8	6	•	•	•		•	•		114

Farmhouse Accommodation

Name Address	Tel. No.	Working Farm	No. of Rooms	En-Suite	TV/Tea	Disabled	Children	Pets	Car Park	Page
Broad Oak Farm, Bramfield, Nr. Halesworth.	0986 84232	Yes	3				•	•	•	148
Grange Farm, Woolpit, Bury St. Edmunds.	0359 41143	Yes	4		•		•	•	•	198
King Row Farm, Shipdham, Norfolk.	0362 820212	No	2	2	Just Tea/ Coffee		•	•	•	83

Caravan & Camping Parks

Name Address	Tel. No.	Open	Tents	Caravans	Caravan/ Tent Hire	Showers	Launderette	Shop	Children	Pets	Credit Cards	Page
Beach Holiday Park, Walton Avenue, Felixstowe.	0394 283393	March–October	No	All Vans are Static. No Tourers	•	•	•	•	•	•	•	209
Pakefield Caravan Park, Arbor Lane, Pakefield, Suffolk.	0502 561136	Ring for Details	No	All Static	•	•	•	•	•	•	•	138
Scratby Hall Caravan Park, Scratby, Gt. Yarmouth, Norfolk.	0493 730283	Easter until end of October	•	•		•	•	•	•	•		96

Restaurants & Cafes

Name Address	Tel. No.	Open	Licensed	Children	Smoking/ Non-Smoking	Car Park	Accomm-odation	Disabled Facilities	Credit Cards	Page
Austins Hotel and Restaurant The High Street, Alderburgh, Suffolk.	0728 453932	All Year	•	Over 12	•	On street	•		•	221
Baggy Anne's, Lestrange Terrance, Hunstanton.	04853 2218	All Year	•	•	•				•	4
Bangkok Restaurant, Lodge House, New Road, Banburgh.	0603 742798	All Year	•	•	•	•		•	•	69

Name Address	Tel. No.	Open	Licensed	Children	Smoking/ Non-Smoking	Car Park	Accomm-odation	Disabled Facilities	Credit Cards	Page
The Bankhouse Restaurant and Free House, King Staithe Square, King's Lynn.	0553 765087	All Year	●	●	●	●	●		●	46
Bears Restaurant, 127A Norfolk Street, King's Lynn.	0553 760987	All Year	●	●	●				●	51
Bradfield House Restaurant, Bradfield Combust, Bury St. Edmunds.	028486 301	All Year	●	●	●	●	●		●	175
La Carrozza, Station Road, Hoveton, Wroxham.	0603 783939	All Year	●	●	●	●	●		●	91
Central House Restaurant, The Street, Westleton.	0728 73297	Flexi	●	●	●			●	●	225
Dagmar Hotel Restaurant, 18 Cabbell Road, Cromer, Norfolk.	0263 511500	All Year	●	●	●	●			●	25
Flax Farm, Diss Road, Scole Norfolk.	0379 740379	All Year		●	●	●		●		128
Georgian House Restaurant, 47A The Thoroughfare, Woodbridge.	03943 7292	All Year	●	●	●			●	●	218
Jenta, 25A Smallgate, Beccles, Suffolk.	0502 717772	All Year	●	●	●				●	141

Name Address	Tel. No.	Open	Licensed	Children	Smoking/ Non-Smoking	Car Park	Accomm-odation	Disabled Facilities	Credit Cards	Page
Koh-I-Noor, 25-27 Upper Orwell Street, Ipswich.	0473 212122	All Year	•	•	•				•	187
The Lantern Restaurant, No. 4 Yarmouth Road, Caister-on-Sea, Norfolk.	0493 728930	All Year	•	•	•				•	95
Mary's of Walberswick, Southwold, Suffolk.	0502 723243	All Year	•	•	No Smoking	•		•		145
Nelson House Restaurant, Nelson House, High Street, North Elmham.	036281 233	All Year	•	•	•				•	82
Norfolk Barn & Old Forge, New Road, Belton, Gt. Yarmouth.	0493 780750	All Year	•	•	•	•		•	•	97
The Old Plough Restaurant, 26 High Street, Ashley, Newmarket.	0638 730110	All Year	•	•	•				•	159
Peggotty's Carvery, 30 Guildhall Street, Bury St. Edmunds.	0284 755444	All Year	•	•	•				•	176
Prince of India, 19 Prince of Wales Road, Norwich.	0603 666933	All Year	•	•	•				•	75
The Swiss Restaurant, The Street, Weybourne, Norfolk.	026370 220	All Year	•	•	•				•	29

Riding Centres

Name Address	Tel. No.	Open	Accommodation	Children	Disabled	Indoor School	Tuition	Livery	Credit Cards	Page
Hillcrest Riding School, Hillcrest Farm, Filby Heath, Filby, Great Yarmouth.	0493 730394	All Year	•	•			•	•		100

Tourist Attractions

Name Address	Tel. No.	Open	Hours	Cars/ Coaches	Children	Pets	Disabled	Refreshments	Shop	Page
Boyton Vineyard, Hill Farm, Boyton End, Stoke by Clare.	0440 61893	May–October	10.30–5.00	•	•	•	•	•	•	164
The Cider Place, Cherry Tree Farm, Ilketshall, St. Lawrence.	0986 81353	All Year	9.00–1.00 2.00–6.00	By Appointment (Coach)	•				•	152
Craft Centre & Tea Shop, Craft at the Suffolk Barn, Fornham Rd. Farm, Gt. Barton	0284 87317	March 10–Xmas	12–6 Sunday Closed Mon, Tues Except Bank Hols.	•	•	•	•	•	•	178
Daymond Services (Boat Hire), 4 Spruce Road, Clackclose Park.	0366 383618	Flexible	Flexible	•	•	•				60
Easton Farm Park, Easton, Nr. Woodbridge.	0728 746475	Easter to October	10.30–6.00	•	•	•	•	•	•	214

Name Address	Tel. No.	Open	Hours	Cars/ Coaches	Children	Pets	Disabled	Refresh-ments	Shop	Page
The Fairhaven Garden Trust, The Woodlands, Pilson Green, South Walsham.	0605 49449	Easter to October	2.00–6.00	●	●	●	●	●		93
Fakenham Garden Centre, Mill Road, Hempton, Fakenham.	0328 3380	All Year	9.00–5.30 10.00–5.30 Sunday	Coaches by Appointment	●	●	●		●	18
The Muckleburgh Collection, Weybourne, Miliary Camp.	026 370608	Easter–October	10.00–5.00	●	●		●	●	●	31
Shawsgate Vineyard, Badingham Road, Framlingham.	0728 724060	April–October	10.00–5.00	●	●	●	●	●	●	205
Geo. Smith and Sons (Boat Hire), Riverside Road, Wroxham.	0603 782527	Easter–October	9.00–7.00	●	●		●	●		90
Somerleyton Hall, Somerleyton, Nr. Lowestoft.	0502 730224	Easter–October	2.00–5.30	●	●		●	●	●	103
Suffolk Cider Co., Friday Street, Brandeston, Woodbridge.	0728 82537	All Year: Mon.–Fri. Saturday: April–Sept.	9.30–5.00 10.00–4.00	Coaches by Appointment	●		●		●	212
The Thursford Collection, Thursford, Fakenham.	0328 77477	Easter–October	Varies	●	●		●	●	●	19
The Woolshed Gallery, Clarks Yard, High Street, Cavendish.	0787 281355	March–January	Wed.–Sat.: 10.00–7.00 Sundays: 11.30–5.00	●	●	●			●	167

Places of Interest

Name Address	Tel. No.	Open	Hours	Coaches	Cars	Children	Disabled	Refresh-ments	Shop	Pets	Page
The African Violet Centre, Terrington St. Clement.	0553 828374	All Year	9.00–4.30	For 4 Coaches	•	•	Limited	•	•		49
Alby Crafts & Lace Museum, Cromer Road, Erdingham.	0263 751690	March–December	10.00–5.00	By Appoint-ment	•	•	•	•	•		26
Banham Zoo & Monkey Sanctuary, The Grove, Banham.	095 387 476	All Year	10.00–6.30	•	•	•	•	•	•		125
Beeston Hall, Nr. Wroxham.	0692 630131	PLEASE TELEPHONE FOR DETAILS									92
Blickling Hall, Nr. Cromer.	Aylsham 733084	April–October	1.00–5.00		•	•		•	•	In Park	38
Bressingham Gardens & Steam Museum, Bressingham, Diss.	0379 88382	April–September	10.00–5.30	•	•	•	•	•	•		130
Caithness Crystal Factory, Hardwick Industrial Estate, King's Lynn.	0533 765111	All Year	9.30–4.30	•	•	•		•	•		48
Castle Rising Castle, Castle Rising.	055387 330	March–October	9.30–6.30	•	•	•	•	•	•		54

Name Address	Tel. No.	Open	Hours	Coaches	Cars	Children	Disabled	Refresh-ments	Shop	Pets	Page
Cockthorpe Hall, Cockthorpe, Nr. Stiffkey.	032875 293	Easter–October	10.00–6.00		•	•					33
Colmans Mustard Shop.	0603 627889	All Year	PLEASE TELEPHONE FOR DETAILS								70
Corpus Christi Guildhall, Lavenham.	0787 247646	Flexi	11.00–1.00 2.00–5.30	•	•	•		•	•		174
Crown Pools, Ipswich.	0473 219231	All Year	Mon–Fri: 7.45–9.00 Sat–Sun: 7.45–8.00			•	•	•			188
East Anglia Transport Museum, Chapel Road, Carlton Colville.	0502 518459	May 1 Sundays & Bank Hols June–Sept	11 am Sat. 2pm Sun. 11am W'day 2pm	•	•	•	•	•	•	•	139
Felbrigg Hall, Nr. Cromer.		April–October	1.30–5.30		•	•	•	•	•		37
Forncett Ind. Steam Museum, Forncett St. Mary.	050841 8277	May–October	2.00–6.00	PLEASE TELEPHONE FOR DETAILS							76
Gainsborough House, Sudbury.	0787 72958	PLEASE TELEPHONE FOR DETAILS				•	Notifi-cation needed		•	•	175
Gainsborough Sports & Community Centre, Ipswich.	0473 7130881	All Year	8–11 8.30–6.00 Weekends	•	•	•	•	•			189

Name Address	Tel. No.	Open	Hours	Coaches	Cars	Children	Disabled	Refresh-ments	Shop	Pets	Page
Great Bircham Windmill, Syderstone.	Syder Stone 393	May–September	10–6		•	•		•	•		9
Grimes Graves, Breckland	0223 358911	PLEASE TELEPHONE FOR DETAILS									110
Helmingham Hall, Nr. Stowmarket	0473 39363	30 April to 1 October	2–6	•	•	•	•	•	•	Dogs on Lead	199
Holkham Hall, Wells-next-the-Sea, Norfolk.	0328 710733	May 30–End Sept. Wed–July/Aug.	11.30–5.00	•	•	•		•	•		13
Houghton Hall, Houghton, King's Lynn.	048522 569	Easter–Sept.	Vary	•	•	•	•	•	•		8
Ipswich Museums & Galleries, High Street, Ipswich.	0473 213761	All Year	10–5			•			•		186
Jacobs Farm Museum, of Childhood, Ubbeston.	Ubbeston 657	Sat.–Sun. 12–6	Ring for Details	•	•	•	•	•	•		149
Kentwell Hall, Long Melford.	0787 310207	Ring for details	Ring for details	•	•	•	Ground floor only	•	•		172
Kilverstone Park, Thetford.	0842 755369	All Year	10–6.30		•	•		•	•		109

Name Address	Tel. No.	Open	Hours	Coaches	Cars	Children	Disabled	Refresh-ments	Shop	Pets	Page
Langham Glass House, Holt.	0328 75511	February–November	10–5.15		●	●		●	●		33
Maritime Museum, Lowestoft.	0502 561963	May–September	10–5	●	●	●	●		●	●	137
Mechanical Music Museum, Nr. Stowmarket.	0449 781354	June–September	2.30–5.30	●	●	●	No disabled toilets	●	●		197
Melford Hall, Long Melford, Bury St. Edmunds.	0787 880286	Weekends May 1–October 2	PLEASE TELEPHONE FOR DETAILS								169
Moyses Hall Museum, Bury St. Edmunds.	0284 769834	All Year	10–5 (Mon–Sat) 2–5 Sun.		●	●	Ground floor only		●		176
Museum of East Anglian Life, Stowmarket.	0449 612229	Ring for details	●	●	●	●	●		●	On lead	196
Nicholas Everitt Park, Oulton Broad.	0502 564289	Weekdays-Weekends-	7.30–Dusk 10.00–Dusk	●	●	●	●	●		●	140
Norfolk Lavender Farm, Caley Mill, Heacham.	0485 70384	Easter–October	10–5	●	●	●	●	●	●		6
Norfolk Wildlife Park, Great Witchingham.	0603 872274	All Year	10.30–6.00		●	●	●	●	●	No	79

Name Address	Tel. No.	Open	Hours	Coaches	Cars	Children	Disabled	Refresh-ments	Shop	Pets	Page
North Norfolk Railway.	Sheringham 822045	PLEASE TELEPHONE FOR DETAILS									34
Otter Trust, Nr. Bungay	0986 3470	April–October	10.30–5.30	•	•	•	•	•	•		154
Pleasurewood Hills, Theme Park, Lowestoft.	0502 513626	20 May–17 Sept. Weekends: 29 Apr–23 Oct	10–6 Flexi	•	•	•	•	•	•		137
Park Farm, Snettisham.	0485 41244	All Year	10–5	•	•	•	•	•	•		7
Sandringham Estate, Estate Office, Sandringham	0553 772675	March–Sept. 11–4.45 Dates and times vary when the Royal Family are in residence		•	•	•	•	•	•		52
Sea Life Centre, The Promenade, Hunstanton.	04853 33576	All Year	Vary	•	•	•	•	•	•		5
Sheringham Hall, Sheringham, Norfolk.	0263 733471	PLEASE TELEPHONE FOR DETAILS									35
Suffolk Regimental Museum, Bury St. Edmunds.	Outrisbygate 752394	All Year	10–12 2–4 Mon.–Fri.	•	•	With adult			•		177
Suffolk Wildlife and Rare Breeds Park, Kessingland.	0502 740291	Easter–End Oct.	10–6	•	•	•	•	•	•		138

Name Address	Tel. No.	Open	Hours	Coaches	Cars	Children	Disabled	Refresh-ments	Shop	Pets	Page
Swannington Manor House and Gardens, Nr. Swannington.		April–Sept.	Write for details		●	●		●	●		78
Titchwell Marsh RSPB, 3 Horseshoe Cottage, Titchwell.	Bran-caster 210432	April–October	10–5	●	●	●	●		●		11
Upper Sheringham Park, Sheringham.		All Year	Dawn–Dusk		●	●	●				33
Welney Wildlife Trust Reserve.	0353 860711	All Year	10–5	●	●	●	●	●			59
West Stow Anglo-Saxon Village, Nr. Bury St. Edmunds.	028484 718	All Year	10–5 Daily	●	●	●	●		●	●	182
Whitton Sports & Community Centre, Ipswich.	0473 462711	All Year Ex't. Xmas & Boxing Day	Weekdays: 9am–11pm Weekends: 9am–6pm	●	●	●	●	●			189

A–Z Index

to

Cities, Towns, Villages and Hamlets

A–Z Index to Cities, Towns, Villages and Hamlets

M&M

Publishing Limited

Dear Reader,

We have enjoyed compiling this book. Constantly have we been amazed at the places we have visited. It brought home to us how little we knew of this county of ours. We hope you too have found the book pleasurable and informative.

It would be very helpful to hear from you, the reader, of any interesting places that we have not mentioned and that will add to the enjoyment of the next edition. We will be happy to repay this kindness, by sending you a complimentary copy of any one of the books in this series you may care to choose.

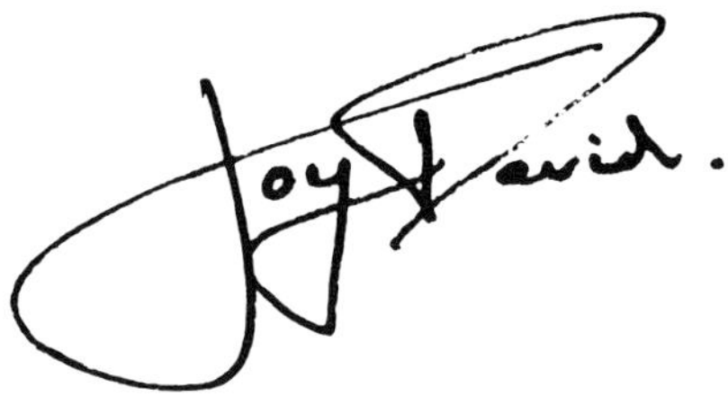

Please write to:

Joy David,
M & M Publishing Ltd.
Dolphin House, Sutton Harbour, Plymouth PL4 0DW.

Notes